Vera Nevil

Or, Poor Wisdom's C.

Mrs. H. Lovett Cameron

Alpha Editions

This edition published in 2024

ISBN : 9789362920249

Design and Setting By
Alpha Editions
www.alphaedis.com
Email - info@alphaedis.com

Contents

CHAPTER I.

THE VICAR'S FAMILY.

With that regal indolent air she had
So confident of her charm.

OWEN MEREDITH.

Beauty too rich for use, for earth too dear.

SHAKESPEARE.

Amongst the divers domestic complications into which short-sighted man is prone to fall there is none which has been more conclusively proved to be an utter and egregious failure than that family arrangement which, for lack of a better name, I will call a "composite household."

No one could have spoken upon this subject with greater warmth of feeling, nor out of the depths of a more painful experience, than could the Rev. Eustace Daintree, sometime vicar of the parish of Sutton-in-the-Wold.

Mr. Daintree's family circle consisted of himself, his mother, his wife, and his wife's sister, and I should like to know how a man could expect to lead a life of peace and tranquillity with such a combination of inharmonious feminine elements!

There were two children also, who were a fruitful source of discord and disunion. It is certain that, had he chosen to do so, the Rev. Eustace might have made many heart-rending and harrowing revelations concerning the private life and customs of the inhabitants of his vicarage. It is equally certain, however, that he would not have chosen to do so, for he was emphatically a man of peace and gentleness, kind hearted and given to good works; and was, moreover, sincerely anxious to do his duty impartially to those whom Providence or fate, or a combination of chances and changes, had somehow contrived to bring together under his roof.

Things had not always been thus with him. In the early days of their married life Eustace Daintree and Marion his wife had had their home to themselves, and right well had they enjoyed it. A fairly good living backed up by independent means, a small rural parish, a pleasant neighbourhood, a pretty and comfortable vicarage-house—what more can the hearts of a clergyman of the Church of England and his wife desire? Mr. and Mrs. Daintree, at all events, had wished for nothing better. But this blissful state of things was not destined to last; it was, perhaps, hardly to be expected that it should, seeing that man is born to trouble, and that happiness is known to be as fleeting as time or beauty or any other good thing.

When Eustace Daintree had been married five years, his father died, and his mother, accepting his warmly tendered invitation to come to Sutton-in-the-Wold upon a long visit, took up her abode in the pleasant vicarage-house.

Her visit was long indeed. In a weak moment her son consented to her urgent request to be allowed to subscribe her quota to the household expenses—this was as good as giving her a ninety-nine years' lease of her quarters. The thin end of the wedge thus inserted, Mrs. Daintree *mère* became immovable as the church tower or the kitchen chimney, and the doomed members of the family began to understand that nothing short of death itself was likely to terminate the old lady's residence amongst them. For the future her son's house became her home.

But, even thus, things were not at their worst. Marion Daintree was a soft-hearted, gentle-mannered little woman. It cannot be said that she regarded the permanent instalment of her mother-in-law in her home with pleasurable feelings; she would have been more than human had she done so. But then she was unfeignedly fond of her husband, and desired so earnestly to make his home happy that, not seeing her way to oust the intruder without a warfare which would have distressed him, she determined to make the best of the situation, and to preserve the family peace and concord at all risks.

She succeeded in her praiseworthy efforts, but at what cost no one but herself ever knew. Marion's whole life became one propitiatory sacrifice to her mother-in-law. To propitiate Mrs. Daintree was a very simple matter. Bearing in mind that her leading characteristics were a bad temper and an ungovernable desire to ride rough-shod over the feelings of all those who came into contact with her, in order to secure her favour it was only necessary to study her moods, and to allow her to tread you under foot as much as her soul desired. Provided that she had her own way in these little matters, Mrs. Daintree became an amiable old lady. Marion did all that was needful; figuratively speaking, she laid down in the dust before her, and the Juggernaut of her fate consented to be appeased by the lowly attitude, and crushed its way triumphantly over her fallen body.

Thus Marion accepted her fate, and peace was preserved in her husband's house. But by-and-by there came somebody into the family who would by no manner of means consent to be so crushed and trodden under foot. This somebody was Vera Nevill.

In order duly to set forth who and what was this young woman, who thus audaciously set at defiance the powers that were, it will be necessary that I should take a brief survey of Marion's family history.

Marion, then, be it known, was the eldest of three sisters; so much the eldest, that when Mr. Daintree had met her and married her in Rome during one of his brief holidays, the two remaining sisters had been at the time hardly more than children. Colonel Nevill, their father, had married an Italian lady, long since dead, and had lived a nomad life ever since he had become a widower; moving about chiefly between Nice, Rome, and Malta. Wherever pleasant society was to be found, there would Colonel Nevill and his daughters instinctively drift, and year after year they became more and more enamoured of their foreign life, and less and less disposed to venture back to the chill fogs and cloudy skies of their native land.

Three years after Marion had left them, and gone away with her husband to his English vicarage; Theodora, the second daughter, had at eighteen married an Italian prince, whose lineage was ancient, but whose acres were few; and Colonel Nevill, dying rather suddenly almost immediately after, Vera, the youngest daughter, as was most natural, instantly found a home with Princess Marinari.

All this time Marion lived at Sutton-in-the-Wold, and saw none of them. She wept copiously at the news of her father's death, regretting bitterly her inability to receive his parting blessing; but, her little Minnie being born shortly after, her thoughts were fortunately diverted into a happier channel, and she suffered from her loss less keenly and recovered from it more quickly than had she had no separate life and no separate interests of her own to engross her. Still, being essentially affectionate and faithful, she clung to the memory of the two sisters now separated so entirely from her. For some years she and Theodora kept up a brisk correspondence. Marion's letters were full of the sayings and doings of Tommy and Minnie, and Theodora's were full of nothing but Vera.

What Vera had looked like at her first ball, how Prince this and Marquis so-and-so had admired her; how she had been smothered with bouquets and bonbons at Carnival time; how she had sat to some world-famed artist, who had entreated to be allowed to put her face into his great picture, and how the house was literally besieged with her lovers. By all this, and much more in the same strain, Marion perceived that her young sister, whom she had last seen in all the raw unformed awkwardness of early girlhood, had developed somehow into a beautiful woman.

And there came photographs of Vera occasionally, fully confirming the glowing accounts Princess Marinari gave of her; fantastic photographs, portraying her in strange and different ways. There was Vera looking out through clouds of her own dark hair hanging loosely about her face; Vera as a Bacchante crowned with vine leaves, laughing saucily; Vera draped as a *dévote*, with drooping eyes and hands crossed meekly upon her bosom. Sometimes she would be in a ball-dress, with lace about her white shoulders; sometimes muffled up in winter sables, her head covered with a fur cap. But always she was beautiful, always a young queen, even in these poor, fading photographs, that could give but a faint idea of her loveliness to those who knew her not.

"She must be very handsome," Eustace Daintree would say heartily, as his wife, with a little natural flush of pride, handed some picture of her young sister across the breakfast-table to him. "How I wish we could see her, she must be worth looking at, indeed. Mother, have you seen this last one of Vera?"

"Beauty is a snare," the old lady would answer viciously, hardly deigning to glance at the lovely face; "and your sister seems to me, Marion, to be dressed up like an actress, most unlike my idea of a modest English girl."

Then Marion would take her treasure away with her up into her own room, out of the way of her mother-in-law's stern and repelling remarks.

But one day there came sad news to the vicarage at Sutton. Theodora, Princess Marinari, caught the Roman fever in its worst form, and after a few agonizing letters and telegrams, that came so rapidly one upon the other that she had hardly time to realize the dreadful truth, Marion learnt that her sister was dead.

After that, the elder sister's English home became naturally the right and fitting place for Vera to come to. So she left her gay life and her lovers, her bright dresses and all that had hitherto seemed to her worth living for, and came back to her father's country and took up her abode in Eustace Daintree's quiet vicarage, where she became shortly her sister's idol and her sister's mother-in-law's mortal foe.

And then it was that the worthy clergyman came to discover that to put three grown-up women into the same house, and to expect them to live together in peace and amity, is about as foolhardy an experiment as to shut up a bulldog, a parrot, and a tom-cat in a cupboard, and expect them to behave like so many lambs.

It is now rather more than a year since Vera Nevill came to live in her brother-in-law's house. Let me waste no further time, but introduce her to you at once.

The time of the year is October—the time of day is five o'clock. In the vicarage drawing-room the afternoon tea-table has just been set out, and the fire just lit, for it is chilly; but one of the long French windows leading into the garden is still open, and through it Vera steps into the room.

There is a background of brown and yellow foliage behind her, across the garden, all aglow with the crimson light of the western sky, against which the outlines of her figure, in its close-fitting dark dress, stand out clearly and distinctly. Vera has the figure, not of a sylph, but of a goddess; it is the absolute perfection of the female form. She is tall—very tall, and she carries her head a little proudly, like a young queen conscious of her own power.

She comes in with a certain slow and languid grace in her movements, and pauses for an instant by the hearth, holding out her hand, that is white and well-shaped, though perhaps a trifle too long-fingered, to the warmth.

The glow of the newly-lit fire flickers up over her face—her face, with its pure oval outlines, its delicate, regular features, and its dreamy eyes, that are neither blue nor gray nor hazel, but something vague and indistinctly beautiful, entirely peculiar to themselves. Her hair, a soft dusky cloud, comes down low over her broad forehead, and is gathered up at the back in some strange and thoroughly un-English fashion that would not suit every one, yet that somehow makes a fitting crown to the stately young head it adorns.

"Tea, Vera?" says Marion, from behind the cups and saucers.

Old Mrs. Daintree sits darning socks, severely, by the fading light. There is a sound of distant whimpering from the shadowy corner behind the piano; it is Tommy in disgrace. Vera turns round; Marion's kind face looks troubled and distressed; the old lady compresses her lips firmly and savagely.

Vera takes the cup from her sister's hands, and putting it down again on the table, proceeds to cut a slice of bread from the loaf, and to spread it thickly with strawberry jam.

"Come here, Tommy, and have some of Auntie's bread and jam."

Out comes a small person, with a very swollen face and a very dirty pinafore, from the distant seclusion of the corner, and flies swiftly to Vera's sheltering arm.

Mrs. Daintree drops her work angrily into her lap.

"Vera, I must beg of you not to interfere with Tom; are you aware that he is in the corner by my orders?"

"Perfectly, Mrs. Daintree; and also that he was there before I went out, exactly three-quarters of an hour ago; there are limits to all human endurance."

"I consider it extremely impertinent," begins the old lady, nodding her head violently.

"Darling Vera," pleads Marion, almost in tears; "perhaps you had better let him go back."

"Tommy is quite good now," says Vera, calmly passing her hand over the rough blonde head. Master Tommy's mouth is full of bread and jam, and he looks supremely indifferent to the warfare that is being carried on on his account over his head.

His crime having been the surreptitious purloining of his grandmamma's darning cotton, and the subsequent immersion of the same in the inkstand, Vera feels quite a warm glow of approval towards the little culprit and his judiciously-planned piece of mischief.

"Vera, I *insist* upon that child being sent back into the corner!" exclaims Mrs. Daintree, angrily, bringing her large fist heavily down upon her knee.

"The child has been over-punished already," she answers, calmly, still administering the soothing solace of strawberry jam.

"Oh, Vera, *pray* keep the peace!" cries Marion, with clasped hands.

"Here, I am thankful to say, comes my son;" as a shadow passes the window, and Eustace's tall figure with the meekly stooping head comes in at the door. "Eustace, I beg that you will decide who is to be in authority in this house— your mother or this young lady. It is insufferable that every time I send the children into the corner Vera should call them out and give them cakes and jam."

Eustace Daintree looks helplessly from one to the other.

"My dear mother—my dear girls—what is it all about? I am sure Vera does not mean——"

"No, Vera only means to be kind, grandmamma," cries Marion, nervously; "she is so fond of the children——"

"Hold your tongue, Marion, and don't take your sister's part so shamelessly!"

Meanwhile Vera rises silently and pushes Tommy and all his enormities gently by the shoulders out of the room. Then she turns round and faces her foe.

"Judge between us, Eustace!" the old lady is crying; "am I to be defied and set at nought? are we all to bow down and worship Miss Vera, the most useless, lazy person in the house, who turns up her nose at honest men and prefers to live on charity, a burden to her relations?"

"Vera is no burden, only a great pleasure to me, my dear mother," said the clergyman, holding out his hand to the girl.

"Oh, grandmamma, how unkind you are," says Marion, bursting into tears. But Vera only laughs lazily and amusedly, she is so used to it all! It does not disturb her.

"Is she to be mistress here, I ask, or am I?" continues Mrs. Daintree, furiously.

"Marion is the mistress here," says Vera, boldly; "neither you nor I have any authority in her house or over her children." And then the old lady gathers up her work and sails majestically from the room, followed by her weak, trembling daughter-in-law, bent on reconciliation, on cajolement, on laying herself down for her own sins, and her sister's as well, before the avenging genius of her life.

The clergyman stands by the hearth with his head bent and his hands behind him. He sighs wearily.

Vera creeps up to him and lays her hand softly upon his coat sleeve.

"I am a firebrand, am I not, Eustace?"

"My dear, no, not that; but if you could try a little to keep the peace!" He stayed the caressing hand within his own and looked at her tenderly. His face is a good one, but not a handsome one; and, as he looks at his wife's young sister, it is softened into its best and kindest. Who can resist Vera, when she looks gentle and humble, with that rare light in her dark eyes?

"Vera, why don't you look like that at Mr. Gisburne?" he says, smiling.

"Oh, Eustace! am I indeed a burden to you, as your mother says?" she exclaims, evasively.

"No, no, my dear, but it seems hard for you here; a home of your own might be happier for you; and Gisburne is a good man."

"I don't like good men who are poor!" says Vera, with a little grimace.

Her brother-in-law looks shocked. "Why do you say such hard worldly things, Vera? You do not really mean them."

"Don't I? Eustace, look at me: do I look like a poor clergyman's wife? Do survey me dispassionately." She holds herself at arm's length from him, and looks comically up and down the length of her gray skirts. "Think of the yards and yards of stuff it takes to clothe me; and should not a woman as tall as I am be always in velvet and point lace, Eustace? What is the good of condemning myself to workhouse sheeting for the rest of my days?"

Mr. Daintree looks at her admiringly; he has learnt to love her; this beautiful southern flower that has come to blossom in his home. Women will be hard enough on Vera through her life—men, never.

"You have great gifts and great temptations, my child," he says, solemnly. "I pray that I may be enabled to do my duty to you. Do not say you do not like good men, Vera, it pains me to hear you say it."

"I like *one* good man, and his name is Eustace Daintree!" she answers, softly; "is not that a hopeful sign?"

"You are a little flatterer, Vera," he says, kissing her; but, though he is a middle-aged clergyman and her brother-in-law, he is by no means impervious to the flattery.

Meanwhile, upstairs, Marion is humbling herself into the dust, at the footstool of her tyrant. Mrs. Daintree is very angry with Marion's sister, and Mr. Gisburne is also the text whereon she hangs her sermon.

"I wish her no harm, Marion; why should I? She is most impertinent to me, but of that I will not speak."

"Indeed, grandmamma, you do not understand Vera. I am sure she——"

"Oh, yes, excuse me, my dear, I understand her perfectly—the impertinence to myself I waive—I hope I am a Christian, but I cannot forgive her for turning up her nose at Mr. Gisburne—a most excellent young man; what can a girl want more?"

"Dear Mrs. Daintree, does Vera look like a poor clergyman's wife?" said Marion, using unconsciously Vera's own arguments.

"Now, Marion, I have no patience with such folly! Whom do you suppose she is to wait for? We haven't got any Princes down at Sutton to marry her; and I say it's a shame that she should go on living on her friends, a girl without a penny! when she might marry a respectable man, and have a home of her own."

And then even Marion said that, if Vera could be brought to like Mr. Gisburne, it might possibly be happier for her to marry him.

CHAPTER II.

KYNASTON HALL.

Only the wind here hovers and revels
In a round where life seems barren as death.
Here there was laughing of old, there was weeping,
Haply of lovers none ever will know.

SWINBURNE, "A Forsaken Garden."

It seemed to be generally acknowledged by the Daintree family that if Vera would only consent to yield to the solicitations of the Reverend Albert Gisburne, and transfer herself to Tripton Rectory for life, it would be the simplest and easiest solution of a good many difficult problems concerning her.

In point of fact, Vera Nevill was an incongruous element in the Daintree household. In that quiet humdrum country clergyman's life she was as much out of her proper place as a bird of paradise in a chicken yard, or a Gloire de Dijon rose in a field of turnips.

It was not her beauty alone, but her whole previous life which unfitted her for the things amongst which she found herself suddenly transplanted. She was no young unformed child, but a woman of the world, who had been courted and flattered and sought after; who had learnt to hold her own, and to fight her battles single-handed, and who knew far more about the dangers and difficulties of life than did the simple-hearted brother-in-law, under whose charge she now found herself, or the timid, gentle sister who was so many years her senior.

But if she was cognizant of the world and its ways, Vera knew absolutely nothing about the life of an English vicarage. Sunday schools and mothers' meetings were enigmas to her; clothing clubs and friendly societies, hopeless and uninteresting mysteries which she had no desire to solve. She had no place in the daily routine. What was she to do amongst it all?

Vera did what was most pleasant and also most natural to her—she did nothing. She was by habit and by culture essentially indolent. The southern blood she inherited, the life of the Italian fine lady she had led, made her languid and fond of inaction. To lie late in bed, to sip chocolate, and open her letters before she rose; to be dressed and re-dressed by a fashionable lady's maid; to recline in luxurious carriages, and to listen lazily to the flattery and adulation that had surrounded her—that had been Vera's life from morning till night ever since she grew up.

How, with such antecedents, was she to enter suddenly into all the activity of an English clergyman's home? There were the schools, and the vestry meetings, and the sick and the destitute to be fretted after from Monday morning till Saturday night—Eustace and Marion hardly ever had a moment's respite or a leisure hour the whole week; whilst Sunday, of course, was the hardest day's work of all.

But Vera could not turn her life into these things. She would not have known how to set about them, and assuredly she had no desire to try.

So she wandered about the garden in the summer time, or sat dreamily by the fire in winter. She gathered flowers and decorated the rooms with them; she spoilt the children, she quarrelled with their grandmother, but she did nothing else; and the righteous soul of Eustace Daintree was disquieted within him on account of her. He felt that her life was wasted, and the responsibility of it seemed, to his over-sensitive conscience, to rest upon himself.

"The girl ought to be married," he would say to his wife, anxiously. "A husband and a home of her own is what she wants. If she were happily settled she would find occupation enough."

"I don't see whom she could marry, Eustace; men are so scarce, and there are so many girls in the county."

"Well, she might have had Barry." Barry was a curate whom Vera had lately scorned, and who had, in consequence of the crushed condition of his affections, incontinently fled. "And then there is Gisburne. Why couldn't she marry Gisburne? He is quite a catch, and a good young man too."

"Yes, it is a pity; perhaps she may change her mind, and he will ask her again after Christmas; he told me as much."

"You must try and persuade her to think better of it by then, my dear. Now I must be off to old Abraham, and be sure you send round the port to Mary Williams; and you will find the list for the blanket club on my study table, love."

Her husband started on his morning rounds, and Marion, coming down into the drawing-room, found old Mrs. Daintree haranguing Vera on the same all-important topic.

"I am only speaking for your good, Vera; what other object could I have?" she was saying, as she dived into the huge basket of undarned socks on the floor before her, and extracted thereout a ragged specimen to be operated upon. "It is sheer obstinacy on your part that you will not accept such a good offer. And there was poor Mr. Barry, a most worthy young man, and his second cousin a bishop, too, quite sure of a living, I should say."

"Another clergyman!" said Vera, with a soft laugh, just lifting up her hands and letting them fall down again upon her lap, with a little, half-foreign movement of impatience. "Are there, then, no other men but the clergy in this country?"

"And a very good thing if there were no others," glared the old lady, defiantly, over her spectacles.

"I do not like them," said Vera, simply.

"Not like them! Considering that I am the daughter, the widow, and the mother of clergymen, I consider that remark a deliberate insult to me!"

"Dear Mrs. Daintree, I am sure Vera never meant——" cried Marion, trembling for fear of a fresh battle.

"Don't interrupt me, Marion; you ought to have more proper pride than to stand by and hear the Church reviled."

"Vera only said she did not like them."

"No more I do, Marion," said Vera, stifling a yawn—"not when they are young; when they are old, like Eustace, they are far better; but when they are young they are all exactly alike—equally harmless when out of the pulpit, and equally wearisome when in it!"

A few moments of offended silence on the part of the elder lady, during which she tugs fiercely and savagely at the ragged sock in her hands—then she bursts forth again.

"You may scorn them as much as you like, but let me tell you that the life of a clergyman's wife—honoured, respected, and useful—is a more profitable one than the idle existence which you lead, utterly purposeless and lazy. You never do one single thing from morning till night."

"What shall I do? Shall I help you to darn Eustace's socks?" reaching at one of them out of the basket.

Mrs. Daintree wrenched it angrily from her hand.

"Good gracious! as if you could! What a bungle it would be. Why, I never saw you with a piece of work in your hand in my life. I dare say you could not even thread a needle."

"I am quite sure I have never threaded one yet," laughed Vera, lazily. "I might try; but you see you won't let me be useful, so I had better resign myself to idleness." And then she rose and took her hat, and went out through the French window, out among the fallen yellow leaves, leaving the other women to discuss the vexed problem of her existence.

She discussed it to herself as she walked dreamily along under the trees in the lane beyond the garden, her head bent, and her eyes fixed upon the ground; she swung her hat idly in her hand, for it was warm for the time of year, and the gold-brown leaves fluttered down about her head and rustled under the dark, trailing skirts behind her.

About half a mile up the lane, beyond the vicarage, stood an old iron gateway leading into a park. It was flanked by square red-brick columns, upon whose summits two stone griffins, "rampant," had looked each other in the face for the space of some two hundred years or so, peering grimly over the tops of the shields against which they stood on end, upon which all the family arms and quarterings of the Kynastons had become softly coated over by an indistinct veil of gray-green moss.

Vera turned in at this gate, nodding to the woman at the lodge within, who looked out for a minute at her as she passed. It was her daily walk, for Kynaston was uninhabited and empty, and any one was free to wander unreproved among its chestnut glades, or to stand and gossip to its ancient housekeeper in the great bare rooms of the deserted house.

Vera did so often. The square, red-brick building, with its stone copings, the terrace walk before the windows, the peacocks sunning themselves before the front door, the fountain plashing sleepily in the stone basin, the statues down the square Italian garden—all had a certain fascination for her dreamy poetical nature. Then turning in at the high narrow doorway, whose threshold Mrs. Eccles, the housekeeper, had long ago given her free leave to cross, she would stroll through the deserted rooms, touching the queer spindle-legged furniture with gentle reverent fingers, gazing absorbedly at the dark rows of family portraits, and speculating always to herself what they had been like, these dead and gone Kynastons, who had once lived and laughed, and sorrowed and died, in the now empty rooms, where nothing was left of them save those dim and faded portraits, and where the echo of her own footsteps was the only sound in the wilderness of the carpetless chambers where once they had reigned supreme.

She got to know them all at last by name—whole generations of them. There was Sir Ralph in armour, and Bridget, his wife, in a ruff and a farthingale; young Sir Maurice, who died in boyhood, and Sir Penrhyn, his brother, in long love-locks and lace ruffles. A whole succession of Sir Martins and Sir Henrys; then came the first Sir John and his wife in powder and patches, with their fourteen children all in a row, whose elaborate marriages and family histories, Vera, although assisted by Mrs. Eccles, who had them all at her fingers' ends, had considerable difficulty in clearly comprehending. It was a relief to be firmly landed with Sir Maurice, in a sad-coloured suit and full-bottomed wig, "the present baronet's grandfather," and, lastly, Sir John, "the present baronet's father," in a deputy-lieutenant's scarlet uniform, with a cocked hat under his arm—by far the worst and most inartistic painting in the whole collection.

It was all wonderful and interesting to Vera. She elaborated whole romances to herself out of these portraits. She settled their loves and their temptations, heart-broken separations, and true lovers' meetings between them. Each one had his or her history woven out of the slender materials which Mrs. Eccles could give her of their real lives. Only one thing disappointed her, there was no portrait of the present Sir John. She would have liked to have seen what he was like, this man who was unmarried still, and who had never cared to live in the house of his fathers. She wondered what the mystery had been that kept him from it. She could not understand that a man should deliberately prefer dark, dirty, dingy London, which she had only once seen in passing from one station to the other on her way to Sutton, to a life in this quiet old-world red-brick house, with the rooks cawing among trees, and the long chestnut glades stretching away into the park, and all the venerable associations of those portraits of his ancestors. Some trouble, some sorrow, must have kept him away from it, she felt.

But she would not question Mrs. Eccles about him; she encouraged her to talk of the dead and gone generations as much as she pleased, but of the man who was her master Vera would have thought it scarcely honourable to have spoken to his servant. Perhaps, too, she preferred her dreams. One day, idly opening the drawer of an old bureau in the little room which Mrs. Eccles always called religiously "My lady's morning room," Vera came upon a modern photograph that arrested her attention wonderfully.

It represented, however, nothing very remarkable; only a broad-shouldered, good-looking young man, with an aquiline noise and a close-cropped head. On the reverse side of the card was written in pencil, "My son—for Mrs. Eccles." Lady Kynaston, she supposed, must therefore have sent it to the old housekeeper, and of course it was Sir John. Vera pushed it back again into the drawer with a little flush, as though she had been guilty of an indiscretion in looking at it, and she said no word of her discovery to the housekeeper. A day or two later she sought for it again in the same place, but it had been taken away.

But the face thus seen made an impression upon her. She did not forget it; and when Sir John Kynaston's name was mentioned, she invested him with the living likeness of the photograph she had seen.

On this particular October morning that Vera strolled up idly to the old house she did not feel inclined to wander among the deserted rooms; the sunshine came down too pleasantly through the autumn leaves; the air was too full of the lingering breath of the dying summer for her to care to go indoors. She paused a minute by the open window of the housekeeper's room, and called the old lady by name.

The room, however, was empty and she received no answer, so she wandered on to the terrace and leant over the stone parapet that looked over the gardens and the fountains, and the distant park beyond, and she thought of the photograph in the drawer.

And then and there there came into Vera Neville's mind a thought that, beginning with nothing more than an indistinct and idle fancy, ended in a set and determined purpose.

The thought was this:—

"If Sir John Kynaston ever comes down here, I will marry him."

She said it to herself, deliberately and calmly, without the slightest particle of hesitation or bashfulness. She told herself that what her relations were perpetually impressing upon her concerning the desirableness of her marrying and making a home of her own, was perfectly just and true. It would undoubtedly be a good thing for her to marry; her life was neither very pleasant nor very satisfactory to herself or to any one else. She had never intended to end her days at Sutton Vicarage; it had only been an intermediate condition of things. She had no vocation for visiting the poor, or for filling that useful but unexciting family office of maiden aunt; and, moreover, she felt that, with all their kindness to her, her brother-in-law and his wife ought not to be burdened with her support for longer than was necessary. As to turning governess, or companion, or lady-help, there was an incongruity in the idea that made it too ludicrous to contemplate even for an instant. There is no other way that a handsome and penniless woman can deliver her friends of the burden of her existence than by marriage.

Marriage decidedly was what Vera had to look to. She was in no way averse to the idea, only she intended to look at the subject from the most practical and matter-of-fact point of view.

She was not going to render herself wretched for life by rashly consenting to marry Mr. Gisburne, or any other equally unsuitable husband that her friends might choose to press upon her. Vera differed in one important respect from the vast majority of young ladies of the present day—she had no vague and indistinct dreams as to what marriage might bring her. She knew exactly what she wanted from it. She wanted wealth and position, because she knew what they were and what life became without them; and because she knew that she was utterly unfitted to be the wife of any one but a rich man.

And therefore it was that Vera looked from the square red house behind her over the wide gardens and broad lawns, and down the noble avenues that spread away into the distance, and said to herself, "This is what will suit me, to be mistress of a place like this; I should love it dearly; I should find real happiness and pleasure in the duties that such a position would bring me. If Sir John Kynaston comes here, it is he whom I will marry, and none other."

As to what her feelings might be towards the man whom she thus proposed to marry it cannot be said that Vera took them into consideration at all. She was not, indeed, aware whether or no she possessed any feelings; they had never incommoded her hitherto. Probably they had no existence. Such vague fancy as had been ever roused within her had been connected with a photograph seen once in a writing-table drawer. The photograph of Sir John Kynaston! The reflection did not influence her in the least, only she said to herself also, "If he is like his photograph, I should be sure to get on with him."

She was an odd mixture, this Vera. Ambitious, worldly-wise, mercenary even, if you will; conscious of her own beauty, and determined to exact its full value; and yet she was tender and affectionate, full of poetry and refinement, honest and true as her own fanciful name.

The secret of these strange contradictions is simply this. Vera has never loved. No one spark of divine fire has ever touched her soul or warmed the latent energies of her being. She has lived in the thick of the world, but love has passed her scatheless. Her mind, her intellect, her brain, are all alive, and sharpened acutely; her heart slumbers still. Happier for her, perhaps, had it never awakened.

She leant upon the stone parapet, supporting her chin upon her hand, dreaming her dreams. Her hat lay by her side, her long dark dress fell in straight heavy folds to her feet. The yellow leaves fluttered about her, the peacocks strutted up and down, the gardeners in the distance were sweeping up the dead leaves on the lawns, but Vera stirred not; one motionless, beautiful figure giving grace, and life, and harmony to the deserted scene.

Some one was passing along among the upper rooms of the house, followed by Mrs. Eccles, panting and exhausted.

"I am sure, Sir John, I am quite ashamed that you should see the place so choked up with dust and lumber. If you had only let me have a day's notice, instead of being took all of a sudden like, I'd have had the house tidied up a bit; but what with not expecting to see any of the family, and my being old, and not so quick at the cleaning as I used to be——"

"Never mind, Mrs. Eccles; I had just as soon see it as it is. I only wanted to see if you could make three or four rooms tolerably habitable in case I thought of bringing my horses down for a month or so. The stables, I find, are in good repair."

"Yes, Sir John, and so is the house; though the furniture is that old-fashioned, that it is hardly fit for you to use."

"Oh! it will do well enough; besides, I have not made up my mind at all. It is quite uncertain whether I shall come——Who is that?" stopping suddenly short before the window.

"That! Oh, bless me, Sir John, it's Miss Vera, from the vicarage. I hope you won't object to her being here; of course, she could not know you was back. I had given her leave to walk in the grounds."

"The vicarage! Has Mr. Daintree a daughter so old as that?"

"Oh, law! no, Sir John. It is Mrs. Daintree's sister. She came from abroad to live with them last year. A very nice young lady, Sir John, is Miss Nevill, and seems lonely like, and it kind of cheers her up to come and see me and walk in the garden. I am sure I hope you won't take it amiss that I should have allowed her to come."

"Take it amiss—good gracious, no! Pray, let Miss—Miss Nevill, did you say?—come as often as she likes. What about the cellars, Mrs. Eccles?"

"I will get the key, Sir John." The housekeeper precedes him out of the room, but Sir John stands still by the window.

"What a picture," he says to himself below his breath; "how well she looks there. She gives to the old place just the one thing it lacks—has always lacked ever since I have known it—the presence of a beautiful woman. Yes, Mrs. Eccles, I am coming." This last aloud, and he hastens downstairs.

Five minutes later, Sir John Kynaston says to his housekeeper,

"You need not scare that young lady away from the place by telling her I was here to-day and saw her. And you may get the rooms ready, Mrs. Eccles, and order anything that is wanted, and get in a couple of maids, for I have made up my mind to bring my horses down next month."

CHAPTER III.

FANNING DEAD ASHES.

Weep no more, nor sigh, nor groan,
Sorrow calls no time that's gone,
Violets plucked, the sweetest rain
Makes not fresh, nor grow again.

FLETCHER.

"Have you heard of Sir John's latest vagary, grandpapa? He is gone down to Kynaston to hunt—so there's an end of *him*."

"Humph! Where did you hear that?"

"I've been lunching at Lady Kynaston's."

The speaker stood by the window of one of the large houses at Prince's Gate overlooking the Horticultural Gardens. She was a small, slight woman, with fair pale features and a mass of soft yellow hair. She had a delicate complexion and very clear blue eyes. Altogether she was a pretty little woman. A stranger would have guessed her to be a girl barely out of her teens. Helen Romer was in reality five-and-twenty, and she had been a widow four years.

Of her brief married life few people could speak with any certainty, although there were plenty of surmises and conjectures concerning it. All that was known was that Helen had lived with her grandfather till she was nineteen; that one fine morning she had walked out of the house and had been married to a man whom her grandfather disapproved of, and to whom she had always professed perfect indifference. It was also known that eighteen months later her husband, having rapidly wasted his existence by drink and other irregular courses, had died in miserable poverty; and that Helen, not being able to set up a home of her own, upon her slender fortune of some five or six thousand pounds, had returned to her grandfather's house in Prince's Gate, where she had lived ever since.

Why she had married William Romer no one ever exactly knew—perhaps Helen herself least of any one. It certainly was not for love; it could hardly have been from any worldly motive. Some people averred, and possibly they were not far wrong, that she had done so out of pique because the man she loved did not want her.

However that might be, Mrs. Romer returned a widow, and not a very disconsolate one, to her grandfather's house.

It is certain that she would not have lived there could she have helped it. She did not love old Mr. Harlowe, neither did Mr. Harlowe love her. A sense of absolute duty to his dead daughter's child on the one side, a sense of absolute necessity on the other, kept the two together. Their natures were inharmonious. They kept up a form of affection and intimacy openly; in reality, they had not one single thought in common.

It is not too much to say that Mr. Harlowe positively disliked his grand-daughter. He had, perhaps, good reason for it. Helen had been nothing but a trouble to him. He had not desired to bring up a young lady in his house; he had not wished for the society which her presence entailed, nor for the dissipations of London life into which he was dragged more or less against his will. Added to which, Helen had not striven to please him in essential matters. She had married a gambling, drinking blackguard, whom he had forbidden to enter his doors; and now, when she might retrieve her position, and marry well and creditably, she refused to make the slightest effort to meet his views.

Helen's life was a mystery to all but herself. To the world she was a pretty, lively little widow, with a good house to live in, and sufficient money of her own to spend to very good effect upon her back, with not a single duty or responsibility in her existence, and with no other occupation in life than to amuse herself. At her heart Helen knew herself to be a soured and disappointed woman, who had desired one thing all her life, and who, having attained with great pains and toil that forbidden fruit which she had coveted, had found it turn, as such fruits too often do, to dust and ashes between her teeth. It was to have been sweet as honeydew—and behold, it was nothing but bitterness!

She stood at the window looking out at the waning light of the November afternoon. She was handsomely dressed in dark-green velvet, with a heavy old-fashioned gold chain round her neck; every now and then she looked at her watch, and a frown passed over her brow. The old man was bending over the fire behind her.

"Gone to Kynaston, is he? Humph! that is your fault, you frightened him off."

"Did I set my cap at him so palpably then?" said Helen, with a short, hard laugh.

"You know very well what I mean," answered her grandfather, sulkily. "Set your cap! No, you only do that to the men you know I don't approve of, and who don't want you."

Helen winced a little. "You put things very coarsely, grandpapa," she said, and laughed again. "I am sorry I have been unable to make love to Sir John Kynaston to please you. Is that what you wanted me to do?"

"I want you to look after a respectable husband, who can afford to keep you. What is the meaning of that perpetual going to Lady Kynaston's then? And why have you dragged me up to town at this confounded time of the year if it wasn't for that? You have played your cards badly as usual. You might have had him if you had chosen."

"I have never had the least intention of casting myself at Sir John's head," said Helen, scornfully.

"You can cast yourself, as you call it, at that good-for-nothing young spendthrift's head fast enough if you choose it."

"I don't in the least know whom you mean," she said, shortly.

The old man chuckled. "Oh, yes, you know well enough—the brother who spends his time racing and betting. You are a fool, Helen; he doesn't want you; and if he did, he couldn't afford to keep you."

"Suppose we leave Captain Kynaston's name out of the discussion, grandpapa," she said, quietly, but her face flushed suddenly and her hands twisted themselves nervously in and out of her heavy chain. "Are you not going to your study this evening?"

"Oh yes, I'm going, fast enough. You want me out of the way, I suppose. Somebody coming to tea, eh? Oh yes, I'll clear out. I don't want to listen to your rubbish."

The old man gathered up his books and papers and shuffled out of the room, muttering to himself as he went.

The servant came in, bringing the lamp, replenished the fire and drew the curtains, shutting out the light of day.

"Any one to tea, ma'am?" he inquired, respectfully.

"One gentleman—no one else. Bring up tea when he comes."

"Very well, ma'am;" and the servant withdrew. Mrs. Romer paced impatiently up and down the room, stopping again and again before the clock.

"Late again! A whole half-hour behind his time! It is insufferable that he should treat me like this. He would go quickly enough to see some new face—some fresh fancy that had attracted him."

She took out her watch and laid it on the table. "Let me see if he will come before the minute-hand touches the quarter; he *must* be here by then!"

She continued to pace steadily up and down the room. The clock ticked on, the minute-hand of the watch crept ever stealthily forward over the golden dial; now and then a passing vehicle without made her heart beat with sudden hope, and then sink down again with disappointment, as the sound of the wheels went by and died away in the distance.

Suddenly she sank into an arm-chair, covering her face with her hands.

"Oh, what a fool—what a fool I am!" she exclaimed aloud. "Why have I not strength of mind to go out before he comes, to show him that I don't care? Why, at least, can I not call up grandpapa, and pretend I had forgotten he was coming? That would be the best way to treat him; the way to show him that I am not the miserable slave he thinks me. Why can I, who know so well how to manage all other men, never manage the one man whose love I want? That horrid old man was right—he does not want me—he never did. Oh, if I only could be proud, and pretend I do not care! But I can't, I can't—there is always this miserable sickening pain at my heart for him, and he knows it. I have let him know it!"

A ring at the bell made her spring to her feet, whilst a glad flush suddenly covered her face.

In another minute the man she loved was in the room.

"Nearly three-quarters of an hour late!" she cried, angrily, as he entered. "How shamefully you treat me!"

He stood in front of the fire, pulling off his dogskin gloves: a broad-shouldered, handsome fellow, with an aquiline nose and a close-cropped head.

"Am I late?" he said, indifferently. "I really did not know it. I have had fifty places to go to in as many minutes."

"Of course I shall forgive you if you have been so busy," she said, softening at once. "Maurice, darling, are you not going to kiss me?" She stood up by his side upon the hearthrug, looking at him with all her heart in her eyes, whilst his were on the fire. She wound her arms round his neck, and drew his head down. He leant his cheek carelessly towards her lips, and she kissed him passionately; and he—he was thinking of something else.

"Poor little woman," he said, almost with an effort recalling himself to the present; he patted her cheek lightly and turned round to toss his gloves into his hat on the table behind him. "How cold it has turned—aren't you going to give me some tea?" And then he sat down on the further side of the fire and stretched himself back in his arm-chair, throwing his arms up behind his head.

Helen rang the bell for the tea.

"Is that all you have to say to me?" she said, poutingly.

Maurice Kynaston looked distressed.

"Upon my word, Helen, I am sure I don't know what you expect. I haven't heard any particular news. I saw you only yesterday, you know. I don't know what you want me to say."

Helen was silent. She knew very well what she wanted, she wanted him to say and do things that were impossible to him—to play the lover to her, to respond to her caresses, to look glad to see her.

Maurice was so tired of it all! tired alike of her reproaches and her caresses. The first irritated him, the second gave him no pleasure. There was no longer any attraction to him about her, her love was oppressive to him. He did not want it, he had never wanted it; only somehow she had laid it so openly and freely at his feet, that it had seemed almost unmanly to him not to put forth his hand and take it. And now he was tired of his thraldom, sick of her endearments, satiated with her kisses. And what was it all to end in? He could not marry her, he would not have desired to do so had he been able; but as things were, there was no money to marry on either side. At his heart Maurice Kynaston was glad of it, for he did not want her for a wife, and yet he feared that he was bound to her.

Man-like, he had no courage to break the chains that bound him, and yet to-night he had said to himself that he would make the effort—the state of his affairs furnished him with a sufficiently good pretext for broaching the subject.

"There is something I wanted to say to you," he said, after the tea had been brought in and they were alone again. He sat forward in his chair and stroked his moustache nervously, not looking at her as he spoke.

Helen came and sat on the hearthrug at his feet, resting her cheek caressingly against his knee.

"What is it, Maurice?"

"Well, it's about myself. I have been awfully hard hit this last week at Newmarket, you know."

"Yes, so you told me. I am so sorry, darling." But she did not care much as long as he was with her and was kind to her—nothing else signified much to her.

"Yes, but I am pretty well broke this time—I had to go to John again. He is an awfully good fellow, is old John; he has paid everything up for me. But I've had to promise to give up racing, and now I've got to live on my pay."

"I could lend you fifty pounds."

"Fifty pounds! pooh! what nonsense! What would be the good of fifty pounds to me?"

He said it rather ungraciously, perhaps, and her eyes filled with tears. When a man does not love a woman, her little childish offers of help do not touch him as they would if he loved her. He would not have taken five thousand from her, yet he was angry with her for talking of fifty pounds.

"What I wanted to say to you, Helen, was that, of course, now I am so hard up it's no good thinking of—of marrying—or anything of that kind; and don't you think it would be happiest if you and I—I mean, wisest for us both—for you, of course, principally——"

"*What!*" She lifted her head sharply. She saw what he meant at once. A wild terror filled her heart. "You mean that you want to throw me over!" she said, breathlessly.

"My dear child, do be reasonable. Throw you over! of course not—but what is it all to lead to? How can we possibly marry? It was bad enough before, when I had my few hundreds a year. But now even that is gone. A captain in a line regiment is not exactly in a position to marry. Why, I shall hardly be able to keep myself, far less a wife too. I cannot drag you down to starvation, Helen; it would not be right or honourable to continue to bind you to my broken fortunes."

She was standing up now before him very white and very resolute.

"Why do you make so many excuses? You want to be rid of me."

"My dear child, how unjust you are."

"Am I unjust? Wait! let me speak. How have we altered things? Could you marry me any more before you lost this money? You know you could not. Have we not always agreed to wait till better times? Why cannot we go on waiting?"

"It would not be fair to tie you."

He had not the courage to say, "I do not love you—money or no money, I do not wish to marry you." How indeed is a man who is a gentleman to say such a discourteous thing to a lady for whom he has once professed affection? Maurice Kynaston, at all events, could not say so.

"It would not be fair to tie you; it would be better to let you be free:" that was all he could find to say. And then Helen burst forth impetuously,

"I wish to be tied—I do not want to be free—I will not marry any other man on earth but you. Oh! Maurice, my love, my darling!" casting herself down again at his feet and clasping her arms wildly round him. "Whom else do I want but you—whom else have I ever loved? You know I have always been yours—always—long ago, in the old days when you never even gave me a look, and I was so maddened with misery and despair that I did not care what became of me when I married poor Willie, hardly knowing what I was doing, only because my life was so unbearable at home. And now that I have got you, do you think I will give you up? And you love me—surely, surely, you *must* love me. You said so once, Maurice—tell me so again. You do love me, don't you?"

What was a man to do? Maurice moved uneasily under her embrace as though he would withdraw her arms from about his neck.

"Of course," he said, nervously; "of course, I am fond of you, and all that, but we can't marry upon less than nothing. You must know that as well as I do."

"No; but we can wait."

"What are we to wait for?" he said, irritably.

"Oh, a hundred things might happen—your brother might die."

"God forbid!" he said, pushing her from him, in earnest this time.

"Well, we will hope not that, perhaps; but grandpapa can't live for ever, and he ought to leave me all his money, and then we should be rich."

"It is horrible waiting for dead people's shoes," said Maurice, with a little shudder; "besides, Mr. Harlowe is just as likely as not to leave his money to a hospital, or to the British Museum, or the National Gallery—you could not count upon anything."

"We could at all events wait and see."

"And be engaged all that time on the off-chance?" he said, drearily; "that is a miserable prospect."

"Then you do wish to get rid of me!" she said, looking at him suspiciously; "you have seen some other woman."

"Pooh! what a little fool you are!" He jumped up angrily from his chair, leaving her there upon the hearthrug. A woman makes a false move when she speaks of "another woman" to the man whose affection for her is on the wane. In the present instance the accusation was utterly without foundation.

Many as were his self-reproaches on her account, that one had never been amongst them. If he did not love her, neither had he the slightest fancy for any other woman. Her remark irritated him beyond measure; it seemed to annul and wipe out the score of his own shortcomings towards her, and to make himself, not her, the injured one.

"Women are the most irrational, the most unjust, the most thoroughly pig-headed set of creatures on the face of the earth!" he burst forth, angrily.

She saw her mistake by this time. She was no fool; she was quick enough—sharp as a needle—where her love did not, as love invariably does, warp and blind her judgment.

"I am sorry, Maurice," she said, humbly. "I did not mean to doubt you, of course. Have you not said you love me? Sit down again, please."

He sat down only half appeased, looking glum and sulky. She felt that some concession on her part was necessary. She took his hand and stroked it softly. She knew so well that he did not love her, and yet she clung so desperately to the hope that she could win him back; she would not own to herself even in the furthermost recesses of her own heart that his love was dead. She would not believe it; to put it in words to herself even would have half killed her; but still she was forced to acknowledge that unless she met him half-way she might lose him altogether.

"I will tell you what I will do, Maurice," she said thoughtfully. "I will consent to let our engagement be in abeyance for the present; I will cease to write to you unless I have anything particular to say, and I will not expect you to write to me. If people question us, we will deny any engagement between us—we will say that we are each of us free—but on one condition only, that you will promise me most solemnly, on your honour as a gentleman, that should either of us be left any money—should there be, say, a clear thousand a year between us, within the next five years——"

"My dear Helen, I am as likely to have a thousand a year as to be presented with the regalia."

"Never mind. If it is unlikely, so much the worse—or the better, whichever you may like to call it. But if such a thing does happen, give me your word of honour that you will come to me at once—that, in fact, our engagement shall be renewed. If things are no better, our prospects no brighter, in five years from now—well, then, let us each be free to marry elsewhere."

There was a moment or two of silence between them. Maurice bent forward in his chair, leaning his arms upon his knees, and staring moodily into the fire. He was weighing her proposition. It was something; but it was not enough. It virtually bound him to her for five years, for, of course, an engagement that is to be tacitly consented to between the principal contractors is an engagement still, though the whole world be in ignorance of it. But then it gave him a chance, and a very good chance too, of perfect liberty in five years' time. It was something, certainly; though, as he had wanted his freedom at once, it could hardly be said to be altogether satisfactory.

Helen knelt bolt upright in front of him, watching his face. How passionately she desired to hear him indignantly repudiate the half-liberty she offered him! How ardently she desired that he should take her in his arms, and swear to her that he would never consent to her terms, no one but herself could know. It had been her last expedient to revive the old love, to rekindle the dead ashes of the smouldering fire. Surely, if there was but a spark of it left, it must leap up into life and vitality again at her words. But, as she watched him, her heart, that had beat so wildly, sank cold and colder within her. She felt that his heart was gone from her; she had cast her last die and lost. But, for all that, she was not minded to let him go free—her wild, ungoverned passion for him was too deeply rooted within her; since he would not be hers willingly, he should be hers by force.

"Surely," she said, wistfully, "you cannot find my terms too hard to consent to—you who—who love me?"

He turned to her quickly and took her hands, every feeling of gentleman-like honour, every spark of manly courtesy towards her, aroused by her gentle words.

"Say no more, Helen—you are too good—too generous to me. It shall be as you say."

And then he left, thankful to escape from her presence and to be alone again with his thoughts in the raw darkness of the November evening.

———

CHAPTER IV.

THE LAY RECTOR.

Or art thou complaining
Of thy lowly lot,
And, thine own disdaining,
Dost ask what thou hast not?
Of the future dreaming,
Weary of the past,
For the present scheming
All but what thou hast.

L. E. LANDON.

In the churchyard at Sutton-in-the-Wold was a monument which, for downright ugliness and bad taste, could hardly find its fellow in the whole county. It was a wonderful and marvellous structure of gray granite, raised upon a flight of steps, and consisted of an object like unto Cleopatra's Needle surmounting a family tea-urn. It had been erected by one Nathaniel Crupps, a well-to-do farmer in the parish, upon the death of his second wife. The first partner of his affections had been previously interred also in the same spot, but it was not until the death of the second Mrs. Crupps, who was undoubtedly his favourite, that Nathaniel bethought him of immortalizing the memory of both ladies by one bold stroke of fancy, as exemplified by this portentous granite monstrosity. On it the virtues of both wives were recorded, as it was touchingly and naïvely stated, by their "sorrowing husband with strict impartiality."

It was upon this graceful structure that Vera Nevill leant one foggy morning in the first week of November, and surveyed the church in front of her. She was not engaged in any sentimental musings appropriate to the situation. She was neither meditating upon the briefness of life in general, nor upon the many virtues of the ladies of the Crupps family, over whose remains she was standing. She was simply waiting for Jimmy Griffiths, and looking at the church because she had nothing else to look at. The church, indeed, afforded her some food for reflection, purely, I regret to state, of a practical and mundane character. It was a large and handsome building, with a particularly fine old tower, that was sadly out of repair; but the chancel was a modern and barn-like structure of brick and plaster, which ought, of course, to be entirely swept away, and a new and more appropriate one built in its stead. The chancel belonged, as most chancels do, to the lay rector, and the lay rector was Sir John Kynaston.

As soon as it became bruited abroad that Sir John was coming down to the old house for the winter, there was a general excitement throughout the parish, but no one partook of the excitement to a greater degree than did its worthy vicar.

It was the dream of Eustace Daintree's life to get his church restored, and more especially to get the chancel rebuilt. There had been a restoration fund accumulating for some years, and could he have had the slightest assistance from the lay rector concerning the chancel, Mr. Daintree would assuredly have sent for the architect, and the builders, and the stone-cutters, and have begun his church at once with that beautiful disregard of the future chances of being able to get the money to pay for it, and with that sparrow-like trust in Providence, which is usually displayed by those clerical gentlemen who, in the face of an estimate which tells them that eight thousand pounds will be the sum total required, are ready to dash into bricks and mortar upon the actual possession of eight hundred. But there was the chancel! To leave it as it was whilst restoring the nave would have been too heart-rending; to touch it without Sir John Kynaston's assistance, impossible and illegal. Several times Eustace Daintree had applied to Sir John in writing upon the subject. The answers had been vague and unsatisfactory. He would promise nothing at all; he would come down and see it some day possibly, and then he would be able to say more about it; meanwhile, for the present, things must remain as they were.

When, therefore, the news was known that Sir John was actually coming down, Mr. Daintree's thoughts flew at once to his beloved church.

"Now we shall get the chancel done at last," he said to his wife gleefully, rubbing his hands. And the very day after Sir John's arrival Eustace went up to the Hall after dinner to see him upon the subject.

"Had you not better wait a day or two?" counselled his more prudent wife. "Wait till you meet him, naturally. You don't very well know what kind of man he is, nor how he will take it."

"What is the use of waiting? I knew him well enough eight years ago; he was a pleasant fellow enough then. He won't kill me, I suppose, and the chancel is a disgrace—a positive disgrace to him. It is my duty to point it out to him; the thing can't afford to wait, it ought to be done at once."

So he disregarded Marion's advice, and Vera helped him on with his great-coat in the hall, and wound his woollen comforter round his neck, and bade him good luck on his expedition to Kynaston.

He came back sorrowful and abashed. Sir John had been civil, very civil; he had insisted on his sitting down at his table—for he had apparently not finished his dinner—and had opened a bottle of fine old port in his honour.

He had inquired about many of the old people, and had expressed a friendly interest in the parish generally; but with regard to the chancel, he had been as adamant.

He did not see, he had said, why it could not go on well enough as it was. If it was in bad repair, Davis should see to it; a man with a barrowful of bricks and a shovelful of mortar should be sent down. That, of course, it was his duty to do. Sir John did not understand that more could possibly be expected of him. The chancel had been good enough for his father, it would probably be good enough for him; it would last his time, he supposed, in any case.

But the soul of the Rev. Eustace became as water within him. It was not of a barrowful of bricks and shovelful of mortar that he had been dreaming, but of lancet windows and stone mouldings; of polished oak rafters within, and of high gables and red tiles without.

He came down from the Hall disheartened and discomfited, with all the spirit crushed out of him; and the ladies of his family, for once, were of one mind about the matter. There arose about him a storm of indignation and a gush of sympathy, which could not fail to soothe him somewhat. Eustace went to rest that night sore and heavy-hearted, it is true, but with all the damnatory verses in the Scriptures concerning the latter end of the "rich man" ringing in his head; a course of meditation which, upon the whole, afforded him a distinct sensation of consolation and comfort.

And the next morning in the churchyard Vera leant against the Cruppsian sarcophagus, and thought about it.

"Poor old Eustace," she said to herself; "how I wish I were very rich, and could do his chancel for him! How pleased he would be; and what a good fellow he is! How odd it is to think what different aims there are in people's lives! There are Eustace and Marion simply miserable this morning because of that hideous barn they can't get rid of. Well, it *is* hideous certainly; but it doesn't disturb my peace of mind in the least. What a mean curmudgeon Sir John must be, by the way! I should not have thought it from his photograph; such a frank, open, generous face he seemed to have. However, we all know how photographs can mislead one. I wonder where that wretched boy can be!"

The "wretched boy" was Jimmy Griffiths afore-mentioned; he was the youth who was in the habit of blowing the organ. The schoolmaster, who was also the organist, was ill, and had sent word to Mr. Daintree that he would be unable to be at the church on the morrow. Eustace had asked Vera to take his place. Now Vera was not accomplished; she neither sang, nor played, nor painted in water-colours; but she had once learnt to play the organ a little— a very little. So she professed herself willing to undertake the office of organ-player for once, that is to say, if she found she could do it pretty well, only she must go into church and try all the chants over. So Jimmy Griffiths was sent for from the village, and Vera, with the church key in her pocket, strolled idly into the churchyard, and, whilst awaiting him, meditated upon the tomb of the two Mrs. Crupps.

She had come in from the private gate of the vicarage, and the vicarage garden—very bleak and very desolate by this time—lay behind her. To the right, the public pathway led down through the lych-gate into the village. Anybody coming up from the village could have seen her as she stood against the granite monument. She wore a long fur cloak down almost to her feet, and a round fur cap upon her head; they were her sister Theodora's sables, which she had left to her. Old Mrs. Daintree always told her she ought to sell them, a remark which made Vera very angry. Her back was turned to the village and to the lych-gate, and she was looking up at poor Eustace's bug-bear—the barn-like chancel.

Suddenly somebody came up close behind her and spoke to her.

"Can you tell me, please, where the keys of the church are kept?"

A gentleman stood beside her, lifting his hat as he spoke. Vera started a little at being so suddenly spoken to, but answered quite quietly and unconfusedly,

"They are generally kept at the vicarage, or else in the clerk's cottage."

"Thank you; then I will go and fetch them."

"But they are not there now," said Vera, as though finishing her former remark.

"If you will kindly tell me where I can find them," continued the stranger, very politely, "I will go and get them."

"I am afraid you can't do that," said Vera, with just the vestige of a smile playing upon her face, "because they are at present in my pocket."

"Oh, I beg your pardon;" and the stranger smiled outright.

"But I will let you into the church, if you like; if that is what you wish?" she said, quite simply.

"Yes, if you please." Vera moved up the path to the porch, the gentleman following her. She turned the key in the heavy door and held it open. "If you will go in, please, I will take the keys; I must not leave them in the door." The gentleman went in, and Vera looked at him as he passed by.

Most uninteresting! was her verdict as he passed her; forty at the very least! What a beautiful situation for an adventure! What a romantic incident! And how excessively tame is the *dénouement*! A middle-aged gentleman, tall and slightly bald, with close-cropped whiskers and grave, set features; who on earth could he be? A stranger, evidently; perhaps he was staying at some neighbouring country house, and had walked over to Sutton for the sake of exercise; but what on earth could he want to see the church for!

The stranger stood just inside the door with his hat off, looking at her.

"Won't you come in and show it to me?" he asked, rather hesitatingly.

"The church? oh, certainly, if you like, but there is nothing to see in it." She came in, closing the door behind her, and stood beside him. It did not strike her as unusual or interesting, or as anything, in fact, but the most common-place and unexciting proceeding, that she should do the honours of the church to this middle-aged stranger.

They stood side by side in the centre of the small nave with all the ugly, high, red-cushioned pews around them. Vera looked up and down the familiar place as though she and not he were seeing it for the first time; from the row of whitewashed pillars to the staring white windows; from the hatchment on the plastered walls to the disfiguring gallery along the west end.

"It is very hideous," she said, almost apologetically, "especially the chancel; Mr. Daintree wants to have it restored, but I suppose that can't be done at all now."

"Why can't it be done?"

"Oh, because nothing can be done unless the chancel is pulled down; that belongs to the lay rector, and he has refused to restore it."

"Sir John Kynaston is the lay rector."

"Yes!" Vera looked a little startled; "do you know him?"

The gentleman passed his hand over his chin.

"Slightly," he answered, not looking at her.

"It is a pity he cannot be brought to see how necessary it is, for he certainly ought to do it," continued Vera. "You see I cannot help being interested in it because Mr. Daintree is such a good man, and has worked so hard to get up money to begin the rest of the church. He had quite counted upon the chancel being done, and now he is so much disappointed; but, I beg your pardon, this cannot interest you."

"But it interests me very much. Why does not somebody put it in this light to Sir John; he would not surely refuse?"

"My brother-in-law, Mr. Daintree, I mean, did ask him last night, and he would not promise to do anything."

The stranger suddenly left her side and walked up the church by himself into the chancel. He went straight up to the east end and made a minute examination apparently of the wall; after that, he came slowly down again, looking carefully into every corner and cranny from the whitewashed ceiling down to the damp and uneven stone paving at his feet; Vera thought him a very odd person, and wondered what he was thinking about.

He came back to her and stood before her looking at her for a minute. And then he made this most remarkable speech:

"If *you* were to ask Sir John Kynaston this he would restore the chancel!" he said.

For half-a-second Vera stared at him in blank amazement. Then she turned haughtily round, and flushed hotly with angry indignation.

"There is nothing more to see in the church," she said, shortly, and walked straight out of it.

The stranger had followed her; when they reached the churchyard he said to her, quite humbly,

"I beg your pardon; Miss Nevill; how unlucky I am to have made you angry, to begin with."

Vera looked at him in astonishment. How did he know her name; who was he? He was looking at her with such a penitent and distressed expression, that for the first time she noticed what a kind face it was. Then, before she could answer him, she saw her brother-in-law over the paling of the vicarage garden, coming towards them.

The stranger saw him, too, and lifted his hat to her.

"Good-bye," he said, rather hastily; "I did not mean to offend you; don't be angry about it;" and, before she could say a word, he turned quickly down the churchyard through the lych-gate into the road, and was gone.

"Vera," said Eustace Daintree, coming leisurely up to her through the garden gate, "how on earth do you come to be talking to Sir John; has he been saying anything to you about the chancel?"

"*Who* was it? *who* did you say?" cried Vera, aghast.

"Why, Sir John Kynaston, to be sure. Did you not know it was he?"

She was thunderstruck. "Are you quite sure?" she faltered.

"Why, of course! I saw him only last night, you know. I wonder why he went off in such a hurry when he saw me?"

Vera was walking silently down the garden towards the house by his side. The thought in her mind was, "If that was Sir John Kynaston, who then is the photograph I found in the writing-table drawer?"

"What did he say to you, Vera? How came you to be talking to him?" pursued her brother-in-law.

"I only let him into the church. I did not know who he was. I told him the chancel ought to be restored—by himself."

Eustace Daintree looked dismayed.

"How very unfortunate. It will, perhaps, make him still more decided to do nothing."

Vera smiled a little to herself. "I hope not, Eustace," was all she said. But although she said no word of it to him, she knew at her heart that his chancel would be restored for him.

Late that night Vera sat alone by her fireside, and thought over her morning's adventure; and once again she said to herself, with a little regretful sigh, "Whose, then, was the photograph?" But she put the thought away from her.

After all, she said to herself, it made no difference. He was still Sir John Kynaston of Kynaston Hall, and just as well worth a woman's while to marry. She had made some mistake, that was all; and the real Sir John was not the least romantic or interesting to look at, but Kynaston Hall belonged to him all the same.

They were not very exalted or very much to be admired, these dreams of Vera's girlhood. But neither were they quite so coarse and unlovely as would have been those of a purely mercenary woman. She was free from the vulgarity of desiring the man's money and his name from any desire to raise herself above her relations, or to feed her own vanity and ambition at their expense. It was only that, marriage being a necessity for her, to marry anything but a rich man would have been, with her tastes and the habits to which she had been brought up, the sheerest and rankest folly. She thought she could make a good wife to any man whose life she would like to share— that is to say, a life of ease and affluence. She knew she would make a very bad wife to a poor man. Therefore she determined upon so carving out her own fortunes that she should not make a failure of herself. It was worldly wisdom of the purest and simplest character.

She was as much determined as ever upon winning Kynaston's owner if he was to be won. Only she wished, with a little sigh, that he had happened to be the man in the photograph. She hardly knew why she wished it—but the wish was there.

She sat bending over her fire, with all her soft, dark hair loose about her face and flowing down her back, and her eyes fixed dreamily upon the flames. Her past life came back to her, her old life in the whirl and turmoil of pleasure which had suited her so well. She compared it, a little drearily, with the present; with the humdrum routine of the vicarage; with the parish talk about the old women and the schools; and the small tittle-tattle about the schoolmaster and the choir, going on around her all day; with old Mrs. Daintree's sharp tongue and her sister's meek rejoinders. She was very tired of it. It did not amuse her. She was not exactly discontented with her lot. Eustace and her sister were very kind to her, and she loved them dearly; but she did not live their life—she was with them, but not of them. As for herself, for her interests and her delights, they stagnated amongst them all. How long was it to last?

And Kynaston, by contrast, appeared very fair, with its smooth lawns and its terrace walks, and its great desolate rooms, that she would so well understand how to fill with life and brightness; but Kynaston's master counted for very little to her. She knew the power of her own beauty so well. Experience had taught her that Vera Nevill had but to smile and to win; it had been so easy to her to be loved and wooed.

"Only," she said to herself, as she stood up before her fire, and stretched up her arms so that her long hair fell back like a cloud around her, "only he is a different sort of man to what I had pictured him. It will, perhaps, not be such an easy matter to win a man like that."

She went to bed and dreamt—not of Sir John Kynaston—but of the man whose pictured face once seen had haunted her ever since.

CHAPTER V.

"LITTLE PITCHERS."

Once at least in a man's life, if only for a brief space, he reverencesthe saint in the woman he desires. He may love and pursue again and again, but she who has power to hold him back, who can make him tremble instead of woo, who can make him silent when he feels eloquent, and restrained when most impassioned, has won from him what never again can be given.

It was an easier matter to win him than Vera thought.

A week later Sir John Kynaston sat alone by his library fire, after breakfast, and owned to himself that he had fallen hopelessly and helplessly in love with Vera Nevill.

This was all the more remarkable because Sir John was not a very young man, and that he was, moreover, not of a nature to do things rashly or impulsively.

He was, on the contrary, of a slow and hesitating disposition. He was in the habit of weighing his words and his actions before he spoke or acted, his mind was tardy to take in new thoughts and new ideas, and he was cautious and almost sluggish in taking any steps in a strange and unaccustomed direction.

Nevertheless, in this matter of Vera, he had succumbed to his fate with all the uncalculating blindness of a boy in his teens.

Vera was like no other woman he had ever seen; she was as far removed above common young-ladyhood as Raphael's Madonnas are beyond and above Greuze's simpering maidens; there could be no other like her—she was a queen, a goddess among women.

From the very first moment that he had caught sight of her on the terrace outside his house her absolute mastery over him had begun. Her rare beauty, her quiet smile, her slow, indolent movements, the very tones of her rich, low voice, all impressed him in a strange and wonderful manner. She seemed to him to be the incarnation of everything that was pure and elevated in womanhood. To have imagined that such a one as she could have thought of his wealth or his position would have been the rankest blasphemy in his eyes.

He raised her up on a pedestal of his own creating, and then he fell down before her and adored her.

John Kynaston had but little knowledge of women. Shy and retiring in manner—somewhat suspicious and distrustful also—he had kept out of their way through life. Once, in very early manhood, he had been deceived; he had become engaged to a girl whom he afterwards discovered to have accepted him only for his money and his name, whilst her heart really belonged to another and a poorer man. He had shaken himself free of her, with horror and disgust, and had sworn to himself that he would never be so betrayed again. Since then he had been suspicious—and not without just cause—of the young ladies who had smiled upon him, and of their mothers, who had pressed him with gracious invitations to their houses. He was a rich man, but he did not mean to be loved for his wealth; he said to himself that, sooner than be so, he would die unmarried and leave to Maurice the task of keeping up the old name and the old family.

But he had seen Vera; and all at once all the old barriers of pride and reserve were broken down! Here was the one woman on earth who realized his dreams, the one woman whom he would wait and toil for, even as Jacob waited and toiled for Rachel!

He had come down to Kynaston to hunt; but hitherto hunting had been very little in his thoughts. He had been down to the vicarage once or twice, he had met her once in the lanes, and he had longed for a glimpse of her daily; as yet he had done nothing else. He opened his letters on this particular morning slowly and abstractedly, tossing them into the fire, one after the other, as he read them, and not paying very much attention to their contents.

There was one, however, from his brother, "I wish you would ask me down to Kynaston for a week or two, old fellow," wrote Maurice. "I know you would mount me—now I have got rid of all my horses to please you—and I should like a glimpse of the old country. Write and tell me if I shall come down on Monday."

This letter Sir John did pay attention to. He rose hastily, as though not a moment was to be lost, and answered it:—

"Dear Maurice,—I can't possibly have you down here yet. My own plans are very uncertain, and if you are going to take your leave after Christmas, you had far better not go away from your work now. If I am still here in January, I shall be delighted if you will come down, and will mount you as much as you like."

He was happier when he had written and directed this letter.

"I must be alone just now," he murmured. "I could not bear Maurice's chatter—it would jar upon me."

Then he put on his hat and strolled out. He looked in at the stables one minute, and called the head groom to him.

"Wright, did not Mr. Beavan say, when I bought that new bay mare of him, that she had carried a lady to hounds?"

"Yes, Sir John; Miss Beavan rode her last season."

"Ah, she is a good rider. Well, I wish you would put a side-saddle and a skirt on her, and exercise her this morning. I might want to—to lend her to a lady; but she must be perfectly quiet. You can take her out every day this week."

Sir John went on his way, leaving the worthy Wright a prey to speculation as to who the mysterious lady might be for whom the bay mare was to be exercised.

His master, meanwhile, bent his steps almost instinctively to the vicarage.

Vera was undergoing a periodical persecution concerning Mr. Gisburne at the hands of old Mrs. Daintree. She was standing up by the table arranging some scarlet berries and some long trails of ivy which the children had brought to her in a vase. Tommy and Minnie stood by watching her intently; Mrs. Daintree sat at a little distance, her lap full of undarned socks, and rated her.

"It is not as if you were a girl who could earn her living in case of need. There is not one single thing you can do."

"Aunt Vera can make nosegays of berries boofully, grandma," interpolates Tommy, earnestly; "can't she, Minnie?"

"Yes, she do," assented the smaller child, with emphasis.

"I wasn't speaking to you, Tom; little boys should be—"

"Heard and not seen," puts in Tommy, rapidly; "you always say that, grandma."

Vera laughs softly. Mrs. Daintree goes on with her lecture.

"Many girls in your position are very accomplished; can teach the piano, and history, and the elements of Latin; but it seems to me you have been brought up in idleness."

"Idleness is not to be despised in its way," answers Vera, composedly. "Another bit of ivy, Tommy. What shall I do, Mrs. Daintree?" she continues, whilst her deft fingers wind the trailing greenery round and round the glass stem of the vase. "Shall I go down to the village school and sit at the feet of Mr. Dee? I have no doubt he could teach me a great many things I know nothing about."

"That is nonsense; of course I don't mean that you can educate yourself to any purpose now; it is too late for that; but you need not, at all events, turn up your nose at the blessings that Providence sets before you; and I must say, that for a young woman deliberately to choose to remain a burden upon her friends, betokens an amount of servility and a lack of the spirit of independence which I should not have supposed possible even in you!"

"What do you want me to do?" said Vera, without a sign of impatience. "Shall I walk over to Tripton this afternoon, and make a low curtsey to Mr. Gisburne, and say to him very politely, 'Here is an idle and penniless young woman who would be very pleased to stop here and marry you!' Would that be the way to do it, Mrs. Daintree?"

"No, no, *no!*" imperatively from Tommy, who was listening with rapidly crimsoning cheeks; "you shall *not* go and stop at Tripton, and tell Mr. Gisburne you will marry him!"

Vera laughed. "No, Tommy, I don't think I will; not, that is to say, if you are a good boy. I think I can do something better than that with myself!" she added, softly, as if to herself. Mrs. Daintree caught the words.

"And *what* better, pray? What better chance are you ever likely to have? Let me tell you, bachelors who want penniless wives don't grow on the blackberry bushes down here! If you were not so selfish and so conceited, you would see where your duty to my son, who is supporting you, lay. You would see that to be married to an honest, upright man like Albert Gisburne is a chance that most girls would catch at only too thankfully."

The old lady had raised her voice; she spoke loud and angrily; she was rapidly working herself into a passion. Tommy, accustomed to family rows, stood on the hearthrug, looking excitedly from his grandmother to his aunt. He was a precocious child; he did not quite understand, and yet he understood partly. He knew that his grandmother was scolding Vera, and telling her she was to go away and marry Mr. Gisburne. That Vera should go away! That, in itself, was sufficiently awful. Tommy adored Vera with all the intensity of his childish soul; that she should go away from him to Mr. Gisburne seemed to him the most terrible visitation that could possibly happen. His little heart swelled within him; the tears were very near his eyes.

At this very minute the door softly opened, and Sir John Kynaston, whose ring had been unheard in the commotion, was ushered in.

Tommy thought he saw a deliverer, specially sent in by Providence for the occasion. He made one spring at him and caught him round the legs, after the manner of enthusiastic small boys.

"Please—please—don't let grandmamma send aunt Vera away to Tripton to marry Mr. Gisburne! He has red hair, and I hate him; and aunt Vera doesn't want to go, she wants to stop at home and do something better!"

A moment of utter confusion on all sides; then Vera, crimson to the roots of her hair, stepped forward and held out her hand.

"Little pitchers have long ears!" she said, laughing: "and Tommy is a very silly little boy."

"No, but, aunt Vera, you said—you said," cried the child. What further revelations he might have made were fortunately not destined to be known. His aunt placed her hand unceremoniously over his small, eager mouth, and hustled both children in some haste out of the room.

Meanwhile, Sir John, looking the picture of distress and embarrassment, had shaken hands with the old lady, and inquired if he could speak with her son.

"Mr. Daintree is in his study; I will take you to him," she said, rising, and led him away out of the room. She looked at him sharply as she showed him into the study; and it did come across her mind, "I wonder what you come so often for." Still, no thought of Vera entered into her head. Sir John was the great man of the place, the squire, the potentate in the hollow of whose hand lay Sutton-in-the-Wold and all its inhabitants, and Vera was a nobody in the old lady's eyes,—a waif, whose presence was of no account at all. Sir John was no more likely to notice her than any of the village girls; except, indeed, that he would speak politely to her because she was Eustace's sister-in-law. Still, it did come across her mind to wonder what he came so often for.

Five minutes later the two gentlemen were seen going across the vicarage garden towards the church.

They remained there a very long time, more than half an hour. When they came back Marion had finished her housekeeping and was in the room busy cutting out unbleached calico into poor men's shirts, on the grand piano, an instrument which she maintained had been specially and originally called into existence for no other purpose. Mrs. Daintree still sat in her chimney corner. Vera was at the writing-table with her back to the room, writing a letter.

The vicar came in with his face all aglow with excitement and delight; his wife looked up at him quickly, she saw that something unusual and of a pleasant character had happened.

"My dear Marion, we must both thank our good friend, Sir John. I am happy to tell you that he has consented to restore the chancel."

"Oh, Sir John, how can we ever thank you enough!" cried Marion, coming forward breathlessly and pressing his hands in eager gratitude. Sir John looked as if he didn't want to be thanked, but he glanced towards the writing-table. Vera's back was turned; she made no sign of having heard.

"I am sure I had given up all hopes of it altogether," continued the vicar. "You gave such an unqualified refusal when I spoke to you about it before, I never dreamt that you would be induced to change your mind."

"Some one—I mean—I thought it over—and—and it was presented to my notice—in another light," stammered Sir John, somewhat confusedly.

"And it is most kind, most generous of you to allow it to be done in my own way, according to the plans I had wished to follow."

"Oh, I am quite sure you will understand it much better than I am likely to do. Besides, I have no time to attend to it; it will suit me better to leave it entirely in your hands."

"Would you not like to see the plans Mr. Woodley drew for us last year?"

"Not now, I think, thank you; I must be going; another time, Mr. Daintree; I can't wait just now."

He was standing irresolute in the middle of the room. He looked again wistfully at Vera's back. Was it possible that she was not going to give him one word, one look, when surely she must know by whose influence he had been induced to consent to rebuild the chancel!

Almost in despair he moved to the door, and just as he reached it, when his hand was already on the handle, she looked up. Her eyes, all softened with pleasure and gratitude, nay, almost with tenderness, met his. He stopped suddenly short.

"Miss Nevill, might I ask you to walk with me as far as the clerk's cottage? I—I forget which it is!"

It was the lamest and most blundering excuse. Any six-year-old child in the village could have pointed out the cottage to him. Mrs. Daintree looked up in astonishment. Vera blushed rosy red; Eustace, man-like, saw nothing, and began eagerly,

"I am walking that way myself; we can go together——" Suddenly his coat tails were violently pulled from behind. "Quite impossible, Eustace; I want you at home for the next hour," says Marion, quietly standing by his side, with a look of utter innocence upon her face. The vicar, almost throttled by the violence of the assault upon his garments, perceived that, in some mysterious manner, he had said something he ought not to have said. He deemed it wisest to subside into silence.

Vera rose from the writing-table. "I will go and put my hat on," she said, quietly, and left the room.

Three minutes later she and Sir John went out of the front door together.

"Well, that is the oddest fellow I ever came across in my life," said Eustace, fairly puzzled as soon as he was gone. "It is my belief," tapping his forehead significantly, "that he is a little touched *here*. I don't believe he quite knows what he is talking about. Why, the other night he would have nothing to say to the chancel, wouldn't even listen to me, cut me so short about it I really couldn't venture to pursue the subject; and here he comes, ten days later, all of his own accord, and proposes to do it exactly as it ought to be done, in the best and most expensive way—purbeck columns round the lancet windows, and all, Marion, just what I wanted; gives me absolute *carte blanche* about it. I only hope he won't take a fresh fancy into his head and change his mind again."

"Perhaps he found he would make himself unpopular if he did not do it," suggested his mother.

Marion held her tongue, and snipped away at her unbleached calico.

"And then, again, about old Hoggs' cottage," pursued Mr. Daintree. "What on earth could make him forget where it was? He might as well forget the way to his own house. I really do think he must be a little gone in the upper storey, poor fellow! Marion, what have you to say about it?"

"I have to say that if you stand chattering here all the morning, we shall never get anything done. I want to speak to you immediately, Eustace, in the other room."

She hurried her husband out into the study, and carefully closed the door upon them.

What then was the Rev. Eustace's amazement to behold his wife suddenly execute a series of capers round the room, which would not have disgraced a *coryphée* at a Christmas pantomime, but were hardly in keeping with the demure and highly respectable bearing of the wife of the vicar of Sutton-in-the-Wold!

Mr. Daintree began to think that everybody was going mad this morning.

"My dear Marion, what on earth is the matter?"

"Oh, you dear, stupid, blunder-headed old donkey!" exclaimed his wife, finishing her *pas seul* in front of him, and hugging him vehemently as a finale to the entertainment. "Do you mean to say that you don't see it?"

"See it? See what?" repeated the unfortunate clergyman, in mortal bewilderment, staring at her hard.

"Oh, you dear, stupid old goose! why, it's as plain as daylight. Can't you guess?"

Eustace shook his head dolefully.

"Why, Sir John Kynaston has fallen in love with Vera!"

"*Marion!* impossible!" in an awe-struck whisper. "What can make you imagine such a thing?"

"Why, everything—the chancel, of course. She must have spoken to him about it; it is to be done for her; did you not see him look at her? And then, asking her to go down the village with him; he knows where Hoggs' cottage is as well as you do, only he couldn't think of anything better."

Eustace literally gasped with the magnitude of the revelation.

"Great Heavens! and I offered to go with him instead of her."

"Yes, you great blundering baby!"

"Oh, my dear, are you sure—are you quite sure? Remember his position and Vera's."

"Well, and isn't Vera good enough, and beautiful enough, for any position?" answered her sister, proudly.

"Yes, yes; that is true; God bless her!" he said, fervently. "Marion, what a clever woman you are to find it out."

"Of course I am clever, sir. But, Eustace, it is only beginning, you know; so we must just let things take their course, and not seem to notice anything. And, mind, not a word to your mother."

Meanwhile Vera and Sir John Kynaston were walking down the village street together. The man awkward and ill at ease, the woman calm and composed, and thoroughly mistress of the occasion.

"It is very good of you about the chancel," said Vera, softly, breaking the embarrassment of the silence between them.

"You *knew* I should do it," he said, looking at her.

She smiled. "I thought perhaps you would."

"You know *why* I am going to do it—for whose sake, do you not?" he pursued, still keeping his eyes upon her downcast face.

"Because it is the right thing to do, I hope; and for the sake of doing good," she answered, sedately; and Sir John felt immediately reproved and rebuked, as though by the voice of an angelic being.

"Tell me," he said, presently, "is it true that they want you to marry—that parson—Gisburne, of Tripton? Forgive me for asking."

Vera coloured a little and laughed.

"What dreadful things little boys are!" was all she said.

"Nay, but I want to know. Are you—are you *engaged* to him?" with a sudden painful eagerness of manner.

"Most decidedly I am not," she answered, earnestly.

Sir John breathed again.

"I don't know what you will think of me; you will, perhaps, say I am very impertinent. I know I have no right to question you."

"I only think you are very kind to take an interest in me," she answered, gently, looking at him with that wonderful look in her shadowy eyes that came into them unconsciously when she felt her softest and her best.

They had passed through the village by this time into the quiet lane beyond; needless to say that no thought of Hoggs, the clerk, or his cottage, had come into either of their heads by the way.

Sir John stopped short, and Vera of necessity stopped too.

"I thought—it seemed to me by what I overheard," he said, hesitatingly, "that they were tormenting you—persecuting you, perhaps—into a marriage you do not wish for."

"They have wished me to marry Mr. Gisburne," Vera admitted, in a low voice, rustling the fallen brown leaves with her foot, her eyes fixed on the ground.

"But you won't let them over-persuade you; you won't be induced to listen to them, will you? Promise me you won't?" he asked, anxiously.

Vera looked up frankly into his face and smiled.

"I give you my word of honour I will not marry Mr. Gisburne," she answered; and then she added, laughingly, "You had no business to make me betray that poor man's secrets."

And then Sir John laughed too, and, changing the subject, asked her if she would like to ride a little bay mare he had that he thought would carry her. Vera said she would think of it, with the air of a young queen accepting a favour from a humble subject; and Sir John thanked her as heartily as though she had promised him some great thing.

"Now, suppose we go and find Hoggs' cottage," she said, smiling. And they turned back towards the village.

CHAPTER VI.

A SOIRÉE AT WALPOLE LODGE.

When the lute is broken,
Sweet notes are remembered not;
When the lips have spoken,
Loved accents are soon forgot.
As music and splendour
Survive not the lamp and the lute,
The heart's echoes render
No song when the spirit is mute.

SHELLEY.

About three miles from Hyde Park Corner, somewhere among the cross-roads between Mortlake and Kew, there stands a rambling, old-fashioned house, within about four acres of garden, surrounded by a very high, red-brick wall. It is one of those houses of which there used to be scores within the immediate neighbourhood of London—of which there still are dozens, although, alas! they are yearly disappearing to make room for gay rows of pert, upstart villas, whose tawdry flashiness ill replaces the sedate respectability of their last-century predecessors. But, uncoveted by the contractor's lawless eye, untouched by the builder's desecrating hand, Walpole Lodge stands on, as it did a hundred years ago, hidden behind the shelter of its venerable walls, and half smothered under masses of wisteria and Virginia creeper. On the wall, in summer time, grow countless soft green mosses, and brown, waving grasses. Thick masses of yellow stonecrop and tufts of snapdragon crown its summit, whilst the topmost branches of the long row of lime-trees within come nodding sweet-scented greetings to the passers-by along the dusty high road below.

But in the winter the wall is flowerless and the branches of the lime-trees are bare, and within, in the garden, there are only the holly-trees and the yew-hedge of the shrubbery walks, and the empty brown flower-beds set in the faded grass. But winter and summer alike, old Lady Kynaston holds her weekly receptions, and thither flock all the wit, and the talent, and the fashion of London. In the summer they are garden parties, in the winter they become evening receptions. How she manages it no one can quite tell; but so it is, that her rooms are always crowded, that no one is ever bored at her house, that people are always keen to come to her, and that there are hundreds who would think it an effort to go to other people's parties across the street who think it no trouble at all to drive nearly to Richmond, to hers. She has the rare talent of making society a charm in itself. No one who is not clever, or beautiful, or distinguished in some way above his or her fellows ever gains a footing in her drawing-rooms. Every one of any note whatever is sure to be found there. There are savants and diplomatists, poets and painters, foreign ambassadors, and men of science. The fashionable beauty is sure to be met there side by side with the latest type of strong-minded woman; the German composer, with the wild hair, whose music is to regenerate the future, may be seen chatting to a cabinet minister; the most rising barrister of the day is lingering by the side of a prima-donna, or discoursing to an Eastern traveller. Old Lady Kynaston herself has charming manners, and possesses the rare tact of making every one feel at home and happy in her house.

It was not done in a day—this gathering about her of so brilliant and delightful a society. She had lived many years at Walpole Lodge, ever since her widowhood, and was now quite an old lady. In her early life she had written several charming books—chiefly biographies of distinguished men whom she had known, and even now she occasionally put pen again to paper, and sent some delightful social essay or some pleasantly written critique to one or other of the Reviews of the day.

Her married life had been neither very long nor very happy. She had never learnt to love her husband's country home. At his death she had turned her back thankfully upon Kynaston, and had never seen it again. Of her two sons, she stood in some awe of the elder, whose cold and unresponsive character resembled her dead husband's, whilst she adored Maurice, who was warm-hearted and affectionate in manner, like herself. There were ten years between them, for she had been married twelve years; and at her secret heart Lady Kynaston hoped and believed that John would remain unmarried, so that the estates and the money might in time become Maurice's.

It is the second Thursday in December, and Lady Kynaston is "at home" to the world. Her drawing-rooms—there are three of them, not large, but low, comfortable rooms, opening one out of the other—are filled, as usual, with a mixed and brilliant crowd.

Across the square hall is the dining-room, where a cold supper, not very sumptuous or very *recherché*, but still sufficient of its kind for the occasion, is laid out; and beyond that is Lady Kynaston's boudoir, where there is a piano, and which is used on these occasions as a music-room, so that those who are musical may retire there, and neither interfere, nor be interfered with, by the rest of the company. Some one is singing in the music-room now—singing well, you may be sure, or he would not be at Walpole Lodge—but the strains of the song can hardly be heard at all across dining-room and hall, in the larger of the three rooms, where most of the guests are congregated.

Lady Kynaston, a small, slight woman in soft gray satin and old lace, moves about graciously and gracefully still, despite her seventy years, among her guests—stopping now at one group, now at another, talking politics to one, science to a second, whispering a few discreet words about the latest scandal to this great lady, murmuring words of approval upon her clever book or her charming poem to another. Her smiles are equally dispensed, no one is passed over, and she has the rare talent of making every single individual in the crowded room feel himself to be the one particular person whom Lady Kynaston is especially rejoiced to see. She has tact, and she has sympathy— two invaluable gifts in a woman.

Conspicuous among the crowd of well-dressed and handsome women is Helen Romer. She sits on an ottoman at the further end of the room, where she holds a little court of her own, dispensing her smiles and pleasant words among the little knot of men who linger admiringly by her side.

She is in black, with masses of gold embroidery about her, and she carries a large black and gold feather fan in her hands, which she moves rapidly, almost restlessly, up and down; her eyes wander often to the doorway, and every now and then she raises her hand with a short, impatient action to her blonde head, as though she were half weary of the talk about her.

Presently, Lady Kynaston, moving slowly among her guests, comes near her, and, leaning for a moment on the back of the ottoman, presses her hand as she passes.

Mrs. Romer is a favourite of hers; she is pretty, and she is piquant in manner and conversation; two very good things, which she thinks highly of in any young woman. Besides that, she knows that Helen loves her younger son; and, although she hardly understands how things are between them, nor how far Maurice himself is implicated, she believes that Helen will eventually inherit her grandfather's money, and, liking her personally, she has seen no harm in encouraging her too plainly displayed affection. Moreover, the love they both bear to him has been a link between them. They talk of him together almost as a mother and a daughter might do; they have the same anxieties over his health, the same vexations over his debts, the same rejoicings when his brother comes forward with his much-needed help. Lady Kynaston does not want her darling to marry yet, but when the time shall come for him to take unto himself a wife, she will raise no objection to pretty Helen Romer, should he bring her to her, as a daughter-in-law.

As the old lady stoops over her, Helen's upturned wistful eyes say as plainly as words can say it—

"Is he coming to-night?"

"Maurice will be here presently, I hope," says his mother, answering the look in her eyes; "he was to come up by the six o'clock train; he will dine at his club and come on here later." Helen's face became radiant, and Lady Kynaston passed on.

Maurice Kynaston's regiment was quartered at Northampton; he came up to town often for the day or for the night, as he could get leave; but his movements were never quite to be depended upon.

Half-an-hour or so more of feverish impatience. Helen watches the gay crowd about her with a feeling of sick weariness. Two members of Parliament are talking of Russian aggression and Turkish misrule close to her; they turn to her presently and include her in the conversation; Mrs. Romer gives her opinion shrewdly and sensibly. An elderly duchess is describing some episode of Royalty's last ball; there is a general laugh, in which Helen joins heartily; a young attaché bends over her and whispers some admiring little speech in her ear, and she blushes and smiles just as if she liked it above all things; while all the time her eyes hardly stray for one second from the open doorway through which Maurice will come, and her heart is saying to itself, over and over again,

"Will he come, will he come?"

He comes at last. Long before the servant, who opens the door to him, has taken his coat and hat from him, Helen catches sight of his handsome head and his broad shoulders through an opening in the crowd. In another minute he is in the room standing irresolute in the doorway, looking round as if to see who is and who is not there to-night.

He is, after all, only a very ordinary type of a good-looking soldierly young Englishman, just such a one as may be seen any day in our parks or our drawing-rooms. He has clearly-cut and rather *prononcé* features, a strong-built, well made figure, a long moustache, close-shaven cheeks, and eyes that are rather deep-set, and are, when you are near enough to see them well, of a deep blue-gray. In all that Maurice Kynaston is in no way different from scores of other good-looking young men whom we may have met. But there is just something that makes his face a remarkable one: it is a strong-looking face—a face that looks as if he had a will of his own and knew how to stick to it; a face that looks, too, as if he could do and dare much for truth and honour's sake. It is almost stern when he is silent; it can soften into the tenderness of a woman when he speaks.

Look at him now as he catches sight of his mother, and steps forward for a minute to press her loving hands. All the hardness and all the strength are gone out of his face now; he only looks down at her with eyes full of love and gentleness—for life as yet holds nothing dearer or better for him than that little white-haired old woman. Only for a minute, and then he leaves go of her hands, and passes on down the room, speaking to the guests whom he knows.

"He does not see me," says Helen, bitterly, to herself; "he will go on into the next room, and never know that I am here."

But he had seen her perfectly. Next to the woman he most wishes to see in a room, the one whom a man first catches sight of is the woman he would sooner were not there. He had seen Helen the very instant he came in, but he had noticed thankfully that some one was talking to her, and he said to himself that there was no occasion for him to hurry to her side; it was not as if they were openly engaged; there could be no necessity for him to rush into slavery at once; he would speak to her, of course, by-and-by; and whenever he came to her he well knew that he would be equally welcomed: he was so sure of her. Nothing on earth or under Heaven is so fatal to a man's love as that. There was no longer any uncertainty; there was none of the keenness of pursuit dear to the old hunting instinct inherent in man; there was not even the charm of variety in her moods. She was always the same to him; always she pouted a little at first, and looked ill-tempered, and reproached him; and always she came round again at his very first kind word, and poured out her heart in a torrent of worship at his feet. Maurice knew it all by heart, the sulks and the cross words, and then the passionate denials, and the wild protestations of her undying love. He was sorry for her, too, in his way; he was too tender-hearted, too chivalrous, to be anything but kind to her; but though he was sorry, he could not love her; and, oh! how insufferably weary of her he was!

Presently he did come up to her, and took the seat by her side just vacated by the attaché. The little serio-comedy instantly repeated itself.

A little pout and a little toss of the head.

"You have been as long coming to speak to me as you possibly could be."

"Do you think it would look well if I had come rushing up to you the instant I came in?"

"You need not, at all events, have stood talking for ten minutes to that great black-eyed Lady Anderleigh. Of course, if you like her better than me, you can go back to her."

"Of course I can, if I choose, you silly little woman; but seeing that I am by you, and not by her, I suppose it is a proof that I prefer your society, is it not?"

Very polite, but not strictly true, Captain Maurice! At his heart he preferred talking to Lady Anderleigh, or to any other woman in the room. The admission, however, was quite enough for Helen.

"Dear Maurice," she whispered, "forgive me; I am a jealous, bad-tempered wretch, but," lower still, "it is only because I love you so much."

And had there been no one in the room, Maurice knew perfectly that at this juncture Mrs. Romer would have cast her arms around his neck—as usual.

To his unspeakable relief, a man—a clever lawyer, whose attention was a flattering thing to any woman—came up to Helen at this moment, and took a vacant chair beside her. Maurice thankfully slipped away, leaving his inamorata in a state of rage and disgust with that talented and elderly lawyer, such as no words can describe.

Captain Kynaston took the favourable opportunity of escaping across the hall, where he spent the remainder of the evening, dividing his attention between the music and supper rooms, and Helen saw him no more that night.

She saw, however, some one she had not reckoned upon seeing. Glancing carelessly across to the end of the room, she perceived, talking to Lady Kynaston, a little French gentleman, with a smooth black head, a neat, pointed, little black beard, and the red ribbon of the Légion d'Honneur in his button-hole.

What there was in the sight of so harmless and inoffensive a personage to upset her it may be difficult to say; but the fact is that, when Mrs. Romer perceived this polite little Frenchman talking to her hostess, she turned suddenly so sick and white, that a lady sitting near her asked her if she was going to faint.

"I feel it a little hot," she murmured; "I think I will go into the next room." She rose and attempted to escape—whether from the heat or the observation of the little Frenchman was best known to herself.

Her maneuver, however, was not destined to succeed. Before she could work her way half-way through the crush to the door, the man whom she was bent upon avoiding turned round and saw her. A look of glad recognition flashed into his face, and he instantly left Lady Kynaston's side, and came across the room to speak to her.

"This is an unlooked-for pleasure, madame."

"I certainly never expected to meet you here, Monsieur D'Arblet," faltered Helen, turning red and white alternately.

"Will you not come and have a little conversation with me?"

"I was just going away."

"So soon! Oh, bien! then I will take you to your carriage." He held out his arm, and Helen was perforce obliged to take it.

There was a little delay in the hall, whilst Helen waited for her, or rather for her grandfather's carriage, during which she stood with her hand upon her unwelcome friend's arm. Whilst they were waiting he whispered something eagerly in her ear.

"No, no; it is impossible!" reiterated Helen, with much apparent distress.

Monsieur D'Arblet whispered something more.

"Very well, if you insist upon it!" she said, faintly, and then got into her carriage and was driven away.

Before, however, she had left Walpole Lodge five minutes, she called out to the servants to stop the carriage. The footman descended from the box and came round to the window.

They had drawn up by the side of a long wall quite beyond the crowd of carriages that was waiting at Lady Kynaston's house.

"I want to wait here a few minutes, for—for a gentleman I am going to drive back to town," she said to the servant, confusedly. She was ashamed to give such an order to him.

She was frightened too, and trembled with nervousness lest any one should see her waiting here.

It was a cold, damp night, and Helen shivered, and drew her fur cloak closer about her in the darkness. Presently there came footsteps along the pathway, and a man came through the fog up to the door. It was opened for him in silence, and he got in, and the carriage drove off again.

Monsieur Le Vicomte D'Arblet had a mean, cunning-looking countenance; strictly speaking, indeed, he was rather handsome, his features being decidedly well-shaped, but the evil and vindictive expression of his face made it an unpleasant one to look upon. As he took his seat in the brougham by Helen's side she shrank instinctively away from him.

"So, ma mie!" he said, peering down into her face with odious familiarity, "here I find you again after all this time, beautiful as ever! It is charming to be with you again, once more."

"Monsieur D'Arblet, pray understand that nothing but absolute necessity would have induced me to drive you home to-night," said Helen, who was trembling violently.

"You are not polite, ma belle—there is a charming *franchise* about you Englishwomen, however, which gives a piquancy to your conversation."

"You know very well why it is that I am obliged to speak to you alone," she interrupted, colouring hotly under his bold looks of admiration.

"*Le souvenir du beau passé!*" murmured the Frenchman, laughing softly. "Is that it, ma belle Hélène?"

"Monsieur," she cried, almost in tears, "pray listen to me; for pity's sake tell me what you have done with my letters—have you destroyed them?"

"Destroyed them! What, those dear letters that are so precious to my heart? Ah, madame, could you believe it of me?"

"You have kept them?" she murmured, faintly.

"Mais si, certainement, that I have kept them, every one—every single one of them," he repeated, looking at her meaningly, with a cold glitter in his black eyes.

"Not that—*that* one?" pleaded Helen, piteously.

"Yes—that one too—that charming and delightful letter in which you so generously offered to throw yourself upon my protection—do you remember it?"

"Alas, only too well!" she murmured, hiding her face in her hands.

"Ah!" he continued, with a sort of relish in torturing her, which resembled the feline cruelty of a wild beast playing with its prey. "Ah! it was a delightful letter, that; what a pity it was that I was out of Paris that night, and never received it till, alas! it was too late to rush to your side. You remember how it was, do you not? Your husband was lying ill at your hotel; you were very tired of him—ce pauvre mari! Well, you had been tired of him for some time, had you not? And he was not what you ladies call 'nice;' he did drink, and he did swear, and I had been often to see you when he was out, and had taken you to the theatre and the bal d'Opéra—do you remember?"

"Ah, for Heaven's sake spare me these horrible reminiscences!" cried Helen, despairingly.

He went on pitilessly, as though he had not heard her, "And you were good enough to write me several letters—there were one, two, three, four of them," counting them off upon his fingers; "and then came the fifth—that one you wrote when he was ill. Was it not a sad pity that I had gone out of Paris for the day, and never received it till you and your husband had left for England? But think you that I will part with it ever? It is my consolation, my trésor!"

"Monsieur D'Arblet, if you have one spark of honour or of gentleman-like feeling, you will give me those mad, foolish letters again. I entreat you to do so. You know that I was beside myself when I wrote them, I was so unhappy—do you not see that they compromise me fatally; that it is my good name, my reputation, which are at stake?" In her agony she had half sunk at his feet on the floor of the carriage, clasping her hands entreatingly together.

Monsieur D'Arblet raised her with *empressement.*

"Ah, madame, do not thus humiliate yourself at my feet. Why should you be afraid? Are not your good name and your reputation safe in my hands?"

Helen burst into bitter tears.

"How cruel, how wicked you are!" she cried; "no Englishman would treat a lady in this way."

"Your Englishmen are fools, ma chère—and I—I am French!" he replied, shrugging his shoulders expressively.

"But what object, what possible cause can you have for keeping those wretched letters?"

He bent his face down close to hers.

"Shall I tell you, belle Hélène? It is this: You are beautiful and you have talent; I like you. Some day, perhaps, when the grandpapa dies, you will have money—then Lucien D'Arblet will come to you, madame, with that precious little packet in his hands, and he will say, 'You will marry me, ma chère, or I will make public these letters.' Do you see? Till then, amusez vous, ma belle; enjoy your life and your liberty as much as you desire; I will not object to anything you do. Only you will not venture to marry—because I have these letters?"

"You would prevent my marrying?" said Helen, faintly.

"Mais, certainement that I should. Do you suppose any man would care to be your husband after he had read that last letter—the fifth, you know?"

No answer, save the choking sobs of his companion.

Monsieur D'Arblet waited a few minutes, watching her; then, as she did not raise her head from the cushions of the carriage, where she had buried it, the Frenchman pulled the check-string of the carriage.

"Now," he said, "I will wish you good-night, for we are close to your house. We have had our little talk, have we not?"

The brougham, stopped, and the footman opened the door.

"Good-night, madame, and many thanks for your kindness," said D'Arblet, raising his hat politely.

In another minute he was gone, and Helen, hoping that the darkness had concealed the traces of her agitation from the servant's prying eyes, was driven on, more dead than alive, to her grandfather's house.

CHAPTER VII.

EVENING REVERIES.

For nothing on earth is sadder
Than the dream that cheated the grasp,
The flower that turned to the adder,
The fruit that changed to the asp,
When the dayspring in darkness closes,
As the sunset fades from the hills,
With the fragrance of perished roses,
And the music of parched-up rills.

A. L. GORDON.

It had been the darkest chapter of her life, that fatal month in Paris, when she had foolishly and recklessly placed herself in the power of a man so unscrupulous and so devoid of principle as Lucien D'Arblet.

It had begun in all innocence—on her part, at least. She had been very miserable; she had discovered to the full how wild a mistake her marriage had been. She had felt herself to be fatally separated from Maurice, the man she loved, for ever; and Monsieur D'Arblet had been kind to her; he had pitied her for being tied to a husband who drank and who gambled, and Helen had allowed herself to be pitied. D'Arblet had charming manners, and an accurate knowledge of the weakness of the fair sex; he knew when to flatter and when to cajole her, when to be tenderly sympathetic to her sorrows, and when to divert her thoughts to brighter and pleasanter topics than her own miseries. He succeeded in fascinating her completely. Whilst her husband was occupied with his own disreputable friends, Helen, sooner than remain alone in their hotel night after night, was persuaded to accept Monsieur D'Arblet's escort to theatres and operas, and other public places, where her constant presence with him very soon compromised her amongst the few friends who knew her in Paris.

Then came scenes with her husband; frantic letters of misery to this French vicomte, whom she imagined to be so devotedly attached to her, and, finally, one ever-to-be-repented letter, in which she offered to leave her husband for ever and to come to him.

True, this letter did not reach its destination till too late, and Helen was mercifully saved from the fate which, in her wicked despair, she was ready to rush upon. Twenty-four hours after her return to England she saw the horrible abyss upon which she had stood, and thanked God from the bottom of her heart that she had been rescued, in spite of herself, from so dreadful a deed. But the letter had been written, and was in Lucien D'Arblet's possession. Later on she learnt, by a chance conversation, the true character of the man, and shuddered when she remembered how nearly she had wrecked her whole life for him. And when her husband's death had placed her once more in the security and affluence of her grandfather's house, with fresh hopes and fresh chances before her, she had but one wish with regard to that Parisian episode of her life,—to forget it as though it had never been.

She hoped, and, as time went on, she felt sure, that she would never see Monsieur D'Arblet again. New hopes and new excitements occupied her thoughts. The man to whom in her youth she had given her heart once more came across her life; she was thrown very much into his society; she learnt to love him more devotedly than ever, and when at last she had succeeded in establishing the sort of engagement which existed between them, she had assured him, and also assured herself, that no other man had ever, for one instant, filled her fancy. That stormy chapter of her married life was forgotten; she resolutely wiped it out of her memory, as if it had never existed.

And now, after all this time—it was five years ago—she had met him again—this Frenchman, who had once compromised her name, and who now had possession of her letters.

There was a cruel irony of fate in the fact that she should be destined to meet him again at Lady Kynaston's, the very house of all others where she would least have wished to see him.

There was, however, had she thought of it, nothing at all extraordinary in her having done so. No house in all London society was so open to foreigners as Walpole Lodge, and Monsieur Le Vicomte D'Arblet was no unknown upstart; he bore a good old name; he was clever, had taken an active part in diplomatic life, and was a very well-known individual in Parisian society. He had been brought to Lady Kynaston's by a member of the French Embassy, who was a frequenter of her soirées.

Neither, however, was meeting with Mrs. Romer entirely accidental on Monsieur D'Arblet's part. He had never forgotten the pretty Englishwoman who had so foolishly and recklessly placed herself in his power.

It is true he had lost sight of her, and other intrigues and other pursuits had filled his leisure hours; but when he came to England he had thought of her again, and had made a few careless inquiries after her. It was not difficult to identify her; the Mrs. Romer who was now a widow, who lived with her rich grandfather, who was very old, who would probably soon die and leave her all his wealth, was evidently the same Mrs. Romer whom he had known. The friend who gave him the information spoke of her as lovely and *spirituelle*, and as a woman who would be worth marrying some day. "She is often at Lady Kynaston's receptions," he had added.

"Mon cher, take me to your Lady Kynaston's soirées," had been Lucien D'Arblet's lazy rejoinder as they finished their evening smoke together. "I would like to meet my friend, la belle veuve, again, and I will see if she has forgotten me."

Bitter, very bitter, were Mrs. Romer's remorseful meditations that night when she reached her grandfather's house at Prince's Gate. Every detail of her acquaintance with Lucien D'Arblet came back to her with a horrible and painful distinctness. Over and over again she cursed her own folly, and bewailed the hardness of the fate which placed her once more in the hands of this man.

Would he indeed keep his cruel threats to her? Would he bring forward those letters to spoil her life once more—to prevent her from marrying Maurice should she ever have the chance of doing so?

Stooping alone over her fire, with all the brightness, and all the freshness gone out of her, with an old and almost haggard look in the face that was so lately beaming with smiles and dimples, Helen Romer asked herself shudderingly these bitter questions over and over again.

Had she been sure of Maurice's love, she would have been almost tempted to have confessed her fault, and to have thrown herself upon his mercy; but she knew that he did not love her well enough to forgive her. Too well she knew with what disgust and contempt Maurice would be likely to regard her past conduct; such a confession would, she knew, only induce him to shake himself clear of her for ever. Indeed, had he loved her, it is doubtful whether Maurice would have been able to condone so grave a fault in the past history of a woman; his own standard of honour stood too high to allow him to pass over lightly any disgraceful or dishonourable conduct in those with whom he had to do. But, loving her not, she would have been utterly without excuse in his eyes.

She knew it well enough. No, her only chance was in silence, and in vague hopes that time might rescue her out of her difficulties.

Meanwhile, whilst Helen Romer sat up late into the early morning, thinking bitterly over her past sins and her future dangers, Maurice Kynaston and his mother also kept watch together at Walpole Lodge after all the guests had gone away, and the old house was left alone again to the mother and son.

"Something troubles you, little mother," said Maurice, as he stretched himself upon the rug by her bedroom fire, and laid his head down caressingly upon her knees.

Lady Kynaston passed her hand fondly over the short dark hair. "How well you know my face, Maurice! Yes, something has worried me all day—it is a letter from your brother."

Maurice looked up laughingly. "What, is old John in trouble? That would be something new. Has he taken a leaf out of my book, mother, and dropped his money at Newmarket, too?"

"No, you naughty boy? John has got more sense. No!" with a sigh—"I wish it were only money; I fear it is a worse trouble than that."

"My dear mother, you alarm me," cried Maurice, looking up in mock dismay; "why, whatever has he been and gone and done?"

"Oh, Maurice, it is nothing to laugh at—it is some woman—a girl he has met down at Kynaston; some nobody—a clergyman's daughter, or sister, or something—whom he says he is going to marry!" Lady Kynaston looked the picture of distress and dismay.

Maurice laughed softly. "Well, well, mother; there is nothing very dreadful after all—I am sure I wish him joy."

"My boy," she said, below her breath, "I had so hoped, so trusted he would never marry—it seemed so unlikely—he seemed so completely happy in his bachelor's life; and I had hoped that you—that you——"

"Yes, yes, mother dear, I know," he said, quickly, and twisted himself round till he got her hand between his, kissing it as he spoke; "but I—I never thought of that—dear old John, he has been the best of brothers to me; and, mother dear, I know it is all your love to me; but you and I, dear, we will not grudge him his happiness, will we?"

He knew so well her weakness—how that she had loved him at the expense of the other son, who was not so dear to her; he loved her for it, and yet he did not at his heart think it right.

Lady Kynaston wiped a few tears away. "You are always right, my boy, always, and I am a foolish old woman. But oh, Maurice, that is only half the trouble! Who is this woman whom he has chosen? Some country girl, ignorant of the ways of the world, unformed and awkward—not fitted to be his wife!"

"Does he say so?" laughed Maurice.

"No, no, of course not. Stay, where is his letter? Oh, there, on the dressing-table; give it me, my dear. No, this is what he says: 'Miss Nevill seems to me in every way to fulfil my ideal of a good and perfect woman, and, if she will consent to marry me, I intend to make her my wife.'"

"Well, a good and perfect woman is a *rara avis*, at all events mother."

"Oh, dear! but all men say that of a girl when they are in love—it amounts to very little."

"You see, he has evidently not proposed to her yet; perhaps she will refuse him."

"Refuse Sir John Kynaston, of Kynaston Hall! A poor clergyman's daughter! My dear Maurice, I gave you credit for more knowledge of the world. Besides, John is a fine-looking man. Oh, no, she is not in the least likely to refuse him."

"Then all we have got to do is to make the best of her," said Maurice, composedly.

"That is easily said for you, who need see very little of her. But John's wife is a person who will be of great importance to my happiness. Dear me! and to think he might have had Lady Mary Hendrie for the asking: a charming creature, well born, highly educated and accomplished—everything that a man could wish for. And there were the De Vallery girls—either of them would have married him, and been a suitable wife for him; and he must needs go and throw himself away on a little country chit, who could have been equally happy, and much more suitably mated, with her father's curate. Maurice, my dear," with a sudden change of voice, "I wish you would go down and cut him out; if you made love to her ever so little you could turn her head, you know."

Maurice burst out laughing. "Oh, you wicked, immoral little mother! Did I ever hear such an iniquitous proposition! Do you want *me* to marry her?"

"No, no!" laughed his mother; "but you might make her think you meant to, and then, perhaps, she would refuse John."

"I have not Kynaston Hall at my back, remember, after which you have given her the credit of angling. Besides, mother dear, to speak plainly, I honestly do not think my taste in women is in the least likely to be the same as John's. No, I think I will keep out of the way whilst the love-making is going on. I will go down and have a look at the young woman by-and-by when it is all settled, and let you know what I think of her. I dare say a good, honest country lass will suit John far better than a beautiful woman of the world, who would be sure to be miserable with him. Don't fret, little mother; make the best of her if you can."

He rose and stretched himself up to his full height before the fire. Lady Kynaston looked up at him admiringly. Oh, she thought, if the money and the name could only have been his! How well he would have made use of it;

how proud she would have been of him—her handsome boy, whom all men liked, and all women would gladly love.

"A good son makes a good husband," she said aloud, following her own thoughts.

"And John has been a good son, mother," said Maurice, cordially.

"Yes, yes, in his way, perhaps; but I was thinking of you, my boy, not of him, and how lucky will be the woman who is your wife, Maurice—will it be———"

Maurice stooped quickly, and laid his hand playfully over her lips.

"I don't know, mother dear—never ask me—for I don't know it myself." And then he kissed her, and wished her good-night, and left her.

She sat long over her fire, dreaming, by herself, thinking a little, perhaps, of the elder son, and the bride he was going to bring her, whom she should have to welcome whether she liked her or no, but thinking more of the younger, whose inner life she had studied, and who was so entirely dear and precious to her. It was very little to her that he had been extravagant and thoughtless, that he had lost money in betting and racing—these were minor faults—and she and John between them had always managed to meet his difficulties; they had not been, in truth, very tremendous. But for that, he had never caused her one day's anxiety, never given her one instant's pain. "God grant he may get a wife who deserves him," was the mother's prayer that night. "I doubt if Helen be worthy of him; but if he loves her, as I believe he must do, no word of mine shall stand between him and his happiness."

And then she went to bed, and dreamed, as mothers dream of the child they love best.

CHAPTER VIII.

THE MEMBER FOR MEADOWSHIRE.

Honour and shame from no condition rise;
Act well your part, there all the honour lies.

POPE, "Essay on Man."

About five miles from Kynaston Hall, as the crow flies, across the fields, stood, as the house-agents would have described it, "a large and commodious modern mansion, standing in about eighty acres of well-timbered park land."

I do not know that any description that could be given of Shadonake would so well answer to the reality as the above familiar form of words.

The house was undoubtedly large, very large, and it was also modern, very modern. It was a handsome stone structure, with a colonnade of white pillars along the entrance side, and with a multiplicity of large plate-glass windows stretching away in interminable vistas in every direction. A broad gravel sweep led up to the front door; to the right were the stables, large and handsome too, with a clock-tower and a belfry over the gateway; and to the left were the gardens and the shrubberies.

There had been an old house once at Shadonake, old and picturesque and uncomfortable; but when the property had been purchased by the present owner—Mr. Andrew Miller—after he had been returned as Conservative member for the county, the old house was swept away, and a modern mansion, more suited to the wants and requirements of his family, arose in its place.

The park was flat, but well wooded. The old trees, of course, remained intact; but the gardens of the first house, being rambling and old-fashioned, had been done away with, to make room for others on a larger and more imposing scale; and vineries and pineries, orchid-houses, and hot-houses of every description arose rapidly all over the site of the old bowling-green and the wilderness, half kitchen garden, half rosary, that had served to content the former owners of Shadonake, now all lying dead and buried in the chancel of the village church.

The only feature of the old mansion which had been left untouched was rather a remarkable one. It was a large lake or pond, lying south of the gardens, and about a quarter of a mile from the house. It lay in a sort of dip in the ground, and was surrounded on all four sides—for it was exactly square—by very steep high banks, which had been cut into by steep stone steps, now gray, and broken, and moss-grown, which led down straight into the water. This pool was called Shadonake Bath. How long the steps had existed no one knew; probably for several hundred years, for there was a ghost story connected with them. Somebody was supposed, before the memory of any one living, to have been drowned there, and to haunt the steps at certain times of the year.

It is certain that but for the fact of a mania for boating, and punting, and skating indulged in by several of his younger sons, Mr. Miller, in his energy for sweeping away all things old, and setting up all things new, would not have spared the Bath any more than he had spared the bowling-green. He had gone so far, indeed, as to have a plan submitted to him for draining it, and turning it into a strawberry garden, and for doing away with the picturesque old stone steps altogether in order to encase the banks in red brick, suitable to the cultivation of peaches and nectarines; but Ernest and Charley, the Eton boys, had thought about their punts and their canoes, and had pleaded piteously for the Bath; so the Bath was allowed to remain untouched, greatly to the relief of many of the neighbours, who were proud of its traditions, and who, in the general destruction that had been going on at Shadonake, had trembled for its safety.

Where Mr. Miller had originally come from nobody exactly knew. It was generally supposed that he had migrated early in life from northern and manufacturing districts, where his father had amassed a large fortune. In spite, however, of his wealth, it is doubtful whether he would ever have achieved the difficult task of being returned for so exclusive and aristocratic a county as Meadowshire had he not made a most prudent and politic marriage. He had married one of the Miss Esterworths, of Lutterton.

Now, everybody who has the slightest knowledge of Meadowshire and its internal politics will see at once that Andrew Miller could not have done better for himself. The Esterworths are the very oldest and best of the old county families; there can be no sort of doubt whatever as to their position and standing. Therefore, when Andrew Miller married Caroline Esterworth, there was at once an end of all hesitation as to how he was to be treated amongst them. Meadowshire might wonder at Miss Caroline's taste, but it kept its wonder to itself, and held out the right hand of fellowship to Andrew Miller then and ever after.

It is true that there were five Miss Esterworths, all grown up, and all unmarried, at the time when Andrew came a-wooing to Lutterton Castle; they were none of them remarkable for beauty, and Caroline, who was the eldest of the five, less so than the others. Moreover, there were many sons at Lutterton, and the daughters' portions were but small. Altogether the love-making had been easy and prosperous, for Caroline, who was a sensible young woman, had readily recognized the superior advantages of marrying an excellent man of no birth or breeding, with twenty thousand a year, to remaining Miss Esterworth to her dying day, in dignified but impecunious spinsterhood. Time had proved the wisdom of her choice. For some years the Millers had rented a small but pretty little house within two miles of Lutterton, where, of course, everybody visited them, and got used to Andrew's squat, burly figure, and agreed to overlook his many little defects of speech and manner in consideration of his many excellent qualities—and his wealth—and where, in course of time, all their children, two daughters and six sons, were born.

And then, a vacancy occurring opportunely, Mrs. Miller determined that her husband should stand in the Conservative interest for the county. She would have made a Liberal of him had she thought it would answer better. How she toiled and how she slaved, and how she kept her Andrew, who was not by any means ambitious of the position, up to the mark, it boots not here to tell. Suffice it to say, that the deed was accomplished, and that Andrew Miller became M.P. for North Meadowshire.

Almost at the same time Shadonake fell into the market, and Mrs. Miller perceived that the time had now come for her husband's wealth to be recognized and appreciated; or, as he himself expressed it, in vernacular that was strictly to the point if inelegant in diction, the time was come for him "to cut a splash."

She had been very clever, this daughter of the Esterworths. She had kept a tight rein over her husband all through the early years of their married life. She would have no ostentation, no vulgar display of wealth, no parading and flaunting of that twenty thousand per annum in their neighbours' faces. And she had done what she had intended; she had established her husband's position well in the county—she had made him to be accepted, not only by reason of his wealth, but also because he was her husband; she had roused no one's envy—she had never given cause for spite or jealousy—she had made him popular as well as herself. They had lived quietly and unobtrusively; they had, of course, had everything of the best; their horses and carriages were irreproachable, but they had not had more of them than their neighbours. They had entertained freely, and they had given their guests well-cooked dinners and expensive wines; but there had been nothing lavish in their entertainments, nothing that could make any of them go away and say to themselves, with angry discontent, that "those Millers" were purse-proud and vulgar in their wealth. When she had gone to her neighbours' houses Mrs. Miller had been handsomely but never extravagantly dressed; she had praised their cooks, and expressed herself envious of their flowers, and had bemoaned her own inability to vie with their peaches and their pineapples; she had never talked about her own possessions, nor had she ever paraded her own eight thousand pounds' worth of diamonds before the envious eyes of women who had none.

In this way she had made herself popular—and in this way she had won the county seat for her husband.

When, however, that great end and aim of her existence was accomplished, Caroline Miller felt that she might now fairly launch out a little. The time was come when she might reap the advantage of her long years of repression and patient waiting. Her daughters were growing up, her sons were all at school. For her children's sake, it was time that she should take the lead in the county which their father's fortune and new position entitled them to, and which no one now was likely to grudge them. Shadonake therefore was bought, and the house straightway pulled down, and built up again in a style, and with a magnificence, befitting Mr. Miller's wealth.

Bricks and mortar were Andrew Miller's delight. He was never so happy as during the three years that Shadonake House was being built; every stone that was laid was a fresh interest to him; every inch of brick wall a keen and special delight. He had been disappointed not to have had the spoliation of Shadonake Bath; it had been a distinct mortification to him to have to forego the four brick walls which would have replaced its ancient steps; but then he had made it up to himself by altering the position of the front door three times before it was finally settled to his satisfaction.

But all this was over by this time, and when my story begins Shadonake new House, as it was sometimes called, was built, and furnished and inhabited in every corner of its lofty rooms, and all along the spacious length of its many wide corridors.

One afternoon—it is about a week later than that soirée at Walpole Lodge, mentioned in a previous chapter—Mrs. Miller and her eldest daughter are sitting together in the large drawing-room at Shadonake. The room is furnished in that style of high artistic decoration that is now the fashion. There are rich Persian rugs over the polished oak floor; a high oak chimney-piece, with blue tiles inserted into it in every direction, and decorated with old Nankin china bowls and jars; a wide grate below, where logs of wood are blazing between brass bars; quantities of spindle-legged Chippendale furniture all over the room, and a profusion of rich gold embroidery and "textile fabrics" of all descriptions lighting up the carved oak "dado" and the sombre sage green of the walls. There are pictures, too, quite of the best, and china of every period and every style, upon every available bracket and shelf and corner where a cup or a plate can be made to stand. Four large windows on one side open on to the lawn; two, at right angles to them, lead into a large conservatory, where there is, even at this dead season of the year, a blaze of exotic blossoms that fill the room with their sweet rich odour.

Mrs. Miller sits before a writing bureau of inlaid satin-wood of an ancient pattern. She has her pen in her hand, and is docketing her visiting list. Beatrice Miller sits on a low four-legged stool by her mother's side, with a large Japanese china bowl on her knees filled with cards, which she takes out one after the other, reading the names upon them aloud to her mother before tossing them into a basket, also of Japanese structure, which is on the floor in front of her.

Beatrice is Mrs. Miller's eldest daughter, and she is twenty. Guy is only eleven months older, and Edwin is a year younger—they are both at Oxford; next comes Geraldine, who is still in the school-room, but who is hoping to come out next Easter; then Ernest and Charley, the Eton boys; and lastly, Teddy and Ralph, who are at a famous preparatory school, whence they hope, in process of time, to be drafted on to Eton, following in the footsteps of their elder brothers.

Of all this large family it is Beatrice, the eldest daughter, who causes her mother the most anxiety. Beatrice is like her mother—a plain but clever-looking girl, with the dark swart features and colouring of the Esterworths, who are not a handsome race. Added to which, she inherits her father's short and somewhat stumpy figure. Such a personal appearance in itself is enough to cause uneasiness to any mother who is anxious for her daughter's future; but when these advantages of looks are rendered still more peculiar by the fact that her hair had to be shaved off some years ago when she had scarlet fever, and that it has never grown again properly, but is worn short and loose about her face like a boy's, with its black tresses tumbling into her eyes every time she looks down—and when, added to this, Mrs. Miller also discovered to her mortification that Beatrice possessed a will of her own, and so decided a method of expressing her opinions and convictions, that she was not likely to be easily moulded to her own views, you will, perhaps, understand the extent of the difficulties with which she has to deal.

For, of course, so clever and so managing a woman as Mrs. Miller has not allowed her daughter to grow up to the age of twenty without making the most careful and judiciously-laid schemes for her ultimate disposal. That Beatrice is to marry is a matter of course, and Mrs. Miller has well determined that the marriage is to be a good one, and that her daughter is to strengthen her father's position in Meadowshire by a union with one or other of its leading families. Now, when Mrs. Miller came to pass the marriageable men of Meadowshire under review, there was no such eligible bachelor amongst them all as Sir John Kynaston, of Kynaston Hall.

It was on him, therefore, that her hopes with regard to Beatrice were fixed. Fortune hitherto had seemed to smile favourably upon her. Beatrice had had one season in town, during which she had met Sir John frequently, and he had, contrary to his usual custom, asked her to dance several times when he had met her at balls. Mrs. Miller said to herself that Sir John, not being a very young man, did not set much store upon mere personal beauty; that he probably valued mental qualities in a woman more highly than the transient glitter of beauty; and that Beatrice's good sense and sharp, shrewd conversation had evidently made a favourable impression upon him.

She never was more mistaken in her life. True, Sir John did like Miss Miller, he found her unconventional and amusing; but his only object in distinguishing her by his attentions had been to pay a necessary compliment to the new M.P.'s daughter, a duty which he would have fulfilled equally had she been stupid as well as plain: moreover, as we have seen, few men were so intensely sensitive to beauty in a woman as was Sir John Kynaston. Mrs. Miller, however, was full of hopes concerning him. To do her justice, she was not exactly vulgarly ambitious for her daughter; she liked Sir John personally, and had a high respect for his character, and she considered that Beatrice's high spirit and self-willed disposition would be most desirably moderated and kept in check by a husband so much older than herself. Lady Kynaston, moreover, was one of her best and dearest friends, and was her beau-idéal of all that a clever and refined lady should be. The match, in every respect, would have been a very acceptable one to her. Whether or no Miss Beatrice shared her mother's views on her behalf remains to be seen.

The mother and daughter are settling together the preliminaries of a week's festivities which Mrs. Miller has decided shall be held at Shadonake this winter. The house is to be filled, and there are to be a series of dinner parties, culminating in a ball.

"The Bayleys, the Westons, the Foresters, and two daughters, I suppose," reads Mrs. Miller, aloud, from the list in her hand, "Any more for the second dinner-party, Beatrice?"

"Are you not going to ask the Daintrees, of Sutton, mother?"

"Oh, dear me, another parson, Beatrice! I really don't think we can; I have got three already. They shall have a card for the ball."

"You will ask that handsome girl who lives with them, won't you?"

"Not the slightest occasion for doing so," replied her mother, shortly. Beatrice lifted her eyebrows.

"Why, she is the best-looking woman in all Meadowshire; we cannot leave her out."

"I know nothing about her, not even her name; she is some kind of poor relation, I believe—acts as the children's governess. We have too many women as it is. No, I certainly shall not ask her. Go on to the next, Beatrice."

"But, mother, she is so very handsome! Surely you might include her."

"Dear me, Beatrice, what a stupid girl you are! What is the good of asking handsome girls to cut you out in your own house? I should have thought you would have had the sense to see that for yourself," said Mrs. Miller, impatiently.

"I think you are horribly unjust, mamma," says Miss Beatrice, energetically; "and it is downright unkind to leave her out because she is handsome—as if I cared."

"How can I ask her if I do not know her name?" said her mother, irritably, with just that amount of dread of her daughter's rising temper to make her anxious to conciliate her. "If you like to find out who she is and all about her——"

"Yes, I will find out," said Beatrice, quietly; "give me the note, I will keep it back for the present."

"Now, for goodness sake, go on, child, and don't waste any more time. Who are coming from town to stay in the house?"

"Well, there will be Lady Kynaston, I suppose."

"Yes. She won't come till the end of the week. I have heard from her; she will try and get down in time for the ball."

"Then there will be the Macpherson girls and Helen Romer. And, as a matter of course, Captain Kynaston must be asked?"

"Yes. What a fool that woman is to advertise her feelings so openly that one is obliged to ask her attendant swain to follow her wherever she goes!"

"On the contrary, I think her remarkably clever; she gets what she wants, and the cleverest of us can do no more. It is a well-known fact to all Helen's acquaintances that not to ask Captain Kynaston to meet her would be deliberately to insult her—she expects it as her right."

"All the same, it is in very bad taste and excessively underbred of her. However, I should ask Captain Kynaston in any case, for his mother's sake, and because I like him. He is a good shot, too, and the coverts must be shot that week. Who next?"

"Mr. Herbert Pryme."

"Goodness me! Beatrice, what makes you think of *him*? We don't know anything about him—where he comes from or who are his belongings—he is only a nobody!"

"He is a barrister, mamma!"

"Yes, of course, I know that—but, then, there are barristers of all sorts. I am sure I do not know what made you fix upon him; you only met him two or three times in town."

"I liked him," said Beatrice, carelessly; "he is a gentleman, and would be a pleasant man to have in the house."

Her mother looked at her sharply. She was playing with the gold locket round her neck, twisting it backwards and forwards along its chain, her eyes fixed upon the heap of cards on her lap. There was not the faintest vestige of a blush upon her face.

"However," she continued, "if you don't care about having him, strike his name out. Only it is a pity, because Sophy Macpherson is rather fond of him, I fancy."

This was a lie; it was Miss Beatrice herself who was fond of him, but not even her mother, keen and quick-scented as she was, could have guessed it from her impassive face. Mrs. Miller was taken in completely.

"Oh," she said, "if Sophy Macpherson likes him, that alters the case. Oh, yes, I will ask him by all means—as you say, he is a gentleman and pleasant."

"Look, mamma!" exclaimed Beatrice, suddenly; "there is uncle Tom riding up the drive."

Now, Tom Esterworth was a very important personage; he was the present head of the Esterworth family, and, as such, the representative of its ancient honours and traditions. He was a bachelor, and reigned in solitary grandeur at Lutterton Castle, and kept the hounds as his fathers had done before him.

Uncle Tom was thought very much of at Shadonake, and his visits always caused a certain amount of agitation in his sister's mind. To her dying day she would be conscious that in Tom's eyes she had been guilty of a *mésalliance*. She never could get that idea out of her head; it made her nervous and ill at ease in his presence. She hustled all her notes and cards hurriedly together into her bureau.

"Uncle Tom! Dear me, what can he have come to-day for! I thought the hounds were out. Ring the bell, Beatrice; he will like some tea. Where is your father?"

"Papa is out superintending the building of the new pigsties," said Beatrice as she rang the bell. "I think uncle Tom has been hunting; he is in boots and breeches I see."

"Dear me, I hope your father won't come in with his muddy feet and his hands covered with earth," said Mrs. Miller, nervously.

Uncle Tom came in, a tall, dark-faced, strong-limbed man of fifty—an ugly man, if you will, but a gentleman, and an Esterworth, every inch of him. He kissed his sister, and patted his niece on the cheek.

"Why weren't you out to-day, Pussy?"

"You met so far off, uncle. I had no one to ride with to the meet. The boys will be back next week. Have you had a good run?"

"No, we've done nothing but potter about all the morning; there isn't a scrap of scent."

"Uncle Tom, will you give us a meet here when we have our house-warming?"

"Humph! you haven't got any foxes at Shadonake," answered her uncle. He had drawn his chair to the fire, and was warming his hands over the blazing logs. Beatrice was rather a favourite with him. "I will see about it, Pussy," he added, kindly, seeing that she looked disappointed. Mrs. Miller was pouring him out a cup of tea.

"Well, I've got a piece of news for you women!" says Mr. Esterworth, stretching out his hand for his tea. "John Kynaston's going to be married!"

Mrs. Miller never knew how it was that the old Worcester tea-cup in her hand did not at this juncture fall flat on the ground into a thousand atoms at her brother's feet. It is certain that only a very strong exercise of self-control and presence of mind saved it from destruction.

"Engaged to be married!" she said, with a gasp.

"That is news indeed," cried Beatrice, heartily, "I am delighted."

"Don't be so foolish, Beatrice," said her mother, quite sharply. "How on earth can you be delighted when you don't even know who it is? Who is it, Tom?"

"Ah, that is the whole pith of the matter," said Mr. Esterworth, who was not above the weakness of liking to be the bearer of a piece of gossip. "I'll give you three guesses, and I'll bet you won't hit it."

"One of the Courtenay girls?"

"No."

"Anna Vivian?"

"I know," says Beatrice, nodding her head sagely; "it is that girl who lives with the Daintrees."

"Beatrice, how silly you are!" cries her mother.

Tom Esterworth turns round in his chair, and looks at his niece.

"By Jove, you've hit it!" he exclaims. "What a clever pussy you are to be sure."

And then the soul of the member's wife became filled with consternation and disgust.

"Well, I call it downright sly of John Kynaston!" she exclaims, angrily; "picking out a nobody like that behind all our backs, and keeping it so quiet, too; he ought to be ashamed of himself for such an unsuitable selection!"

Beatrice laughed. "You know, uncle Tom, mamma wanted him to marry me."

"Beatrice, you should not say such things," said her mother, colouring.

"Whew!" whistled Mr. Esterworth. "So that was the little game, Caroline, was it? John Kynaston has better taste. He wouldn't have looked at an ugly little girl like our pussy here, would he, Puss? Miss Nevill is one of the finest women I ever saw in my life. She was at the meet to-day on one of his horses; and, by Jove! she made all the other women look plain by the side of her! Kynaston is a very lucky fellow."

"I think, mamma, there can be no doubt about sending Miss Nevill an invitation to our ball now," said Beatrice, laughingly.

"She will have to be asked to stay in the house," said Mrs. Miller, with something akin to a groan. "I cannot leave her out, as Lady Kynaston is coming. Oh, dear! oh, dear! what fools men are, to be sure!"

But Beatrice was wicked enough to laugh again over her mother's discomfiture.

CHAPTER IX.

ENGAGED.

I wonder did you ever count
The value of one human fate,
Or sum the infinite amount
Of one heart's treasures, and the weight
Of one heart's venture.

A. Procter.

It was quite true what Mr. Thomas Esterworth had said, that Vera was engaged to Sir John Kynaston.

It had all come about so rapidly, and withal so quietly, that, when Vera came to think of it, it rather took her breath away. She had expected it, of course; indeed, she had even planned and tried for it; but, when it had actually come to her, she felt herself to be bewildered by the suddenness of it.

In the end the climax of the love-making had been prosaic enough. Sir John had not felt himself equal to the task of a personal interview with the lady of his affections, with the accompanying risks of a personal rejection, which, in his modesty and humility with reference to her, he had believed to be quite on the cards. So he had written to her. The note had been taken up to the vicarage by the footman, and had been brought into the dining-room by the vicarial parlour-maid, just as the three ladies were finishing breakfast, and after the vicar himself had left the room.

"A note from Kynaston, please 'm," says rosy-cheeked Hannah, holding it forth before her, upon a small japanned tray, as an object of general family interest and excitement.

"For your master, Hannah?" says old Mrs. Daintree. "Are they waiting for an answer? You will find him in his study."

"No, ma'am, it's for Miss Vera."

"Dear me!" with a suspicious glance across the table; "how very odd!"

Vera takes up the note and opens it.

"May I have the crest, auntie?" clamours Tommy before she had read three words of it.

"Is it about the horse he has offered you to ride?" asks his mother.

But Vera answers nothing; she gets up quietly, and leaves the room without a word.

"Extraordinary!" gasps Mrs. Daintree; "Vera's manners are certainly most abrupt and unlady-like at times, Marion. I think you ought to point it out to her."

Marion murmurs some unintelligible excuse and follows her sister—leaving the unfortunate Tommy a prey to his grandmother's tender mercies. So brilliant an opportunity is not, of course, to be thrown away. Tommy's fingers, having incontinently strayed in the direction of the sugar-basin, are summarily slapped for their indiscretion, and an admonition is straightway delivered to him in forcible language concerning the pains and penalties which threaten the ulterior destiny of naughty little boys in general and of such of them in particular who are specially addicted to the abstraction of lumps of sugar from the breakfast-table.

Meanwhile, Marion has found her sister in the adjoining room standing up alone upon the hearthrug with Sir John Kynaston's letter in her hands. She is not reading it now, she is looking steadfastly into the fire. It has fulfilled—nay, more than fulfilled—her wishes. The triumph of her success is pleasant to her, and has brought a little more than their usual glow into her cheeks, and yet—Heaven knows what vague and intangible dreams and fancies have not somehow sunk down chill and cold within her during the last five minutes.

Gratified ambition—flattered vanity—the joy of success—all this she feels to the full; but nothing more! There is not one single other sensation within her. Her pulses have not quickened, ever so little, as she read her lover's letter; her heart has not throbbed, even once, with a sweeter, purer delight—such as she has read and heard that other women have felt.

"I suppose I have no heart," said Vera to herself; "it must be that I am cold by nature. I am happy; but—but—I wonder what it feels like—this *love*—that there is so much talked and written about?"

And then Marion came in breathlessly.

"Oh, Vera, what is it?"

Vera turns round to her, smiling serenely, and places the note in her hands.

This is what Sir John Kynaston has written:—

"Dear Miss Nevill,—I do not think what I am about to say will be altogether unexpected by you. You must have surely guessed how sincere an affection I have learnt to feel for you. I know that I am unworthy of you, and I am conscious of how vast a disparity there is between my age and your own youth and beauty. But if my great love and devotion can in any way bridge over the gap that lies between us, believe me, that if you will consent to be my wife, my whole life shall be devoted to making you happy. If you can give me an answer to-day, I shall be very grateful, as suspense is hard to bear. But pray do not decide against me in haste, and without giving me every chance in your power.

"Yours devotedly,

"JOHN KYNASTON."

"Oh! Vera, my darling sister, I am so glad!" cries Marion, in tearful delight, throwing her arms up round the neck of the young sister, who is so much taller than she is; "I had guessed it, dearest; I saw he was in love with you; and oh, Vera, I shall have you always near me!"

"Yes, that will be nice," assents Vera, quietly, and a trifle absently, stroking her sister's cheek, with her eyes still fixed on the fire; "and of course," rousing herself with an effort, "of course I am a very lucky woman."

And then Mr. Daintree came in, and his wife rushed to him rapturously to impart the joyful news. There was a little pleasant confusion of broken words and explanations between the three, and then Marion whisked away, brimming over with triumphant delight to wave the flags of victory exultingly in her mother-in-law's face.

Eustace Daintree and Vera were alone. He took her hands within his, and looked steadfastly in her face.

"Vera, are you sure of yourself, my dear, in this matter?"

Her eyes met his for a moment, and then fell before his earnest gaze. She coloured a little.

"I am quite sure that I mean to accept Sir John's proposal," she said, with a little uneasy laugh.

"Child, do you love him?"

Her eyes met his again; there was a vague trouble in them. The man had a power over her, the power of sheer goodness of soul. She could never be untrue to herself with Eustace Daintree; she was always at her very best with him, humble and gentle; and she could no more have told him a lie, or put him off with vague conventionalities, than she could have committed a deadly sin.

What is it about some people that, in spite of ourselves, they thus force out of us the best part of our nature; that base and unworthy thoughts cannot live in us before them,—that they melt out of our hearts as the snow before the rays of the sun? Even though the effect may be transient, such is the power of their faith, and their truth, and their goodness, that it must needs call forth in us something of the same spirit as their own.

Such was Eustace Daintree's influence over Vera. It was not because of his office, for no one was less susceptible than Vera—a Protestant brought up, with but vague ideas of her own faith, in a Catholic land—to any of those recognized associations with which a purely English-bred girl might have felt the character of the clergyman of the parish where she lived to be invested. It was nothing of that sort that made him great to her; it was, simply and solely, the goodness of the man that impressed her. His guilelessness, his simplicity of mind, his absolute uprightness of character, and, with it all, the absence in him of any assumption of authority, or of any superiority of character over those about him. His very humility made her humble with him, and exalted him into something saintly in her eyes.

When Eustace looked at her fixedly, with all his good soul in his earnest eyes, and said to her again, "Do you love him, Vera?" Vera could but answer him simply and frankly, almost against her will, as it were.

"I don't think I do, Eustace; but then I do not quite know what love is. I do not think, however, that it can be what I feel."

"My child, no union can be hallowed without love. Vera, you will not run into so great a danger?" he said anxiously.

She looked up at him smiling.

"I like him better than any one else, at all events. Better than Mr. Gisburne, for instance. And I think, I do really think, Eustace, it will be for my happiness."

The vicar looked grave. "If Sir John Kynaston were a poor man, would you marry him?"

And Vera answered bravely, though with a heightened colour—

"No; but it is not only for the money, Eustace; indeed it is not. But—but— I should be miserable without it; and I must do something with my life."

He drew her near to him, and kissed her forehead. He understood her. With that rare gift of sympathy—the highest, the most God-like of all human attributes—he felt at once what she meant. It was wonderful that this man, who was so unworldly, so unselfish, so pure of the stains of earth himself, should have seen at once her position from her own point of view; that was neither a very exalted one, nor was it very free from the dross of worldliness. But it was so. All at once he seemed to know by a subtle instinct what were the weaknesses, and the temptations, and the aims of this girl, who, with all her faults, was so dear to him. He understood her better, perhaps, than she understood herself. Her soul was untouched by passion; the story of her life was unwritten; there was no danger for her yet; and perchance it might be that the storms of life would pass her by unscathed, and that she might remain sheltered for ever in the safe haven which had opened so unexpectedly to receive her.

"There is a peril in the course you have chosen," he said, gravely; "but your soul is pure, and you are safe. And I know, Vera, that you will always do your duty."

And the tears were in her eyes as he left her.

When he had gone she sat down to write her answer to Sir John Kynaston. She dipped her pen into the ink, and sat with it in her hand, thinking. Her brother-in-law's words had aroused a fresh train of thought within her. There seemed to be an amount of solemnity in what she was about to do that she had not considered before. It was true that she did not love him; but then, as she had told Eustace just now, she loved no one else; she did not rightly understand what love meant, indeed. And is a woman to wait on in patience for years until love comes to her? Would it ever come? Probably not, thought Vera; not to her, who thought herself to be cold, and not easily moved. There must be surely many women to whom this wonderful thing of love never comes. In all her experience of life there was nothing to contradict this. It was not as if she had been a girl who had never left her native village, never tasted of the pleasures of life, never known the sweet incense of flattery and devotion. Vera had known it all. Many men had courted her; one or two had loved her dearly, but she had not loved them. Amongst them all, indeed, there had been never one whom she had liked with such a sincere affection as she now felt for this man, who seemed to love her so much, and who wrote to her so diffidently, and yet so devotedly.

"I love him as well as I am ever likely to love any one," said Vera, to herself. Yet still she leant her chin upon her hand and looked out of the window at the gray bare branches of the elm-trees across the damp green lawn, and still her letter was unwritten.

"Vera!" cries Marion, coming in hurriedly and breaking in upon her reverie, "the footman from Kynaston is waiting all this time to know if there is any answer! Shall I send him away? Or have you made up your mind?"

"Oh yes, I have made up my mind. My note will be ready directly; he may as well take it. It will save the trouble of sending up to the Hall later." For Vera remembers that there is not a superfluity of servants at the vicarage, and that they all of them have plenty to do.

And thus, a mere trifle—a feather, as it were, on the river of life—settled her destiny for her out of hand.

She dipped her pen into the ink once more, and wrote:—

"Dear Sir John,—You have done me a great honour in asking me to be your wife. I am fully sensible of your affection, and am very grateful for it. I fear you think too highly of me; but I will endeavour to prove myself worthy of your good opinion, and to make you as good a wife as you deserve.

"Yours,

"VERA NEVILL."

She was conscious herself of the excessive coldness of her note, but she could not help it. She could not, for the life of her, have made it warmer. Nothing, indeed, is so difficult as to write down feelings that do not exist; it is easier to simulate with our spoken words and our looks; but the pen that is urged beyond its natural inclination seems to cool into ice in our fingers. But, at all events, she had accepted him.

It was a relief to her when the thing was done, and the note sent off beyond the possibility of recall.

After that there had been no longer any leisure for her doubting thoughts. There was her sister's delighted excitement, Mrs. Daintree's oppressive astonishment, and even Eustace's calmer satisfaction in her bright prospects, to occupy and divert her thoughts. Then there came her lover himself, tender and grateful, and with so worshipful a respect in every word and action that the most sensitive woman could scarcely have been ruffled or alarmed by the prospects of so deferential a husband.

In a few days Vera became reconciled to her new position, which was in truth a very pleasant one to her. There were the congratulations of friends and acquaintances to be responded to; the pleasant flutter of adulation that surrounded her once more; the little daily excitement of John Kynaston's visits—all this made her happy and perfectly satisfied with the wisdom of her decision.

Only one thing vexed her.

"What will your mother say, John?" she had asked the very first day she had been engaged to him.

"It will not make much difference to me, dearest, whatever she may say."

Nor in truth would it, for Sir John, as we have seen, had never been a devoted son, nor had he ever given his confidence to his mother; he had always gone his own way independently of her.

"But it must needs make a difference to me," Vera had insisted. "You have written to her, of course."

"Oh, yes; I wrote and told her I was engaged to you."

"And she has not written?"

"Yes, there was a message for you—her love or something."

Sir John evidently did not consider the subject of much importance. But Vera was hurt that Lady Kynaston had not written to her.

"I will never enter any family where I am not welcome," she had said to her lover, proudly.

And then Sir John had taken fright, for she was so precious to him that the fear of losing her was becoming almost as a nightmare to him, and, possibly, at the bottom of his heart he knew how feeble was his hold over her. He had written off to his mother that day a letter that was almost a command, and had told her to write to Vera.

This letter was not likely to prepossess Lady Kynaston, who was a masterful little lady herself, in her daughter-in-law's favour; it did more harm than good. She had obeyed her son, it is true, because he was the head of the family, and because she stood in awe of him; but the letter, thus written under compulsion, was not kind—it was not even just.

"Horrid girl!" had said Lady Kynaston, angrily, to herself, as she had sat down to her writing-table to fulfil her son's mandate. "It is not likely that I can be very loving to her—some wretched, second-rate girl, evidently—for not even Caroline Miller who, goodness knows, rakes up all the odds and ends of society—ever heard of her before!"

It is not to be supposed that a letter undertaken under such auspices could be in any way conciliatory or pleasant in its tone. Such as it was, Vera put it straight into the fire directly she had read it; no one ever saw it but herself.

"I have heard from your mother," she said to Sir John.

"Yes? I am very glad. She wrote everything that was kind, no doubt."

"I dare say she meant to be kind," said Vera; which was not true, because she knew perfectly that there had been no kindness intended. But she pursued the subject no further.

"I hope you will like Maurice," said Sir John, presently; "he is a good-hearted boy, though he has been sadly extravagant, and given me a good deal of trouble."

"I shall be glad to know your brother," said Vera, quietly. "Is he coming to Kynaston?"

"Yes, eventually; but you will meet him first at Shadonake when you go to stay there: they have asked a large party for that week, I hear, and Maurice will be there."

Now, by this time Vera knew that the photograph she had once found in the old writing-table drawer at Kynaston was that of her lover's brother Maurice.

CHAPTER X.

A MEETING ON THE STAIRS.

Since first I saw your face
I resolved to honour and renown you;
If now I be disdained,
I wish my heart had never known you.

The Sun whose beams most glorious are
Rejecteth no beholder,
And your sweet beauty past compare
Made my poor eyes the bolder.

THOMAS FORD.

I have often wondered why, in the ordering of human destinies, some special Providence, some guardian spirit who is gifted with foreknowledge, is not mercifully told off to each of us so to order the trifles of our lives that they may combine to the working together of our weal, instead of conspiring, as they too often and too evidently do, for our woe.

Look back upon your own life, and upon the lives of those whose story you have known the most intimately, and see what straws, what nonentities, what absurd trivialities have brought about the most important events of existence. Recollect how, and in what manner, those people whom it would have been well for you never to have known came across you. How those whose influence over you is for good were kept out of your way at the very crisis of your life. Think what a different life you would have led; I do not mean only happier, but how much better and purer, if some absurd trifle had not seemed to play into the hands, as it were, of your destiny, and to set you in a path whereof no one could at the time foresee the end.

Some one had looked out their train in last month's Bradshaw, unwitting of the autumn alterations, and was kept from you till the next day. You took the left instead of the right side of the square on your way home, or you stood for a minute gossiping at your neighbour's door, and there came by some one who ultimately altered and embittered your whole life, and who, but for that accidental meeting, you would, probably, never have seen again; or some evil adviser was at hand, whilst one whose opinion you revered, and whose timely help would have saved you from taking that false step you ever after regretted, was kept to the house, by Heaven knows what ridiculous trifle—a cold in the head, or finger-ache—and did not see you to warn and to keep you back from your own folly until it was too late.

People say these things are ordered for us. I do not know; it may be so, but sometimes it seems rather as if we were irresponsible puppets, tossed and buffeted about, blindly and helplessly, upon life's river, as fluttering dead leaves are danced wildly along the swift current of a Highland stream. Such a trifle might have saved us! yet there was no pitying hand put forth to avert that which, in our human blindness, appeared to us to be as unimportant as any other incident of our lives.

Life is an unsolvable problem. Shall we ever, in some other world, I wonder, read its riddles aright?

All these moral dissertations have been called forth because Vera Nevill went to stay for a week at Shadonake. If she had known—what we none of us know—the future, she doubtless would have stayed away. Fate—a beneficent fate, indeed—made, I am bound to confess, a valiant effort in her behalf. Little Minnie fell ill the day before her departure; and the symptoms were such that everybody in the house believed that she was sickening for scarlet fever. The doctor, however, having been hastily summoned, pronounced the disease to be an infantile complaint of a harmless and innocuous nature, which he dignified by the delusively poetical name of "Rosalia."

"It is not infectious, Mr. Smee, I hope?" asked Marion, anxiously. "Nothing to prevent my sister going to stay at the Millers' to morrow?"

"Not in the least infectious, Mrs. Daintree, and anybody in the house can go wherever they like, except the child herself, who must be kept in a warm room for two days, when she will probably be quite well again."

"I am glad, dear, there is nothing to put a stop to your visit; it would have been such a pity," said Marion, in her blindness, to her sister afterwards.

So the fates had a game of pitch and toss with Vera's future, and settled it amongst them to their own satisfaction, probably, but not, it will be seen, for Vera's own good or ultimate happiness.

On the afternoon of the 3rd day of January, therefore, Eustace Daintree drove his sister-in-law over to Shadonake in the open basket pony-carriage, and deposited her and her box safely at the stone-colonnaded door of that most imposing mansion, which she entered exactly ten minutes before the dressing-bell rang, and was conducted almost immediately upstairs to her own room.

Some twenty minutes later there are still two ladies sitting on in the small tea-room, where it is the fashion at Shadonake to linger between the hours of five and seven, who alone have not yet moved to obey the mandate of the dressing-bell.

"What *is* the good of waiting?" says Beatrice, impatiently; "the train is often late, and, besides, he may not come till the nine o'clock train."

"That is just what I want to wait for," answers Helen Romer. "I want just to hear if the carriage has come back, and then I shall know for certain."

"Well, you know how frightfully punctual papa is, and how angry it makes him if anybody is late."

"Just two minutes more, Beatrice; I can dress very quickly when once I set to work," pleads Helen.

Beatrice sits down again on the arm of the sofa, and resigns herself to her fate; but she looks rather annoyed and vexed about it.

Mrs. Romer paces the room feverishly and impatiently.

"What did you think of Miss Nevill?" asks Beatrice.

"I could hardly see her in her hat and that thick veil; but she looked as if she were handsome."

"She is *beautiful*!" says Beatrice, emphatically, "and uncle Tom says——"

"Hush!" interrupts Helen, hurriedly. "Is not that the sound of wheels?—Yes, it is the carriage."

She flies to the door.

"Take care, Helen," says Beatrice, anxiously; "don't open the door wide, don't let the servants think we have been waiting, it looks so bad—so—so unlady-like."

But Helen Romer does not even hear her; she is listening intently to the approaching sounds, with the half-opened door in her hand.

The tea-room door opens into a large inner hall, out of which leads the principal staircase; the outer or entrance-hall is beyond; and presently the stopping of the carriage, the opening and shutting of doors from the servants' departments, and all the usual bustle of an arrival are heard.

The two girls stand close together listening, Beatrice hidden in the shadow of the room.

"There are *two* voices!" cries Helen, in a disappointed tone; "he is not alone!"

"I suppose it is Mr. Pryme—mamma said he might come by this train," answers Beatrice, so quietly that no one could ever have guessed how her heart was beating.

"Helen, *do* let us run upstairs; I really cannot stay. Let *me* go, at all events!" she adds, with a sudden agony of entreaty as the guests were heard advancing towards the door of the inner hall. And as Helen made not the slightest sign of moving, Beatrice slipped past her and ran lightly and swiftly across the hall upstairs, and disappeared along the landing above just as Captain Kynaston and Mr. Herbert Pryme appeared upon the scene below.

No such scruples of modesty troubled Mrs. Romer. As the young men entered the inner hall preceded by the butler, who was taking them up to their rooms, and followed by two footmen who were bearing their portmanteaus, Helen stepped boldly forward out of the shelter of the tea-room, and held out her hand to Captain Kynaston.

"How do you do? How late your train is."

Maurice looked distinctly annoyed, but of course he shook hands with her.

"How are you, Mrs. Romer? I did not expect you to be here till to-morrow. Yes, we are late," consulting his watch; "only twenty minutes to dress in—I must look sharp."

Meanwhile the stranger, Mr. Pryme, was following the butler upstairs.

Helen lowered her voice.

"I *must* speak to you a minute, Maurice; it is six weeks since we have met, and to meet in public would be too trying. Please dress as quickly as ever you can; I know you can dress quickly if you choose; and wait for me here at the bottom of the stairs—we might get just three minutes together before dinner."

There were the footmen and the portmanteaus within six yards of them, and Mr. Pryme and the butler still within earshot. What was Maurice to do? He could not really listen to a whole succession of prayers, and entreaties, and piteous appeals. There was neither the time, nor was it the place, for either discussion or remonstrance. All he could do was to nod a hasty assent to her request.

"Then I must make haste," he said, and ran quickly upstairs in the wake of the other guest.

The staircase at Shadonake was very wide and very handsome, and thoroughly in keeping with the spacious character of the house. It consisted of one wide flight of shallow steps, with a richly-carved balustrade on either side of it, leading straight down from a large square landing above. Both landing and steps were carpeted with thick velvet-pile carpet, so that no jarring footfall was ever heard upon them. The hall into which the staircase led was paved in coloured mosaic tiles, and was half covered over with rich Persian rugs. A great many doors, nearly all the sitting-rooms of the house, in fact, opened into it, and the blank spaces of the wall were filled in with banks of large handsome plants, palms and giant ferns, and azaleas in full bloom, which were daily rearranged by the gardeners in every available corner.

At the foot of the staircase, and with his back to it, leaning against the balustrade, stood Captain Kynaston, exactly four minutes before the dinner was announced.

Most people were in the habit of calling Maurice a good-looking man, but if anybody had seen him now for the first time it is doubtful whether they would have endorsed that favourable opinion upon his personal appearance. A thoroughly ill-tempered expression of face seldom enhances any one's good looks, and if ever a man looked in a bad temper, Maurice Kynaston did so at the present moment.

He stood with his hands in his trousers pockets, and his eyes fixed upon his own boots, and he looked as savage as it was well possible for a man to look.

He was waiting here for Helen, because he had told her that he would do so, and when Captain Kynaston promised anything to a lady he always kept his word.

But to say that he hated being there is but a mild term for the rage and disgust he experienced.

To be waylaid and attacked thus, directly he had set foot in the house, with a stranger and three servants looking on so as to render him absolutely helpless; to be uncomfortably hurried over his toilet, and inveigled into a sort of rendezvous at the foot of a public staircase, where a number of people might at any minute enter from any one of the six or eight surrounding doors, was enough of itself to try his temper; but when he came to consider how Helen, in thus appropriating him and making him obey her caprices, was virtually breaking her side of the treaty between them; that she was exacting from him the full amount of servitude and devotion which an open engagement would demand, and yet she had agreed to deny any such engagement between them openly—it was, he felt, more than he could continue to bear with meekness.

Meekness, indeed, was in no way Maurice Kynaston's distinguishing characteristic. He was masterful and imperious by nature; to be the slave of any woman was neither pleasant nor profitable to him. Honour, indeed, had bound him to Helen, and had he loved her she might have led him. Her position gave her a certain hold over him, and she knew how to appeal to his heart; but he loved her not, and to control his will and his spirit was beyond her power.

Maurice said to himself that he would put a stop to this system of persecution once and for all—that this interview, which she herself had contrived, should be made the opportunity of a few forcible words, that should frighten her into submission.

So he stood fretting, and fuming, and raging, waiting for her at the foot of the stairs.

There was a soft rustle, as of a woman's dress, behind him. He turned sharply round.

Halfway down the stairs came a woman whom he had never seen before. A black velvet dress, made high in the throat, with a wide collar of heavy lace upon her shoulders, hung clingingly about the outlines of her tall and perfect figure; her hands, with some lace ruffles falling about her wrists, were simply crossed before her. The light of a distant hanging-lamp shone down upon her, just catching one diamond star that glittered among the thick coils of her hair—she wore no other ornament. She came down the stairs slowly, almost lingeringly, with a certain grace in her movements, and without a shadow of embarrassment or self-consciousness.

Maurice drew aside to let her pass him—looking at her—for how could he choose but look? But when she reached the bottom of the steps, she turned her face towards him.

"You are Maurice—are you not?" she said, and put forth both her hands towards him.

An utter bewilderment as to who she was made him speechless; his mind had been full of Helen and his own troubles; everything else had gone out of his head. She coloured a little, still holding out her hands to him.

"I am Vera," she said, simply, and there was a little deprecating appeal in the words as though she would have added, "Be my friend."

He took the hands—soft slender hands that trembled a very little in his grasp—within his own, and some nameless charm in their gentle touch brought a sudden flush into his face, but no appropriate words concerning his pleasure at meeting her, or his gratification at their future relations, fell from Maurice Kynaston's lips. He only held her thus by her hands, and looked at her—looked at her as if he could never look at her enough—from her head to her feet, and from her feet up again to her head, till a sudden wave of colour flooded her face at the earnestness of his scrutiny.

"Vera—*Vera Nevill!*" was all he said; and then below his breath, as though his absolute amazement were utterly irrepressible: "*By Jove!*" And Vera laughed softly at the thoroughly British character of the exclamation.

"How like an Englishman!" she said. "An Italian would have paid me fifty pretty compliments in half the time you have taken just to stare at me!"

"What a charming *tableau vivant*!" exclaims a voice above them as Mrs. Romer comes down the staircase. "You really look like a scene in a play! Pray don't let me disturb you."

"I am making friends with my sister-in-law that is to be, Mrs. Romer," says Maurice, who has dropped Vera's hands with a guilty suddenness, and now endeavours to look completely at his ease—an effort in which he signally fails.

"Were you? Dear me! I thought you and Miss Nevill were practising the pose of the 'Huguenots'!"

Now the whole armoury of feminine weapons—impertinence, spite, and bad manners, born of jealousy—is utterly beneath the contempt of such a woman as Vera; but she is no untried, inexperienced country girl such as Mrs. Romer imagines her to be disconcerted or stricken dumb by such an attack. She knew instantly that she had been attacked, and in what manner, and she was perfectly capable of taking care of herself.

"I have never seen that picture, the 'Huguenots,' Mrs. Romer," she said, quietly; "do you think there is a photograph or a print of it at Kynaston, Maurice? If so, you or John must show it to me."

And how Mrs. Romer hated her then and there, from that very minute until her life's end, it would not be easy to set forth!

The utter *insouciance*, the lady-like ignoring of Helen's impertinence, the quiet assumption of what she knew her own position in the Kynaston family to be, down to the sisterly "Maurice," whereby she addressed the man whom in public, at least, Mrs. Romer was forced to call by a more formal name—all proved to that astute little woman that Vera Nevill was no ordinary antagonist, no village maiden to be snubbed or patronised at her pleasure, but a woman of the world, who understood how to fight her own battles, and was likely, as she was forced to own to herself, to "give back as good as she got."

Not another single word was spoken between them, for at that very minute a door was thrown open, and the whole of the party in the house came trooping forth in pairs from the drawing-room in a long procession on their way to the dining-room.

First came Mr. Miller with old Mrs. Macpherson on his arm. Then Mr. Pryme and Miss Sophy Macpherson; her sister behind with Guy Miller; Beatrice, looking melancholy, with the curate in charge; and her mother last with Sir

John, who had come over from Kynaston to dinner. Edwin Miller, the second son, by himself brought up the rear.

There was some laughter at the expense of the three defaulters, who, of course, were supposed to have only just hurried downstairs.

"Aha! just saved your soup, ladies!" cried Mr. Miller, laughingly. "Fall in, fall in, as best you can!"

Mrs. Miller came to the rescue, and, by a rapid stroke of generalship, marshalled them into their places.

Miss Nevill, of course, was a stranger; Helen had been on intimate terms with them all for years; Vera, besides, was standing close to Maurice.

"Please take in Miss Nevill, Captain Kynaston; and Edwin, my dear, give your arm to Mrs. Romer."

Edwin, who was a pleasant-looking boy, with plenty to say for himself, hurried forward with alacrity; and Helen had to accept her fate with the best grace she could.

"Well, how did you get on with Vera, and how did you like her?" asked Sir John, coming round to his brother's side of the table when the ladies had left the room. He had noted with pleasure that Vera and Maurice had talked incessantly throughout the dinner.

"My dear fellow!" cried Maurice, heartily, "she is the handsomest woman I ever met in my life! I give you my word that, when she introduced herself to me coming downstairs, I was so surprised, she was so utterly different to what I and the mother have been imagining, that upon my life I couldn't speak a word—I could do nothing but stare at her!"

"You like her, then?" said his brother, smiling, well pleased at his openly expressed admiration.

"I think you are a very lucky fellow, old man! Like her! of course I do; she's a downright good sort!"

And if Sir John was slightly shocked at the irreverence of alluding to so perfect and pure a woman as his adored Vera by so familiar a phrase as "a good sort," he was, at all events, too pleased by Maurice's genuine approval of her to find any fault with his method of expressing it.

CHAPTER XI.

AN IDLE MORNING.

We loved, sir; used to meet;
How sad, and bad, and mad it was;
But then, how it was sweet!

BROWNING.

Leaning against a window-frame at the end of a long corridor on the second floor, and idly looking out over the view of the wide lawns and empty flower-beds which it commands, stands Mr. Herbert Pryme, on the second morning after his arrival at Shadonake House.

It is after breakfast, and most of the gentlemen of the house have dispersed; that is to say, Mr. Miller has gone off to survey his new pigsties, and his sons and a Mr. Nethercliff, who arrived last night, have ridden to a meet some fifteen miles distant, which the ladies had voted to be too far off to attend.

Mr. Pryme, however, is evidently not a keen sports-man; he has declined the offer of a mount which Guy Miller has hospitably pressed upon him, and he has also declined to avail himself of his host's offer of the services of the gamekeeper. Curiously enough, another guest at Shadonake, whose zeal for hunting has never yet been impeached, has followed his example.

"What on earth do they meet at Fretly for!" Maurice Kynaston had exclaimed last night to young Guy, as the morrow's plans had been discussed in the smoking-room; "it's the worst country I ever was in, all plough and woodlands, and never a fox to be found. Your uncle ought to know better than to go there. I certainly shan't take the trouble to get up early to go to that place."

"Not go?" repeated Guy, aghast; "you don't mean to say you won't go, Kynaston?"

"That's just what I do mean, though."

"What the deuce will you do with yourself all day?"

"Lie in bed," answered Maurice, between the puffs of his pipe; "we've had a precious hard day's shooting to-day, and I mean to take it easy to-morrow."

And Captain Kynaston was as good as his word. He did not appear in the breakfast-room the next morning until the men who were bound for Fretly had all ridden off and were well out of sight of the house. What he had stayed for he would have been somewhat puzzled to explain. He was not the kind of man who, as a rule, cared to dawdle about all day with women when there was any kind of sport to be had from hunting down to ratting; more especially was he disinclined for any such dawdling when Helen Romer was amongst the number of the ladies so left to be danced attendance upon. And yet he distinctly told himself that he meant to be devoted for this one day to the fair sex. All yesterday he had been crossed and put out; the men had been out shooting from breakfast till dinner; some of the ladies had joined them with the Irish-stew at lunch time; Helen had been amongst them, but not Miss Nevill. Maurice, in spite of the pheasants having been plentiful and the sport satisfactory, had been in a decidedly bad temper all the afternoon in consequence. In the evening the party at dinner had been enlarged by an influx of country neighbours; Vera had been hopelessly divided from him and absorbed by other people the whole evening; he had not exchanged a single word with her all day.

Captain Kynaston was seized with an insatiable desire to improve his acquaintance with his sister-in-law to be. It was his duty, he told himself, to make friends with her; his brother would be hurt, he argued, and his mother would be annoyed if he neglected to pay a proper attention to the future Lady Kynaston. There could be no doubt that it was his duty; that it was also his pleasure did not strike him so forcibly as it should have done, considering the fact that a man is only very keen to create duties for himself when they are proportionately mingled with that which is pleasant and agreeable. The exigencies of his position, with regard to his elder brother's bride having been forcibly borne in upon him—combined possibly with the certain knowledge that the elder brother himself would be hunting all day—compelled him to stop at home and devote himself to Vera. Mr. Herbert Pryme, however, had no such excuse, real or imaginary, and yet he stands idly by the corridor window, idly, yet perfectly patiently—relieving the tedium of his position by the unexciting entertainment of softly whistling the popular airs from the "Cloches de Corneville" below his breath.

Herbert Pryme is a good-looking young fellow of about six-and-twenty; he looks his profession all over, and is a good type of the average young barrister of the present day. He has fair hair, and small, close-cropped whiskers; his face is retrieved from boyishness by strongly-marked and rather heavy features; he studiously affects a solemn and imposing gravity of face and manner, and a severe and elderly style of dress, which he hopes may produce a favourable effect upon the non-legal minds of his somewhat imaginary clients.

It is doubtful, however, whether Mr. Pryme has not found a shorter and pleasanter road to fortune than that slow and toilsome route along which the legal muse leads her patient votaries.

Ten, fifteen, twenty minutes elapse, and still Mr. Pryme looks patiently out of the window, and still he whistles the Song of the Bells. The only sign of weariness he gives is to take out his watch, which, by the way, is suspended by a broad black ribbon, and lives, not in his waistcoat pocket, but in a "fob," and is further decorated by a very large and old-fashioned seal. Having consulted a time piece which for size and thickness might have belonged to his great-grandfather, he returns it to his fob, and resumes his whistling.

Presently a door at the further end of the corridor softly opens and shuts, and Mr. Pryme looks up quickly.

Beatrice Miller, looking about her a little guiltily, comes swiftly towards him along the passage.

"Mamma kept me such ages!" she says, breathlessly; "I thought I should never get away."

"Never mind, so long as you are here," he answers, holding her by both hands. "My darling, I must have a kiss; I hungered for one all yesterday."

He looks into her face eagerly and lovingly. To most people Beatrice is a plain girl, but to this man she is beautiful; his own love for her has invested her with a charm and a fascination that no one else has seen in her.

Oh! divine passion, that can thus glorify its object. It is like a dash of sunshine over a winter landscape, which transforms it into the loveliness of spring; or the magic brush of the painter, which can turn a ploughed field and a barren common into the golden glories of a Cuyp or a Turner.

Thus it was with Herbert Pryme. He looked at Beatrice with the blinding glamour of his own love in his eyes, and she was beautiful to him. Truth to say, Beatrice was a woman whom to love once was to love always. There was so much that was charming and loveable in her character, so great a freshness of mind and soul about her, that, although from lack of beauty she had hitherto failed to attract love, having once secured it, she possessed that rare and valuable faculty of being able to retain it, which many women, even those who are the most beautiful, are incapable of.

"It is just as I imagined about Mr. Nethercliff," says Beatrice, laughing; "he has been asked here for my benefit. Mamma has just been telling me about him; he is Lord Garford's nephew and his heir. Lord Garford's place, you know, is quite the other side of the county; he is poor, so I suppose I might do for him," with a little grimace. "At all events, I am to sit next to him at dinner to-night, and make myself civil. You see, I am to be offered to all the county magnates in succession."

Herbert Pryme still holds her hands, and looks down with grave vexation into her face.

"And how do you suppose I shall feel whilst Mr. Nethercliff is making love to you?"

"You may make your mind quite easy; it is impossible that there should be another man foolish enough in all England to want to make love to such an 'ugly duckling' as I am!"

"Don't be silly, child, and don't fish for compliments," he answers, fondly, stroking her short dark hair, which he thinks so characteristic of herself.

Beatrice looks up happily at him. A woman is always at her very best when she is alone with the man she loves. Unconsciously, all the charms she possesses are displayed in her glistening eyes, and in the colour which comes and goes in her contented face. There is no philtre which beauty can use, there is neither cosmetic nor rouge that can give that tender, lovely glow with which successful love transforms even a plain face into radiance and fascination.

"I wish, Beatrice, you would let me speak to your father," continued Herbert; "I cannot bear to be here under false pretences. Why will you not let me deal fairly and openly with your parents?"

"And be sent about your business by the evening train. No, thank you! My dear boy, speaking to papa would be as much use as speaking to the butler; they would both of them refer you instantly to mamma; and with an equally lamentable result. Please leave things to me. When mamma has offered me ineffectually to every marriageable man in Meadowshire, she will get quite sick of it, and, I dare say, I shall be allowed to do as I like then without any more fuss."

"And how long is this process to last?"

"About a year; by which time Geraldine will be nearly eighteen, and ready to step into my shoes. Mamma will be glad enough to be rid of me then, and to try her hand upon her instead. Geraldine is meek and tractable, and will be quite willing to do as she is told."

"And, meanwhile, what am I to do?"

"You! You are to make love to Sophy Macpherson. Do you not know that she is the excuse for your having been asked here at all?"

"I don't like it, Beatrice," repeats her lover, gravely—not, however, alluding to the duties relating to Miss Macpherson, which she had been urging upon him. "Upon my life, I don't." He looks away moodily out of the window. "I hate doing things on the sly. And, besides, I am a poor man, and your parents are rich. I could not afford to support a wife at present on my own income."

"All the more reason that we should wait," she interrupts, quickly.

"Yes; but I ought not to have spoken to you; I'd no business to steal your heart."

"You did not steal it," she says, nestling up to his side. "I presented it to you, free, gratis."

Where is the man who could resist such an appeal! Away went duty, prudence, and every other laudable consideration to the winds; and Herbert Pryme straightway became insanely and blissfully oblivious of his own poverty, of Mr. Miller's wealth, and of everything else upon earth and under the sun that was not entirely and idiotically delightful and ecstatic.

"You will do as I tell you?" whispers Beatrice.

"Of course I will," answers her lover. And then there is a complete stagnation of the power of speech on both sides for the space of five minutes, during which the clock ticking steadily on at the far end of the corridor has things entirely its own way.

"There is another couple who are happy," says Herbert Pryme, breaking the charmed silence at length, and indicating, by a sign, two people who are wandering slowly down the garden. Beatrice Miller, following the direction of his eyes, sees Maurice Kynaston and Vera.

"Those two?" she exclaims. "Oh dear, no! They are not happy—not in our way. Miss Nevill is engaged to his brother, you know."

"Umph! if I were Sir John Kynaston, I would look after my brother then."

"Herbert! what *can* you mean?" cries Beatrice, opening her eyes in astonishment. "Why, Captain Kynaston is supposed to be engaged to Mrs. Romer; at any rate, she is desperately in love with him."

"Yes, everybody knows that: but is he in love with her?"

"Herbert, I am sure you must be mistaken!" persists Beatrice, eagerly.

"Perhaps I am. Never mind, little woman," kissing her lightly; "I only said they looked happy. If you will take the trouble to remark them through the day, you will, perhaps, be struck by the same blissful aspect that I have noticed. If they are happy, it won't last long. Why should not one be glad to see other people enjoying themselves? Let them be happy whilst they can."

Herbert Pryme was right. Maurice and Vera wandering side by side along the broad gravel walks in the wintry gardens were happy—without so much as venturing to wonder what it was that made them so.

"I did not want to hunt to-day," Maurice is saying; "I thought I would stop at home and talk to you."

"That was kind of you," answers Vera, with a smile.

If she had known him better, she would have been more sensible of the compliment implied. To give up a day's hunting for a woman's sake is what very few keen sports-men have been known to do; the attraction must be great indeed.

"You will go out, of course, on Monday, the day the hounds meet here? I should like to see you on a horse."

"I shall at all events put on a habit and get up on the mare John has given me. But I know very little of English hunting; I have only ridden in Italy. We used to go out in winter over the Campagna—that is very different to England."

"You must look very well in a habit." He turned to look at her as he spoke. There was no reticence in his undisguised admiration of her.

Vera laughed a little. "You shall look at me if you like when I have it on," she said, blushing faintly under his scrutiny.

"I am grateful to you for the permission; but I am bound to confess that I should look all the same had you forbidden me to do so."

Vera was pleased. She felt glad that he admired her. Was it not quite right and most desirable that her husband's brother should appreciate her beauty and ratify his good taste?

"When does your mother come?" she said, changing the subject quietly, but without effort.

"Only the very night of the ball, I am afraid. Tuesday, is it not?"

"Have you written to her about me? She does not like me, I fear."

"No; I will not write. She shall see you and judge for herself. I am not the least afraid of her not liking you when she knows you; and you will love her."

By this time they had wandered away from the house through the belt of shrubbery, and had emerged beyond upon the margin of the pool of water.

Vera stood still, suddenly struck with the sight.

"Is this Shadonake Bath?" she asked, below her breath.

"Yes; have you never seen it before?" he answered, in some surprise.

"Never. I have not lived in Meadowshire long, you know, and the Millers were moving into the house and furnishing it all last summer. I have never been in the gardens till to-day. How strangely sad the place looks! Let us walk round it."

They went round to the further side.

The pool of water lay dark and silent within its stone steps; not a ripple disturbed its surface; not a dead leaf rested on its bosom. Only the motionless water looked up everlastingly at the gray winter skies above, and reflected them back blackly and gloomily upon its solemn face.

Vera stood still and looked at it. Something in its aspect—she could not have told what—affected her powerfully. She went down two or three steps towards the water, and stooped over it intently.

Maurice, watching her curiously, saw, to his surprise, that she trembled. She turned round to him.

"Does it not look dark and deep? Is it very deep?"

"I believe it is. There are all sorts of stories about it. Come up, Vera; why do you tremble so?"

"How dreadful to be drowned here!" she said, below her breath, and she shuddered.

He stretched out his hand to her.

"Do not say such horrid things! Give me your hand—the steps are slippery. What has put drowning into your head? And—why, how pale you are; what has frightened you?"

She took his hand and came back again to where he stood.

"Do you believe in presentiments?" she said, slowly, with her eyes fixed still, as though by some fascination, upon the dark waters beneath them.

"Not in the very least," he answered, cheerily; "do not think of such things. John would be the first to scold you—and to scold me for bringing you here."

He stood, holding her hand, looking at her kindly and compassionately; suddenly she looked at him, and as their eyes met once more, she trembled from head to foot.

"Vera, you are frightened; tell me what it is!"

"I don't know! I don't know!" she cried, with a sudden wail, like a person in pain; "only—oh! I wish I had not seen it for the first time with *you*!"

Before he could answer her, some one, *beckoning* to them from the further side of the pool, caused them both to turn suddenly round.

It was not only Herbert Pryme who had seen them wander away down the garden from the house. Mrs. Romer, too, had been at another window and had noticed them. To run lightly upstairs, put on her hat and jacket, and to follow them, had been the work of but a very few minutes. Helen was not minded to allow Maurice to wander about all the morning with Vera.

"Are you going for a walk?" she called out to them across the water. "Wait for me; I am coming with you."

Vera turned quickly to her companion.

"Is it true that you are engaged to her?" she asked him rapidly, in a low voice.

Maurice hesitated. Morally speaking, he was engaged to her; but, then, it had been agreed between them that he was to deny any such engagement. He felt singularly disinclined to let Vera know what was the truth.

"People say you are," she said, once more. "Will you tell me if it is true?"

"No; there is no engagement between us," he answered, gravely.

"I am very glad," she answered, earnestly. He coloured, but he had no time to ask her why she was glad—for Helen came up to them.

"How interested you look in each other's conversation!" she said, looking suspiciously at them both. "May I not hear what you have been talking about?"

"Anybody might hear," answered Vera, carelessly, "were it worth one's while to take the trouble of repeating it."

Maurice said nothing. He was angry with Helen for having interrupted them, and angry with himself for having denied his semi-engagement. He stood looking away from them both, prodding his stick into the gravel walk.

For half a minute they stood silently together.

"Let us go on," said Vera, and they began to walk.

Once again in the days that were to come those three stood side by side upon the margin of Shadonake Bath.

CHAPTER XII.

THE MEET AT SHADONAKE.

The desire of the moth for the star,
Of the night for the morrow,
The devotion to something afar.

SHELLEY.

Mrs. Macpherson had brought up her daughters with one fixed and predominant idea in her mind. Each of them was to excel in some one taste or accomplishment, by virtue of which they might be enabled to shine in society. They were taught to do one thing well. Thus, Sophy, the eldest, played the piano remarkably, whilst Jessie painted in water-colours with charming exactitude and neatness. They had both had first-rate masters, and no pains had been spared to make each of them proficient in the accomplishment that had been selected for her. But, as neither of these young ladies had any natural talent, the result was hardly so satisfactory as their fond mother could have desired. They did exactly what they had been taught to do with precision and conscientiousness; no less and no more; and the further result of their entire devotion to one kind of study was, that they could do nothing else.

Mrs. Macpherson began to realize that her system of education had possibly left something to be desired on the Monday morning that Mr. Esterworth brought up his hounds to Shadonake House. It was provoking to see all the other ladies attired in their habits, whilst her own daughters had to come down to breakfast in their ordinary morning dresses, because they had never been taught to ride.

"Are you not going to ride?" she heard Guy Miller ask of Sophy, who was decidedly the best looking and the pleasantest of the sisters.

"No, we have never ridden at all; mamma never thought we had the time for it," answers Sophy.

"I think," said Mrs. Macpherson, turning to her hostess, "that I shall pursue a different course with my younger girls. I feel sorry now that Sophy and Jessie do not ride. Music and painting are, of course, the most charming accomplishments that a woman can have; but still it is not at all times that they are useful."

"No, you cannot be always painting and playing."

"Neither can you be always riding," said Mrs. Macpherson, with some asperity, for there was a little natural jealousy between these ladies on the subject of their girls; "but still——"

"But still, you will acknowledge that I have done right in letting Beatrice hunt. You may be quite sure that there is no accomplishment which brings a girl so much into notice in the country. Look at her now."

Mrs. Macpherson looked and saw Beatrice in her habit at the far end of the dining-room surrounded by a group of men in pink, and she also saw her own daughters sitting neglected by themselves on the other side of the room. She made no observation upon the contrast, for it would hardly have been polite to have done so; but she made a mental note of the fact that Mrs. Miller was a very clever woman, and that, if you want an ugly daughter to marry, you had better let her learn how to ride across country. And she furthermore decided that her third daughter, Alice, who was not blessed with the gift of beauty, should forthwith abandon the cultivation of a very feeble and uncertain vocal organ and be sent to the nearest riding-school the very instant she returned to her home.

Beatrice Miller rode very well indeed; it was the secret of her uncle's affection for her, and many a good day's sport had the two enjoyed side by side across the flat fields and the strong fences and wide ditches of their native country. Her brothers, Guy and Edwin, were fond of hunting too, but they rode clumsily and awkwardly, floundering across country in what their uncle called, contemptuously, a thoroughly "provincial style." But Beatrice had the true Esterworth seat and hand; she looked as if she were born to her saddle, and, in truth, she was never so happy as when she was in it. It was a proof of how great and real was her love to Herbert Pryme that she fully recognized that, in becoming his wife, she would have to live in London entirely and to give up her beloved hunting for his sake.

A woman who rides, as did Beatrice, is sure to be popular on a hunting morning; and, with the consciousness of her lover's hands resting upon the back of her chair, with her favourite uncle by her side, and with several truly ardent admirers of her good riding about her, Miss Miller was evidently enjoying herself thoroughly.

The scene, indeed, was animated to the last degree. The long dining-room was filled with guests, the table was covered with good things, a repast, half breakfast, half luncheon, being laid out upon it. Everybody helped themselves, with much chattering and laughter, and there was a pleasant sense of haste and excitement, and a charming informality about the proceedings, which made the Shadonake Hunt breakfast, which Tom Esterworth had been prevailed upon by his niece's entreaties to allow, a thorough and decided success.

Outside there were the hounds, drawn up in patient expectation on the grass beyond the gravel sweep, the bright coats and velvet caps of the men, and the gray horses—on which it was the Meadowshire tradition that they should be always mounted—standing out well against the dark background of the leafless woods behind. Then there were a goodly company who had not dismounted, and to whom glasses of sherry were being handed by the servants, and who also were chattering to each other, or to those on foot, whilst before the door, an object of interest to those within as to those without, Sir John Kynaston was putting Miss Nevill upon her horse.

There was not a man present who did not express his admiration for her beauty and her grace; hardly a woman who did not instantly make some depreciatory remark. The latter fact spoke perhaps more convincingly for the undoubted success she had created than did the former.

Maurice was standing by one of the dining-room windows, Mrs. Romer, as usual, by his side. He alone, perhaps, of all the men who saw her vault lightly into her saddle, made no audible remark, but perhaps his admiration was all too plainly written in his eyes, for it called forth a contemptuous remark from his companion—

"She is a great deal too tall to look well on a horse; those big women should never ride."

"What! not with a figure so perfect as hers?"

"Yes, that is the third time you have spoken about her figure to-day," said Helen, irritably. "What on earth can you see in it?" for Mrs. Romer, who was slight almost to angularity, was, as all thin women are, openly indignant at the masculine foible for more flowing outlines, which was displayed with greater candour than discretion by her quasi-lover.

"What do I see in it?" repeated Maurice, who was dimly conscious of her jealousy, and was injudicious enough to lose his temper slightly over its exhibition. "I see in it the beauty of a goddess, and the perfection of a woman!"

"Really!" with a sarcastic laugh; "how wonderfully enthusiastic and poetical you become over Miss Nevill's charms; it is something quite new in you, Maurice. Your interest in this 'goddess-like' young lady strikes me as singularly warmly expressed; it is more lover-like than fraternal."

"What do you mean?" he said, looking at her coldly and angrily. Helen had seen that look of hard contempt in his face before; she quailed a little before it, and was frightened at what she had said.

"Of course," she said, reddening, "I know it's all right; but it does really sound peculiar, your admiring her so much; and—and—it is hardly flattering to me."

"I don't see that it has anything to do with you," and he turned shortly away from her.

She made a step or two after him. "You will ride with me, will you not, Maurice? You know I can't go very hard; you might give me a lead or two, and keep near me."

"You must not ask me to make any promises," he said, politely, but coldly. "Guy Miller says there is a groom told off to look after you ladies. Of course, if I can be of any use to you, I shall be happy, but it is no use making rash engagements as to what one will do in a run."

"Come, come, it's time we were off," cries out Tom Esterworth at the further end of the room, and his stalwart figure makes its way in the direction of the door.

In a very few minutes the order "to horse" has gone forth, and the whole company have sallied forth and are busy mounting their horses in front of the house.

Off goes the master, well in front, at a sharp trot, towards the woods on the further slope of the hill, and off go the hounds and the whips, and the riders, in a long and gay procession after him, down the wide avenue.

"Promise me you will not stop out long, Vera," says Sir John to her as they go side by side down the drive. "You look white and tired as it is. Have you got a headache?"

"Yes, a little," confesses Vera, with a blush. "I did not sleep well."

"This sitting up late night after night is not good for you," says her lover, anxiously; "and there is the ball to-morrow night."

"Yes; and I want to look my best for your mother," she said, smiling. "I will take care of myself, John; I will go home early in time for lunch."

"You are always so ready to do what I ask you. Oh, Vera, how good you are! how little I deserve such a treasure!"

"Don't," she answers, almost sharply, whilst an expression of pain contracts her brow for an instant. "Don't say such things to me, John; don't call me good."

John Kynaston looks at her fondly. "I will not call you anything you don't wish," he says, gently, "but I am free to think it, Vera!"

The first covert is successfully drawn without much delay. A fox is found, and breaks away across the open, and a short but sharp burst of fifteen or twenty minutes follows. The field is an unusually large one, and there are many out who are not in it at all. Beatrice, however, is well up, and so is Herbert Pryme, who is not likely to be far from her side. Close behind them follows Sir John Kynaston, and Mrs. Romer, who is well mounted upon one of Edwin Miller's horses, keeps well up with the rest.

Vera never quite knew how it was that somehow or other she got thrown out of that short but exciting run. She was on the wrong side of the covert to begin with; several men were near her, but they were all strangers, and at the time "Gone away!" was shouted, there was no one to tell her which way to take. Two men took the left side of the copse, three others turned to the right. Vera followed the latter, and found that the hounds must have gone in the opposite direction, for when she got round the wood not a trace of them was to be seen.

She did not know the country well, and she hardly knew which way to turn. It seemed to her, however, that by striking across a small field to the left of her she would cut off a corner, and eventually come up with the hounds again.

She turned her mare short round, and put her at a big straggling hedge which she had no fears of her being unable to compass. There was, however, more of a drop on the further side than she had counted upon, and in some way, as the mare landed, floundering on the further side, something gave way, and she found that her stirrup-leather had broken.

Vera pulled up and looked about her helplessly. She found herself in a small spinney of young birch-trees, filling up the extremity of a triangular field into which she had come. Not a sign of the hounds, or, indeed, of any living creature was to be seen in any direction. She did not feel inclined to go on— or even to go back home with her broken stirrup-leather. It occurred to her that she would get off and see what she could do towards patching it together herself.

With some little difficulty, her mare being fidgety, and refusing to stand still, she managed to dismount; but in doing so her wrist caught against the pommel of her saddle, and was so severely wrenched backwards, as she sprang to the ground, that she turned quite sick with the pain.

It seemed to her that her wrist must be sprained; at all events, her right hand was, for the minute, perfectly powerless. The mare, perceiving that nothing further was expected of her, amused herself by cropping the short grass at her feet, whilst Vera stood by her side in dire perplexity as to what she was to do next. Just then she heard the welcome sound of a horse's hoofs in the adjoining field, and in another minute a hat and black coat, followed by a horse's head and forelegs appeared on the top of the fence, and a man dropped over into the spinney just ten yards in front of her.

Vera took it to be her lover, for the brothers both hunted in black, and there was a certain family resemblance between their broad shoulders and the square set of their heads. She called out eagerly,

"Oh, John! how glad I am to see you! I have come to grief!"

"So I see; but I am not John. I hope, however, I may do as well. What is the matter?"

"It is you, Maurice? Oh, yes, you will do quite as well. I have broken my stirrup-leather, and I am afraid I have sprained my wrist."

"That sounds bad—let me see."

In an instant he had sprung from his horse to help her.

She looked up at him as he came, pushing the tall brushwood away as he stepped through it. It struck her suddenly how like he was to the photograph she had found of him at Kynaston long ago, and what a well-made man he was, and how brave and handsome he looked in his hunting gear.

"How have you managed to hurt your wrist? Let me see it."

"I wrenched it somehow in jumping down; but I don't think that it can be sprained, for I find I can move it now a little; it is only bruised, but it hurts me horribly."

She turned back her cuff and held out the injured hand to him. Maurice stooped over it. There was a moment's silence, the two horses stood waiting patiently by, the solitary fields lay bare and lifeless on every side of them, the little birch-trees rustled mysteriously overhead, the leaden sky, with its chill curtain of unbroken gray cloud, spread monotonously above them; there was no living thing in all the winter landscape besides to listen or to watch them.

Suddenly Maurice Kynaston caught the hand that he held to his lips, and pressed half a dozen passionate kisses upon its outstretched palm.

It was the work of half a minute, and in the next Maurice felt as if he should die of shame and remorse.

"For God's sake, forgive me!" he cried, brokenly. "I am a brute—I forgot myself—I must be mad, I think; for Heaven's sake tell me that I have not offended you past forgiveness, Vera!"

His pulses were beating wildly, his face was flushed, the hands that still held hers shook with a nameless emotion; he looked imploringly into her face, as if to read his sentence in her eyes, but what he saw there arrested the torrent of repentance and regret that was upon his lips.

Upon Vera's face there was no flush either of shame or anger. No storm of indignation, no passion of insulted feeling; only eyes wide open and terror-stricken, that met his with the unspeakable horror that one sees sometimes in those of a hunted animal. She was pale as death. Then suddenly the colour flushed hotly back into her face; she averted her eyes.

"Let me go home," she said, in a faint voice; "help me to get on to my horse, Maurice."

There was neither resentment nor anger in her voice, only a great weariness.

He obeyed her in silence. Possibly he felt that he had stood for one instant upon the verge of a precipice, and that miraculously her face had saved him, he knew not how, where words would only have dragged him down to unutterable ruin.

What had it been that had thus saved him? What was the meaning of that terror that had been written in her lovely eyes? Since she was not angry, what had she feared?

Maurice asked himself these questions vainly all the way home. Not a word was spoken between them; they rode in absolute silence side by side until they reached the house.

Then, as he lifted her off her horse at the hall-door, he whispered,

"Have you forgiven me?"

"There was nothing to forgive," she answered, in a low, strained voice. She spoke wearily, as one who is suffering physical pain. But, as she spoke, the hand that he still held seemed almost, to his fancy, to linger for a second with a gentle fluttering pressure within his grasp.

Miss Nevill went into the house, having utterly forgotten that she had sprained her wrist; a fact which proves indisputably, I suppose, that the injury could not have been of a very serious nature.

CHAPTER XIII.

PEACOCK'S FEATHERS.

That practised falsehood under saintly show,
Deep malice to conceal, couched with revenge.

MILTON, "Paradise Lost."

Old Lady Kynaston arrived at Shadonake in the worst possible temper. Her butler and factotum, who always made every arrangement for her when she was about to travel, had for once been unequal to cope with Bradshaw; he had looked out the wrong train, and had sent off his lady and her maid half-an-hour too late from Walpole Lodge.

The consequence was that, instead of reaching Shadonake comfortably at half-past six in the afternoon, Lady Kynaston had to wait for the next train. She ate her dinner alone, in London, at the Midland Railway Hotel, and never reached her destination till half-past nine on the night of the ball.

Before she had half completed her toilette the guests were beginning to arrive.

"I am afraid I must go down and receive these people, dear Lady Kynaston," said Mrs. Miller, who had remained in her guest's room full of regret and sympathy at the *contretemps* of her journey.

"Oh, dear me! yes, Caroline—pray go down. I shall be all the quicker for being left alone. Not *that* cap, West; the one with the Spanish point, of course. Dear me, how I do hate all this hurry and confusion!"

"I am so afraid you will be tired," murmured Mrs. Miller, soothingly. "Would you like me to send Miss Nevill up to your room? It might be pleasanter for you than to meet her downstairs."

"Good gracious, no!" exclaimed the elder lady, testily. "What on earth should I be in such a hurry for! I shall see quite as much of her as I want by-and-by, I have no doubt."

Mrs. Miller retired, and the old lady was left undisturbed to finish her toilette, during which it may fairly be assumed that that dignified personage, Mrs. West, had a hard time of it.

When she issued forth from her room, dressed, like a little fairy godmother, in point lace and diamonds, the dancing downstairs was in full swing.

Lady Kynaston paused for a minute at the top of the broad staircase to look down upon the bright scene below. The hall was full of people. Girls in many-coloured dresses passed backwards and forwards from the ball-room to the refreshment-room, laughing and chatting to their partners; elderly people were congregated about the doorways gossiping and shaking hands with new-comers, or watching their daughters with pleased or anxious faces, according to the circumstances of their lot. Everybody was talking at once. There came up a pleasant confusion of sound—happy voices mingling with the measured strains of the dance-music. In a sheltered corner behind the staircase, Beatrice and Herbert Pryme had settled themselves down comfortably for a chat. Lady Kynaston saw them.

"Caroline is a fool!" she muttered to herself. "All the balls in the world won't get that girl married as she wishes. She has set her heart upon that briefless barrister. I saw it as plain as daylight last season. As to entertaining all this *cohue* of aborigines, Caroline might spare her trouble and her money, as far as the girl is concerned."

And then, coming slowly down the staircase, Lady Kynaston saw something which restored her to good temper at once.

The something was her younger son. She had caught sight of him through an open doorway in the conservatory. His back was turned to her, and he was bending over a lady who was sitting down, and whose face was concealed behind him.

Lady Kynaston stood still with that sudden *serrement de coeur* which comes to us all when we see the creature we love best on earth. He did not see her, and she could not see his face, because it was turned away from her; but she knew, by his very attitude, the way he bent down over his companion, by the eager manner in which he was talking to her, and by the way in which he was evidently entirely engrossed and absorbed in what he was saying—that he was enjoying himself, and that he was happy.

The mother's heart all went out towards him; the mother's eyes moistened as she looked.

The couple in the conservatory were alone. A Chinese lantern, swung high up above, shed down a soft radiance upon them. Tall camellia bushes, covered with waxen blossoms and cool shiny leaves, were behind them; banks of long-fronded, feathery ferns framed them in like a picture. Maurice's handsome figure stood up tall and strong amongst the greenery; the dress of the woman he was with lay in soft diaphanous folds upon the ground beyond him. One white arm rested on her lap, one tiny foot peeped out from below the laces of her skirt. But Lady Kynaston could not see her face.

"I wonder who she is," she said to herself. "It is not Helen. She has peacock's feathers on her dress—bad luck, I believe! Dear boy, he looks thoroughly happy. I will not disturb him now."

And she passed on through the hall into the large drawing-room, where the dancing was going on.

The first person she caught sight of there was her eldest son. He was dancing a quadrille, and his partner was a short young lady in a strawberry-coloured tulle dress, covered with trails of spinach-green fern leaves. This young person had a round, chubby face, with bright apple-hued cheeks, a dark, bullet-shaped head, and round, bead-like eyes that glanced about her rapidly like those of a frightened dickey-bird. Her dress was cut very low, and the charms she exhibited were not captivating. Her arms were very red, and her shoulders were mottled: the latter is considered to be a healthy sign in a baby, but is hardly a beautiful characteristic in a grown woman.

"*That* is my daughter-in-law," said Lady Kynaston to herself, and she almost groaned aloud. "She is *worse* even than I thought! Countrified and common to the last degree; there will be no licking that face or that figure into shape— they are hopeless! Elise and Worth combined could do nothing with her! John must be mad. No wonder she is good, poor thing," added the naughty little old lady, cynically. "A woman with *that* appearance can never be tempted to be anything else!"

The quadrille came to an end, and Sir John, after depositing his partner at the further side of the room, came up to his mother.

"My dear mother, how are you? I am so sorry about your journey; you must be dead beat. What a fool Bates was to make such a mistake." He was looking about the room as he spoke. "I must introduce you to Vera."

"Yes, introduce me to her at once," said his mother, in a resigned and depressed tone of voice. She would like to have added, "And pray get it over as soon as you can." What she did say was only, "Bring her up to me now. The young lady you have just been dancing with, I suppose!"

"What!" cried Sir John, and burst out laughing. "Good Heavens, mother! that was Miss Smiles, the daughter of the parson of Lutterton. You don't mean to say you thought a little ugly chit like *that* was my Vera!"

His mother suddenly laid her hand upon his arm.

"Who is that lovely woman who has just come in with Maurice?" she exclaimed.

Her son followed the direction of her eyes, and beheld Vera standing in the doorway that led from the conservatory by his brother's side.

Without a word he passed his mother's hand through his arm and led her across the room.

"Vera, this is my mother," he said. And Lady Kynaston owned afterwards that she never felt so taken aback and so utterly struck dumb with astonishment in her life.

Her two sons looked at her with amusement and some triumph. The little surprise had been so thoroughly carried out; the contrast of the truth to what they knew she had expected was too good a joke not to be enjoyed.

"Not much what you expected, little mother, is it?" said Maurice, laughingly. But to Vera, who knew nothing, it was no laughing matter.

She put both her hands out tremblingly and hesitatingly—with a pretty pleading look of deprecating deference in her eyes—and the little old lady, who valued beauty and grace and talent so much that she could barely tolerate goodness itself without them, was melted at once.

"My dear," she said, "you are beautiful, and I am going to love you; but these naughty boys made me think you were something like little Miss Smiles."

"Nay, mother, it was your own diseased imagination," laughed Maurice; "but come, Vera, I am not going to be cheated of this waltz—if John does not want you to dance with him, that is to say."

John nodded pleasantly to them, and the two whirled away together into the midst of the throng of dancers.

"Well, mother?"

"My dear, she is a very beautiful creature, and I have been a silly, prejudiced old woman."

"And you forgive her for being poor, and for living in a vicarage instead of a castle?"

"She would be a queen if she were a beggar and lived in a mud hovel!" answered his mother, heartily, and Sir John was satisfied.

Lady Kynaston's eyes were following the couple as they danced: for all her admiration and her enthusiasm, there was a little anxiety in their gaze. She had not forgotten the little picture she had caught a glimpse of in the conservatory, nor had her woman's eyes failed to notice that Vera's dress was trimmed with peacock's feathers.

Where was Helen? Lady Kynaston said to herself; and why was Maurice devoting himself to his future sister-in-law instead of to her?

Mrs. Romer, you may be sure, had not been far off. Her sharp eyes had seen Vera and Maurice disappear together into the conservatory. She could have told to a second how long they had remained there; and again, when they came out, she had watched the little family scene that had taken place at the door. She had seen the look of delighted surprise on Lady Kynaston's face; she had noted how pleased and how proud of Vera the brothers had looked, and then how happily Maurice and Vera had gone off again together.

"What does it mean?" Helen asked herself, bitterly. "Is Sir John a fool or blind that he does not see what is going on under his nose? She has got him, and his money, and his place; what does she want with Maurice too? Why can't she let him alone—she is taking him from me."

She watched them eagerly and feverishly. They stood still for a moment near her; she could not hear what they said, but she could see the look in Maurice's eyes as he bent towards his partner.

Can a woman who has known what love is ever be mistaken about that?

Vera, all wondering and puzzled, might be but dimly conscious of the meaning in the eyes that met hers; her own drooped, half troubled, half confused, before them. But to Helen, who knew what love's signals were, there was no mystery whatever in the passion in his down-bent glance.

"He loves her!" she said to herself, whilst a sharp pang, almost of physical pain, shot through her heart. "She shall never get him!—never! never! Not though one of us die for it! They are false, both of them. I swear they shall never be happy together!"

"Why are you not dancing, Mrs. Romer?" said a voice at her elbow.

"I will dance with you, Sir John, if you will ask me," answers Helen, smiling.

Sir John responds, as in duty bound, by passing his arm around her waist.

"When are you going to be married, Sir John?" she asks him, when the first pause in the dance gives her the opportunity of speech.

Sir John looks rather confused. "Well, to tell you the truth, I have not spoken to Vera yet. I have not liked to hurry her—I thought, perhaps——"

"Why don't you speak to her? A woman never thinks any better of a man for being diffident in such matters."

"You think not? But you see Vera is——"

"Vera is very much like all other women, I suppose; and you are not versed in the ways of the sex."

Sir John demurred in his own mind as to the first part of her speech. Vera was certainly not like other women; but then he acknowledged the truth of Mrs. Romer's last remark thoroughly.

"No, I dare say I don't know much about women's ways," he admitted; "and you think——"

"I think that Vera would be glad enough to be married as soon as she can. An engagement is a trying ordeal. One is glad enough to get settled down. What is the use of waiting when once everything is arranged?"

Sir John flushed a little. The prospect of a speedy marriage was pleasant to him. It was what he had been secretly longing for—only that, in his slow way, he had not yet been able to suggest it.

"Do you really think she would like it?" he asked, earnestly.

"Of course she would; any woman would."

"And how long do you think the preparations would take?"

"Oh, a month or three weeks is ample time to get clothes in."

His pulses beat hotly at the bare possibility of such a thing. To possess his Vera in so short a time seemed something too great and too wonderful to be true.

"Do not lose any more time," continued Helen, following up the impression she saw she had made upon him. "Speak to her this evening; get her to fix your wedding-day within the month; believe me, a man gets no advantage by putting things off too long; and there are dangers, too, in your case."

"Dangers! How do you mean?" he said, quickly.

"Oh, nothing particular—only she is very handsome, and she is young, and not accustomed, I dare say, to admiration. Other men may admire her as well as you."

"If they did, it could do her no harm," he answered, stiffly.

"Oh, no, of course not; but you can't keep other men from looking at her. When once she is your wife you will have her more completely to yourself."

Sir John made no particular answer to this; but when he had done dancing with Mrs. Romer, he led her back to her seat and thanked her gravely and courteously for her suggestions.

"You have done me a great service, Mrs. Romer, and I am infinitely obliged to you," he said, and then went his way to find Vera.

He was not jealous; but there was a certain uneasiness in his mind. It might be, indeed, true that others would admire and love Vera; others more worthy of her, more equally mated with her youth and loveliness; and he, he said to himself in his humility with regard to her, he had so little to offer her— nothing but his love. He knew himself to be grave and quiet; there was nothing about him to enchain her to him. He lacked brilliancy in manner and conversation; he was dull; he was, perhaps, even prosy. He knew it very well himself; but suppose Vera should find it out, and find that she had made a mistake! The bare thought of it was enough to make him shudder.

No; Mrs. Romer was a clever, well-intentioned little woman. She had meant to give him a hint in all kindness, and he would not be slow to take it. What she had meant to say was, "Take her yourself quickly, or some one else will take her from you."

And Sir John said to himself that he would so take her, and that as quickly as possible.

Standing talking to her younger son, later on that evening, Lady Kynaston said to him, suddenly,

"Why does Vera wear peacock's feathers?"

"Why should she not?"

"They are bad luck."

Maurice laughed. "I never knew you to be superstitious before, mother."

"I am not so really; but from choice I would avoid anything that bears an unlucky interpretation. I saw her with you in the conservatory as I came downstairs."

Maurice turned suddenly red. "Did you?" he asked, a little anxiously.

"Yes. I did not know it was her, of course. I did not see her face, only her dress, and I noticed that it was trimmed with peacock's feathers; that was what made me recognize her afterwards."

"That was bad luck, at all events," said Maurice, almost involuntarily.

"Why?" asked Lady Kynaston, looking up at him sharply. But Maurice would not tell her why.

Lady Kynaston asked no more questions; but she pondered, and she watched. Captain Kynaston did not dance again with Vera that night, and he did dance several times with Mrs. Romer; it did not escape her notice, however, that he seemed absent and abstracted, and that his face bore its hardest and sternest aspect throughout the remainder of the evening.

So the ball at Shadonake came to an end, as balls do, with the first gleams of daylight; and nothing was left of all the gay crowd who had so lately filled the brilliant rooms but several sleepy people creeping up slowly to bed, and a great *chiffonade* of tattered laces, and flowers, and coloured scraps littered all over the polished floor of the ball-room.

CHAPTER XIV.

HER WEDDING DRESS.

Those obstinate questionings
Of sense and outward things,
Fallings from us, vanishings,
Blank misgivings—High instincts before which our moral nature
Did tremble like a guilty thing surprised.

WORDSWORTH.

"Vera, are you not coming to look at it?"

"Presently."

"It is all laid out on your bed, and you ought to try it on; it might want alterations."

"Oh, there is plenty of time!"

"It is downright affectation!" says old Mrs. Daintree, angrily, to her daughter-in-law, as she and Marion leave the room together; "no girl can really be indifferent to a wedding dress covered with yards of lovely Brussels lace flounces; she ought to be ashamed of herself for her ingratitude to Lady Kynaston for such a present; she must really want to see it, only she likes playing the fine lady beforehand!"

"I don't think it is that," says Marion, gently; "I don't believe Vera is well."

"Fiddlesticks!" snorts her mother-in-law. "A woman who is going to marry ten thousand a year within ten days is bound to be well."

Vera sits alone; she leans her head against the window, her hands lie idle in her lap, her eyes mechanically follow the rough, gray clouds that rack across the winter sky. In little more than a week she will be Vera Nevill no longer; she will have gained all that she desired and tried for—wealth, position, Kynaston—and Sir John! She should be well content, seeing that it has been her own doing all along. No one has forced or persuaded her into this engagement, no one has urged her on to a course contrary to her own inclination, or her own judgment. It has been her own act throughout. And yet, as she sits alone in the twilight, and counts over on her fingers the few short days that intervene between to-day and her bridal morning, hot miserable tears rise to her eyes, and fall slowly down, one by one, upon her clasped hands. She does not ask herself why she weeps; possibly she dares not. Only her thoughts somehow—by that strange connection of ideas which links something in our present to some other thing in our past, and which apparently is in no way dependent upon it—go back instinctively, as it were, to her dead sister, the Princess Marinari.

"Oh, my poor darling Theodora!" she murmurs, half aloud; "if you had lived, you would have taken care of your Vera; if you had not died, I should never have come here, nor ever have known—any of them."

And then she hears Marion's voice calling to her from the top of the stairs.

"Vera! Vera! do come up and see it before it gets quite dark."

She rises hastily and dashes away her tears.

"What is the matter with me to-day!" she says to herself, impatiently. "Have I not everything in the world I wish for? I am happy—of course I am happy. I am coming, Marion, instantly."

Upstairs her wedding dress, a soft cloud of rich silk and fleecy lace, relieved with knots of flowers, dark-leaved myrtle, and waxen orange blossoms, lies spread out upon her bed. Marion stands contemplating it, wrapt in ecstatic admiration; old Mrs. Daintree has gone away.

"It is perfectly lovely! I am so glad you had silk instead of satin; nothing could show off Lady Kynaston's lace so well: is it not beautiful? you ought to try it on. Why, Vera! what is the matter? I believe you have been crying."

"I was thinking of Theodora," she murmurs.

"Ah! poor dear Theodora!" assents Marion, with a compassionate sigh; "how she would have liked to have known of your marriage; how pleased she would have been."

Vera looks at her sister. "Marion," she says, in a low earnest voice; "if—if I should break it off, what would you say?"

"Break it off!" cries her sister, horror-struck. "Good heavens, Vera! what can you mean? Have you gone suddenly mad? What is the matter with you? Break off a match like this at the last minute? You must be demented!"

"Oh, of course," with a sudden change of manner; "of course I did not mean it, it only came into my head for a minute; of course, as you say, it is a splendid match for me. What should I want to break it off for? What should I gain? what, indeed?" She spoke feverishly and excitedly, laughing a little harshly as she spoke.

Marion looked at her anxiously. "I hope to goodness you will never say such horrid things to anybody else; it sounds dreadful, Vera, as if Eustace and I were forcing you into it; as if you did not want to marry Sir John yourself."

"Of course I want to marry him!" interrupted Vera, with unreasonable sharpness.

"Then, pray don't make a fool of yourself, my dear, by talking about breaking it off."

"It was only a joke. Break it off! how could I? The best match in the county, as you say. I am not going to make a fool of myself; don't be afraid, Marion. It would be so inconvenient, too; the trousseau all bought, the breakfast ordered, the guests invited; even the wedding dress here, all finished and ready to put on, and ten thousand a year waiting for me! Oh, no, I am not going to be such an utter fool!"

She laughed; but her laughter was almost more sad than her tears, and her sister left her, saddened and puzzled by her manner.

It was now nearly two months since the ball at Shadonake; and, soon after that eventful visit, Vera had begun to be employed in preparing for her wedding-day, which had been fixed for the 27th of February; for Sir John had taken Mrs. Romer's hint, and had pressed an early marriage upon her. Vera had made no objection; what objection, indeed, could she have found to make? She had acquiesced readily in her lover's suggestions, and had set to work to prepare herself for her marriage.

All this time Captain Kynaston had not been in Meadowshire at all; he had declined his brother's hospitality, and had gone to spend his leave amongst other friends in Somersetshire, where he had started a couple of hunters, and wrote word to Sir John that the sport was of such a very superior nature that he was unable to tear himself away.

Within a fortnight, however, of Sir John's wedding, Maurice did yield at last to his brother's pressing request, and came up from Somersetshire to Kynaston. Last Sunday he had suddenly appeared in the Kynaston pew in Sutton Church by Sir John's side, and had shaken hands with Vera and her relations on coming out of church, and had walked across the vicarage garden by the side of Mrs. Daintree, Vera having gone on in front with Tommy and Minnie. And it was from that moment that Vera had as suddenly discovered that she was utterly and thoroughly wretched, and that she dreaded her wedding-day with a strange and unaccountable terror.

She told herself that she was out of health, that the excitement and bustle of the necessary preparations had over-tried her, that her nerves were upset, her spirits depressed by reason of the solemnity a woman naturally feels at the approach of so important a change in her life. She assured herself aloud, day after day, that she was perfectly happy and content, that she was the very luckiest and most fortunate of women, and that she would sooner be Sir John's wife than the wife of any one else in the world. And she told it to herself so often and so emphatically, that there were whole hours, and even whole days together, when she believed in these self-assurances implicitly and thoroughly.

All this time she saw next to nothing of Maurice Kynaston; the weather was mild and open, and he went out hunting every day. Sir John, on the other hand, was much with her; a constant necessity for his presence seemed to possess her. She was never thoroughly content but when he was with her; ever restless and ill at ease in his absence.

No one could be more thoroughly convinced than Vera of the entire wisdom of the marriage she was about to make. It was, she felt persuaded, the best and the happiest thing she could have done with her life. Wealth, position, affection, were all laid at her feet; and her husband, moreover, would be a man whose goodness and whose devotion to her could never fail to command her respect. What more could a woman who, like herself, was fully alive to the importance of the good things of this world desire? Surely nothing more. Vera, when she was left alone with the glories of her wedding garment, took herself to task for her foolish words to her sister.

"I am a fool!" she said to herself, half angrily, as she bundled all the white silk and the rich lace unceremoniously away into an empty drawer of her wardrobe. "I am a fool to say such things even to Marion. It looks, as she says, as if I were being forced into a rich marriage by my friends. I am very fond of John; I shall make him a most exemplary wife, and I shall look remarkably well in the family diamonds, and that is all that can possibly be required of me."

Having thus settled things comfortably in her own mind, she went downstairs again, and was in such good spirits, and so radiant with smiles for the rest of the evening, that Mr. Daintree remarked to his wife, when they had retired into their conjugal chamber, that he had never seen Vera look so well or so happy.

"Dear child," he said, "it is a great comfort to me to see it, for just at first I feared that she had been influenced by the money and the position, and that her heart was not in it; but now she has evidently become much attached to Sir John, and is perfectly happy; and he is a most excellent man, and in every way worthy of her. Did I tell you, Marion, that he told me the chancel should be begun immediately after the wedding? It is a pity it could not have been done before; but we shall just get it finished by Easter."

"I am glad of that. We must fill the church with flowers for the 27th, and then its appalling ugliness will not be too visible. Of course, the building could hardly have been begun in the middle of winter."

But if Mrs. Eustace Daintree differed at all from her husband upon the subject of her sister's serene and perfect happiness, she, like a wise woman, kept her doubts to herself, and spoke no word of them to destroy the worthy vicar's peace of mind upon the subject.

The next morning Sir John came down from the Hall to the vicarage with a cloud upon his brow, and requested Vera to grant him a few minutes' private conversation. Vera put on her sable cloak and hat, and went out with him into the garden.

"What is the matter?"

"I am exceedingly vexed with my brother," he answered.

"What has Maurice done?"

"He tells me this morning that he will not stop for the wedding, nor be my best man. He talks of going away to-morrow."

Vera glanced at him. He looked excessively annoyed; his face, usually so kind and placid, was ruffled and angry; he flicked the grass impatiently with his stick.

"I have been talking to him for an hour, and cannot get him to change his mind, or even to tell me why he will not stay; in fact, he has no good reason for going. He *must* stay."

"Does it matter very much?" she asked, gently.

"Of course it matters. My mother is not able to be present; it would not be prudent after her late attack of bronchitis. My only brother surely might make a point of being at my wedding."

"But if he has other engagements——"

"He has no other engagement!" he interrupted, angrily; "He cannot find any but the most paltry excuses. It is behaving with great unkindness to myself, but that is a small matter. What I do mind and will not submit to is, that it is a deliberate insult to you."

"An insult to me! Oh! John, how can that be?" she said, in some surprise; and then, suddenly, she flushed hotly. She knew what he meant. There had been plenty of people to say that Sir John Kynaston was marrying beneath himself—a nobody who was unworthy of him: these murmurs had reached Vera's ears, but she had not heeded them since Lady Kynaston had been on her side. She saw, however, that Sir John feared that the absence of his mother and his brother at his wedding might be misconstrued into a sign that they also disapproved of his bride.

"I don't think Maurice would wish to slight me," she said, gently.

"No; but, then, he must not behave as though he did. I assure you, Vera, if he perseveres in his determination, I shall be most deeply hurt. I have always endeavoured to be a kind brother to him, and, if he cannot do this small thing to please me, I shall consider him most ungrateful."

"That I am sure he is not," she answered, earnestly; "little as I know him, I can assure you that he never loses an occasion of saying how much he feels your goodness and generosity to him."

"Then he must prove it. Look here, Vera, will you go up to the Hall now and talk to him? He is not hunting to-day; you will find him in the library."

"I?" she cried, looking half frightened; "what can I do? You had much better ask him yourself."

"I have asked him over and over again, till I am sick of asking! If you were to put it as a personal request from yourself, I am sure he would see how important to us both it is that he should be present at our wedding."

"Pray don't ask me to do such a thing; I really cannot," she said, hastily.

Sir John looked at her in some surprise; there was an amount of distress in her face that struck him as inadequate to the small thing he had asked of her.

"Why, Vera! have you grown shy? Surely you will not mind doing so small a thing to please me? You need not stay long, and you have your hat on all ready. I have to speak to your brother-in-law about the chancel; I have a letter from the architect this morning; and everything must be settled about it before we go. If you will go up and speak to Maurice now, I will join you— say in twenty minutes from now," consulting his watch, "at the lodge gates. You will go, won't you, dear, just to please me?"

She did not know how to refuse; she had no excuse to give, no reason that she could put into words why she should shrink with such a dreadful terror from this interview with his brother which he was forcing upon her. She told him that she would go, and Sir John, leaving her, went into the house well satisfied to do his business with the vicar.

And Vera went slowly up the lane alone towards the Hall. She did not know what she was going to say to Maurice; she hardly knew, indeed, what it was she had been commissioned to ask of him; nor in what words her request was to be made. She thought no longer of her wedding-day, nor of the lover who had just parted with her. Only before her eyes there came again the little wintry copse of birch-trees; the horses standing by, the bare fields stretching around, and back into her heart there flashed the memory of those quick, hot kisses pressed upon her outstretched hand; the one short—and alas! all too perilous—glimpse that had been revealed to her of the inner life and soul of the man whose lightest touch she had learnt that day to fear as she feared no other living thing.

CHAPTER XV.

VERA'S MESSAGE.

Alas! how easily things go wrong,
A word too much, or a sigh too long;
And there comes a mist and a driving rain,
And life is never the same again.

The library at Kynaston was the room which Sir John had used as his only sitting-room since he had come down to stay in his own house. When his wedding with Miss Nevill had been definitely fixed, there had come down from town a whole army of decorators and painters and upholsterers, who had set to work to renovate and adorn the rest of the house for the advent of the bride, who was so soon to be brought home to it.

They had altered things in various ways, they had improved a few, and they had spoiled a good many more; they had, at all events, introduced a wholesome and thorough system of cleansing and cleaning throughout the house, that had been very welcome to the soul of Mrs. Eccles; but into the library they had not penetrated. The old bookshelves remained untouched; the old books, in their musty brown calf bindings, were undesecrated by profaning hands. All sorts of quaint chairs and bureaus, gathered together out of every other room in the house, had congregated here. The space over the mantelpiece was adorned by a splendid portrait by Vandyke, flanked irreverently on either side by a series of old sporting prints, representing the whole beginning, continuation, and end of a steeple-chase course, and which, it is melancholy to state, were far more highly appreciated by Sir John than the beautiful and valuable picture which they surrounded. Below these, and on the mantelpiece itself, were gathered together a heterogeneous collection of pipes, spurs, horse-shoes, bits, and other implements, which the superintending hands of any lady would have straightway relegated to the stables.

In this library Sir John and his brother fed, smoked, wrote and read, and lived, in fact, entirely in full and disorderly enjoyment of their bachelorhood and its privileges. The room, consequently, was in a condition of untidiness and confusion, which was the despair of Mrs. Eccles and the delight of the two men themselves, who had even forbidden the entrance of any housemaid into it upon pain of instant dismissal. Mrs. Eccles submitted herself with resignation to the inevitable, and comforted herself with the reflection that the time of unchecked masculine dominion was well-nigh over, and that the days were very near at hand when "Miss Vera" was coming to alter all this.

"Ah, well, it won't last long, poor gentleman!" the worthy lady said to herself, in allusion to Sir John's uninvaded sanctum; "let him enjoy his pigstye while he can. When his wife comes she will soon have the place swept clean out for him."

So the papers, and the books, and the pipes, and the tobacco-tins were left heaped up all over the tables and chairs, and the fox-terriers sat in high places on the sofa cushions; and the brothers smoked their pipes after their meals, emptied their ashes on to the tables, threw their empty soda-water bottles into a corner of the room, wore their slippers at all hours, and lapsed, in fact, into all those delightful methods of living at ease practised by the vicious nature inherent in man when he is unchecked by female influence; whilst Mrs. Eccles groaned in silence, but possessed her soul in patience by reason of that change which she knew to be coming over the internal economy of Kynaston Hall.

Maurice Kynaston reclines at ease in the most comfortable arm-chair in the room, his feet reposing upon a second chair; his pipe is in his mouth, and his hands in his trouser pockets; he wears a loose, gray shooting-jacket, and Sir John's favourite terrier, Vic, has curled herself into a little round white ball upon his outstretched legs. Maurice has just been reading his morning's correspondence, and a letter from Helen, announcing that her grandfather is ill and confined to his room by bronchitis, is still in his hand. He looks gloomily and abstractedly into the red logs of the wood fire. The door opens.

"Any orders for the stable, Captain?"

"None to-day, Mrs. Eccles."

"You are not going out hunting?"

"No, I am going to take a rest. By the way, Mrs. Eccles, I shall be leaving to-morrow, so you can see about packing my things."

"Dear me! sir, I hope we shall see you again, at the wedding."

"Very unlikely; I don't like weddings, Mrs. Eccles; the only one I ever mean to dance at is yours. When you get married, you let me know."

"Law! sir, how you do go on!" said the old lady, laughing; not ill-pleased at the imputation. "Dear me," she went on, looking round the room uneasily, "did I ever see such a mess in all my born days. Now Sir John is out, sir, I suppose you couldn't let me——"

"*Certainly not*—if you mean bring in a broom and a dust-pan! Just let me catch you at it, that's all!"

The housekeeper shook her head with a resigned sigh.

"Ah, well! it can't last long; when Miss Vera comes she'll turn the whole place inside-out, and all them nasty pipes, and dogs and things will be cleared away."

"Do you think so?" suddenly sitting upright in his chair. "Wait a bit, Mrs. Eccles; don't go yet. Do you think Miss Vera will have things her own way with my brother?"

"Oh! sir, what do you ask me for?" she answered, with discreet evasiveness. "Surely you must know more about Miss Vera than I can tell you."

Mrs. Eccles went away, and Maurice got up and leant against the mantelpiece looking down gloomily, into the fire. Vic, dislodged from his knee, sat up beside him, resting her little white paws on the edge of the fender, warming her nose.

"What a fool I am!" said Maurice, aloud to himself. "I can't even hear her name mentioned by a servant without wanting to talk about her. Yes, it's clear he loves her—but does she love him? Will she be happy? Yes, of course, she will get her own way. Will that be enough for her? Ah!" turning suddenly round and taking half-a-dozen steps across the room. "It is high time I went. I am a coward and a traitor to linger on here; I will go. Why did I say to-morrow—why have I not settled to go this very day? If I were not so weak and so irresolute, I should be gone by this time. I ought never, knowing what I do know of myself—I ought never to have come back at all." He went back to the fire and sat down again, lifting the little dog back on to his knee. "I shall get over it, I suppose," he murmured. "Men don't die of this sort of thing; she will marry, and she will think me unkind because I shall never come near her; but even if she knew the truth, it would never make any difference to her; and by-and-by I too, I suppose, shall marry." The soliloquy died away into silence. Maurice stroked the dog and looked at the fire dreamily and somewhat drearily.

Some one tapped at the door.

"Come in! What is it, Mrs. Eccles?" he cried, rousing himself.

The door softly opened and there entered, not Mrs. Eccles, but Vera Nevill.

Captain Kynaston sprang hastily to his feet. "Oh, Vera! I beg your pardon—how do you do? I suppose you have come for John? You must have missed him; he started for the vicarage half-an-hour ago."

"No, I have seen him. I have come to see you, Maurice, if you don't mind." She spoke rather timidly, not looking at him.

"I am delighted, of course," he answered, a little constrainedly.

Vera stood up on the hearth divesting herself of her long fur cloak; she flung it over the back of a chair, and then took off her hat and gloves. Maurice was strangely unlike himself this morning, for he never offered to help her in these operations, he only stood leaning against the corner of the mantelpiece opposite her, looking at her.

Vera stooped down and stroked the little fox-terrier; when she had done so, she raised her head and met his eyes.

Did she see, ere he hastily averted them, all the hunger and all the longing that filled them as he watched her? He, in his turn, stooped and replenished the fire.

"John sent me to talk to you, Maurice," began Vera, hurriedly, like one repeating a lesson; "he tells me you will not be with us on the 27th; is that so?"

"I am sorry, but I am obliged to go away," he answered.

"John is dreadfully hurt, Maurice. I hope you will alter your mind."

"Is it John for whom you are speaking, or for yourself?" he asked, looking at her.

"For both of us. Of course it will be a great disappointment if you are not there. You are his only brother, and he will feel it deeply."

"And you; will you feel it?" he persisted. She coloured a little.

"Yes, I shall be very sorry," she answered, nervously. "I should not like John to be vexed on his wedding-day; he has been a kind brother to you, Maurice, and it seems hard that you cannot do this little thing to show your sense of it."

"Believe me, I show my gratitude to my brother just as well in staying away as in remaining," he answered, earnestly. "Do not urge me any further, Vera; I would do anything in the world to please John, but I cannot be present at your wedding."

There was a moment's silence; the fire flickered up merrily between them; a red-hot cinder fell out noisily from the grate; the clock ticked steadily on the chimney-piece; the little terrier sniffed at the edge of Vera's dress.

Suddenly there came into her heart a wild desire *to know*, to eat for once of that forbidden fruit of the tree of Eden, whence the flaming swords in vain beckoned her back; to eat, and afterwards, perchance, to perish of the poisonous food.

A wild conflict of thought thronged into her soul. Prudence, wisdom, her very heart itself counselled her to be still and to go. But something stronger than all else was within her too; and something that was new and strange, and perilously sweet to her; a something that won the day.

She turned to him, stretching out her hands; the warm glow of the fire lit up her lovely face and her eloquent pleading eyes, and flickered over the graceful and beautiful figure, whose perfect outlines haunted his fancy for ever.

"Stay, for my sake, because I ask you!" she cried, with a sudden passion; "or else tell me why you must go."

There came no answering flash into his eyes, only he lowered them beneath hers; he sat down suddenly, as though he was weary, on the chair whence he had risen at her entrance, so that she stood before him, looking down at him.

There was a certain repression in his face which made him look stern and cold, as one who struggles with a mortal temptation. He stooped over the little dog, and became seemingly engrossed in stroking it.

"I cannot stop," he said, in a cold, measured voice; "it is an impossibility. But, since you ask me, I will tell you why. It can make no possible difference to you to know; it may, indeed, excite your interest or your pity for a few moments whilst you listen to me; but when it is over and you go away you will forget it again. I do not ask you to remember it or me; it is, in fact, all I ask, that you should forget. This is what it is. Your wedding-day is very near; it is bringing you happiness and love. I can rejoice in your happiness. I am not so selfish as to lament it; but you will not wish me to be there to see it when I tell you that I have been fool enough to dare to love you myself. It is the folly of a madman, is it not? since I have never had the slightest hope or entertained the faintest wish to alter the conditions of your life; nor have I even asked myself what effect such a confession as this that you have wrung from me can have upon you. Whether it excites your pity or your contempt, or even your amusement, it cannot in any case make any difference to me. My folly, at all events, cannot hurt you or my brother; it can hurt no one but myself: it cannot even signify to you. It is only for my own sake that I am going, because one cannot bear more than a certain amount, can one? I thought I might have been strong enough, but I find that it would be too much; that is all. You will not ask me to stay any more, will you?"

Not once had he looked at her; not by a single sign or token had he betrayed the slightest emotion or agitation. His voice had been steady and unbroken; he spoke in a low and somewhat monotonous manner; it was as though he had been relating something that in no way concerned himself—some story that was of some other, and that other of no great interest either to him who told it or to her who listened to the tale. Any one suddenly coming into the room would have guessed him to be entirely engrossed in the contemplation of the little dog between his hands; that he was relating the story of his own heart would not have been imagined for an instant.

When he had done speaking there was an absolute silence in the room. What he had spoken seemed to admit of no answer of any sort or kind from his listener. He had asked for nothing; he had pleaded neither for her sympathy nor her forgiveness, far less for any definite expression of the effect of his words upon her. He had not, seemingly, cared to know how they affected her. He had simply told his own story—that was all; it concerned no one but himself. She might pity him, she might even be amused at him, as he had said: anyhow, it made no difference to him; he had chosen to present a picture of his inner life to her as a doctor might have described some complicated disease to a chance acquaintance—it was a physiological study, if she cared to look upon it as such; if not, it did not matter. There was no possible answer that she could make to him; no form of words by which she could even acknowledge that she had heard him speak.

She stood perfectly silent for the space of some two or three seconds; she scarcely breathed, her very heart seemed to have ceased to beat; it was as if she had been turned to stone. She knew not what she felt; it was neither pain, nor joy, nor regret; it was only a sort of dull apathy that oppressed her very being.

Presently she put forth her hands, almost mechanically, and reached her cloak and hat from the chair behind her.

The soft rustle of her dress upon the carpet struck his ear; he looked up with a start, like one waking out of a painful dream.

"You are going!" he said, in his usual voice.

"Yes; I am going."

He stood up, facing her.

"There is nothing more to be said, is there?" He said it not as though he asked her a question, but as one asserting a fact.

"Nothing, I suppose," she answered, rather wearily, not looking at him as she spoke.

"I shall not see you again, as I leave to-morrow morning by the early train. You will, at least, wish me good-bye?"

"Good-bye, Maurice."

"Good-bye, Vera; God bless you."

She opened the door softly and went out. She went slowly away down the avenue, wrapping her cloak closely around her; the wind blew cold and chill, and she shivered a little as she walked. Presently she struck aside along a narrow pathway through the grass that led her homewards by a shorter cut. She had forgotten that Sir John was to wait for her at the lodge-gates.

She had forgotten his very existence. For she *knew*. She had eaten of the tree of knowledge, and the scales had fallen for ever from her eyes.

She knew that Maurice loved her—and, alas! for her—she knew also that she loved him. And between them a great gulf was fixed; deep, and wide, and impassable as the waters of Lethe.

Out of the calm, unconscious lethargy of her maidenhood's untroubled dreams the soul of Vera had awakened at length to the realization of the strong, passionate woman's heart that was within her.

She loved! It had come to her at last; this thing that she had scorned and disbelieved in, and yet that, possibly, she had secretly longed for. She had deemed herself too cold, too wise, too much set upon the good things of earth, to be touched by that scorching fire; but now she was no colder than any other love-sick maiden, no wiser than every other foolish woman who had been ready to wreck her life for love in the world's history.

Surely no girl ever learnt the secret of her own heart with such dire dismay as did Vera Nevill. There was neither joy nor gladness within her, only a great anger against herself and her fate, and even against him who, as he had said, had dared to love her. She had courted the avowal from his lips, and yet she resented the words she had wrung from him. But, more than all, she resented the treachery of the heart that was within her.

"Why did I ever see him?" she cried aloud in her bitterness, striking her hands wildly against each other. "What evil fate brought us together? What fool's madness induced me to go near him to-day? I was happy enough; I had all I wanted; I was content with my fate—and now—now!" Her passionate words died away into a wail. In her haste and her abstraction her foot caught against a long, withered bramble trail that lay across her path; she half stumbled. It was sufficient to arrest her steps. She stood still, and leant against the smooth, whitened trunk of a beech tree. Her hands locked themselves tightly together; her face, white and miserable, lifted itself despairingly towards the pitiless winter sky above her.

"How am I to live out my life?" she asked herself, in her anguish.

It had not entered into her head that she could alter it. It did not occur to her to imagine that she could give up anything to which she now stood pledged. To be John Kynaston's wife, and to love his brother, that was what struck upon her with horror; no other possible contingency had as yet suggested itself to her.

Presently, as she moved slowly onwards, still absorbed in her new-found misfortune, a fresh train of thought came into her mind. She thought no longer about herself, but about him.

"How cruel I was to leave him like that," she said to herself, reproachfully; "without a word, or so much as a look, of consolation—for, if I suffer, has not he suffered too!"

She forgot that he had asked her for nothing; she only knew that, little enough as she had to give him, she had withheld that little from him.

"What must he think of me?" she repeated to herself, in dismay. "How heartless and how cold I must be in his eyes to have parted from him thus without one single kind word. I might, at least, have told him that I was grateful for the love I cannot take. I wonder," she continued, half aloud to herself, "I wonder what it is like to be loved by Maurice——" She paused again, this time leaning against the wicket-gate that led out of the park into the high road.

A little smile played for one instant about her lips, a soft, far-away look lingered in her dreaming eyes for just a moment—just the space of time it might take you to count twenty; she let her fancy carry her away—*where?*

Ah, sweet and perilous reverie! too dear and too dangerous to be safely indulged in. Vera roused herself with a start, passing her hand across her brow as though to brush away the thoughts that would fain have lingered there.

"Impossible!" she said aloud to herself, moving on again rapidly. "I must be a fool to stand here dreaming—I, whose fate is irrevocably fixed; and I would sooner die than alter it. The best match in the county, it is called. Well, so it is; and nothing less would satisfy me. But—but—I think I will see him once again, and wish him good-bye more kindly."

CHAPTER XVI.

"POOR WISDOM."

No; vain, alas! the endeavour
From bonds so sweet to sever,
Poor Wisdom's chance against a glance
Is now as weak as ever!

THOS. MOORE.

The station at Sutton stood perched up above the village on a high embankment, upon which the railway crossed the valley from the hills that lay to the north to those that lay to the south of it. Up at the station it was always draughty and generally cold. To-day, this very early morning, about ten minutes before the first up train is due, it is not only cold and draughty, but it is also wet and foggy. A damp, white mist fills the valley below, and curls up the bare hill sides above; it hangs chillingly about the narrow, open shed on the up side of the station, covering the wooden bench within it with thick beads of moisture, so that no man dare safely sit down on it, and clinging coldly and penetratingly to the garments of a tall young lady in a long ulster and a thick veil, who is slowly walking up and down the platform.

The solitary porter on duty eyes her inquiringly. "Going by the up train, Miss?" he says, touching his hat respectfully as he passes her.

"No," says Vera, blushing hotly under the thick shelter of her veil, and then adds with that readiness of explanation to which persons who have a guilty conscience are prone, "I am only waiting to see somebody off." An uncalled-for piece of information which has only the effect of setting the bucolic mind of the local porter agog with curiosity and wonderment.

Presently the few passengers for the early train begin to arrive; a couple of farmers going into the market town, a village girl in a smart bonnet, an old woman in a dirty red shawl, carrying a bundle; that is all. Maurice is very late. Vera remembers that he always puts off starting to catch a train till the very last minute. She stands waiting for him at the further end of the platform, as far away as she can from the knot of rustic passengers, with a beating heart and a fever of impatience within her.

The train is signalled, and at that very minute the dog-cart from Kynaston drives up at last! Even then he has to get his ticket, and to convey himself and his portmanteau across from the other side of the line. Their good-bye will be short indeed!

The train steams up, and Maurice hurries forward followed by the porter bearing his rugs and sticks; he does not even see her, standing a little back, as she does, so as not to attract more attention than need be. But when all his things are put into the carriage, and the porter has been duly tipped and has departed, Captain Kynaston hears a soft voice behind him.

"I have come to wish you good-bye again." He turns, flushing at the sound of the sweet familiar voice, and sees Vera in her long ulster, and her face hidden behind her veil, by his side.

"Good Heavens, Vera! *you*—out on such a morning?"

"I could not let you go away without—without—one kind word," she begins, stammering painfully, her voice shaking so, as she speaks, that he cannot fail to divine her agitation, even though he cannot see the lovely troubled face that has been so carefully screened from his gaze.

"This is too good of you," he begins. That very minute a brougham dashes rapidly up to the station.

"It is the Shadonake carriage!" cried Vera, casting a terrified glance behind her. "Who can it be? they will see me."

"Jump into the train," he answers, hurriedly, and, without a thought beyond an instinct of self-preservation for the moment, she obeys him. Maurice follows her quickly, closing the carriage door behind him. "Nobody can have seen you," he says. "I daresay it is only some visitors going away; they could not have noticed you. Oh! Vera," turning with sudden earnestness to her; "how am I ever to thank you for this great kindness to me?"

"It is nothing; only a five minutes' walk before breakfast. It is no trouble to me; and I did not want you to think me unfeeling, or unkind to you."

Before she could speak another word the carriage door was violently slammed to, and the guard's sharp shrill whistle heralded the departure of the train. With a cry, Vera sprang towards the door; before she could reach it, Maurice, who had perceived instantly what had happened, had let down the window and was shouting to the porter. It was too late. The train was off.

Vera sank back hopelessly upon the seat; and Maurice, according to the manners and customs of infuriated Britons, gave utterance to a very laconic word of bad import below his breath.

"I wouldn't have had this happen for ten thousand pounds!" he said, after a minute, looking at her in blank despair.

Vera was taking off her veil mechanically; when he could see her face, he perceived that she was very white.

"Never mind," she said, with a faint smile; "there is no real harm done. It is unfortunate, that is all. The train stops at Tripton. I can get out there and walk home."

"Five miles! and it is I who have got you into this scrape! What a confounded fool I was to make you get into the carriage! I ought to have remembered how late it was. How are you to walk all that way?"

"Pray don't reproach yourself, Maurice; I shall not mind the walk a bit. I shall have to confess my escapade to Marion, and tell her why I am late for breakfast—that is all; as it is, I can, at all events, finish what I wanted to say to you."

And then she was silent, looking away from him out of the further window. The train, gradually accelerating its pace, sped quickly on through the fog-blotted landscape. Hills, villages, church spires, all that made the country familiar, were hidden in the mist; only here and there, in the nearer hedge-rows, an occasional tree stood out bleak and black against the white veil beyond like a sentinel alone on a limitless plain. Absolute silence—only the train rushing on faster and faster through the white, wet world without.

Then, at last, it was Maurice, not Vera, that spoke.

"I blame myself bitterly for this, Vera," he said in a low, pained voice. "Had it not been for my foolish, unthinking words to you yesterday, you would not have been tempted to do this rash act of kindness. I spoke to you in a way that I had no right to speak, believing that my words would make no impression upon you beyond the fact of showing you that it was impossible for me to stay for your wedding. I never dreamt that your kindly interest in me would lead you to waste another thought upon me. I did not know how good and pitying your nature is, nor give you credit for so much generosity."

She turned round to him sharply and suddenly. "What are you saying?" she cried, with a harsh pain in her voice. "What words are you using to me? *Kindness, pity, generosity!*—have they any place here between you and me?"

There was a moment in which neither of them spoke, only their eyes met, and the secret that was hidden in their souls lay suddenly revealed to each of them.

In another instant Vera had sunk upon her knees before him.

"While you live," she cried, passionately, lifting her beautiful dark eyes, that were filled with a new light and a new glory, to his—"while you live I will never be another man's wife!"

And there was no other word spoken. Only a shower of close, hot kisses upon her lips, and two strong arms that drew her nearer and tighter to the beating heart against which she rested, for he was only human after all.

Oh, swift and divine moment of joy, that comes but once in a man's life, when he holds the woman he loves for the first time to his heart! Once, and once only, he tastes of heaven and forgets life itself in the short and delirious draught. What envious deity shall grudge him those moments of rapture, all too sweet, and, alas! all too short!

To Vera and Maurice, locked in each other's arms, time had no shore, and life was not. It might have been ten seconds, it might have been an eternity— they could not have told—no pang entered that serene haven where their souls were lapped in perfect happiness; no serpent entered into Eden; no harsh note struck upon their enchanted ears, nor jarring sight upon their sun-dazzled vision. Where in that moment was the duty and the honour that was a part of the man's very self? What to Vera was the rich marriage and the life of affluence, and all the glitter and tinsel which it had been her soul's desire to attain? She remembered it not; like a house of cards, it had fallen shattered to the ground.

They loved, and they were together. There was neither duty, nor faith, nor this world's wisdom between them; nothing but that great joy which on earth has no equal, and which Heaven itself cannot exceed.

But brief are the moments whilst joy, with bated breath and folded wings, pauses on his flight; too soon, alas! is the divine elixir dashed away from our lingering lips.

Already, for Maurice and for Vera, it is over, and they have awakened to earth once more.

It is the man who is the first to remember. "Good God, Vera!" he cries, pushing her back from him, "what terrible misfortune is this? Can it be true that you must suffer too, that you love me?"

"Why not?" she answered, looking at him; happy still, but troubled too; for already for her also Paradise is over. "Is it so hard to believe? And yet many women must have loved you. But I—I have never loved before. Listen, Maurice: when I accepted your brother, I liked him, I thought I could be very happy with him; and—and—do not think ill of me—I wanted so much to be rich; it was so miserable being poor and dependent, and I knew life so well, and how hard the struggle is for those who are poor. I was so determined I would do well for myself; and he was good, and I liked him."

At the mention of the brother, whom he had wronged, Maurice hid his face in his hands and groaned aloud.

She laid her hand softly upon his knee; she had half raised herself upon the seat by his side, and her head, from which her hat had fallen, pillowed itself with a natural caressing action against his shoulder.

At the soft touch he shivered.

"It was dreadful, was it not? But then, I am not perfect, and I liked the idea of being rich, and I had never loved—I did not even know what it meant. And then I met you—long ago your photograph had arrested my fancy; and do you remember that evening at Shadonake when I first saw you?"

Could he ever forget one single detail of that meeting?

"You stood at the foot of the staircase, waiting, and I came down softly behind you. You did not see me till I was close to you, and then you turned, and you took my hands, and you looked and looked at me till my eyes could no longer meet yours. There came a vague trouble into my heart; I had never felt anything like it before. Maurice, from that instant I must have loved you."

"For God's sake, Vera!" he cried out wildly, as though the gentle words gave him positive pain, "do not speak of it. Do you not see the abyss which lies between us—which must part us for ever?"

"Loving you, I will never marry your brother!" she answered, earnestly.

"And I will never rob my brother of his bride. Darling, darling, do not tempt me too far, or God knows what I may say and do! To reach you, love, would be to dip my hands in dishonour and basest treachery. Not even for you can I do this vile thing. Kiss me once more, sweet, and let me go out of your life for ever; believe me, it is better so; best for us both. In time you will forget, you will be happy. He will be good to you, and you will be glad that you were not tempted to betray him."

"You do not know what you ask of me," she cried, lifting her face, all wet with tears, to his. "Leave me, if you will—go your way—forget me—it is all the same to me; henceforth there is no other man on earth to me but you. I will never swear vows at God's altar that I cannot keep, or commit the frightful sin of marrying one man whilst I know that I love another. Yes, yes; I know it is a horrible, dreadful misfortune. Have I sought it, or gone out of my way to find it? Have I not struggled to keep it away from me? striven to blind my eyes to it and to go on as I was, and never to acknowledge it to myself? Do I not love wealth above all things; do I not know that he is rich, and you poor? And yet I cannot help loving you!"

He took her clasped, trembling hands within his own, and held them tightly. In that moment the woman was weak, and the man was her master.

"Listen," he said. "Yes, you are right, I am poor; but that is not all. Vera, for Heaven's sake, reflect, and pause before you wreck your whole life. I cannot marry you—not only because I am poor, but also, alas! because I am bound to another woman."

"Helen Romer!" she murmured, faintly; "and you love *her*?" A sick, cold misery rushed into her heart. She strove to withdraw her hands from his; but he only held them the tighter.

"No; by the God above us, I love you, and only you," he answered her, almost roughly; "but I am bound to her. I cannot afford to marry her—we have neither of us any money; but I am bound all the same. Only one thing can set me free; if, in five years, we are, neither of us, better off than now, she has told me that I may go free. Under no other conditions can I ever marry any one else. That is my secret, Vera. At any moment she can claim me, and for five years I must wait for her."

"Then I will wait for you five years too," she cried, passionately. "Is my love less strong, less constant, than hers, do you think? Can I not wait patiently too?" She wound her arms about his neck, and drew his face down to hers.

"Five years," she murmured; "it is but a small slice out of one's life after all; and when it is over, it seems such a little space to look back upon. Dearest, some day we shall remember how miserable, and yet how happy too, we have been this morning; and we shall smile, as we remember it all, out of the fulness of our content."

How was he to gainsay so sweet a prophet? Already the train was slackening, and the moment when they must part drew near. The beautiful head lay upon his breast; the deep, shadowy eyes, which love for the first time had softened into the perfection of their own loveliness, mirrored themselves in his; the flower-shaped, trembling lips were close up to his. How could he resist their gentle pleading? There was no time for more words, for more struggles between love and duty.

"So be it, then," he murmured, and caught her in one last, passionate embrace to his heart.

Five minutes later a tall young lady, deeply veiled as when she had entered the train, got out of it and walked swiftly away from Tripton station down the hill towards the high road. So absorbed was she in her own reflections that she utterly failed to notice another figure, also female and also veiled, who, preceding her through the mist, went on swiftly before her down the road. Nor did she pay the slightest attention to the fact until a turn in the road brought her suddenly face to face with two persons who stood deep in conversation under the shelter of the tall, misty hedge-row.

As Vera approached these two persons sprang apart with a guilty suddenness, and revealed to her astonished eyes—Beatrice Miller and Mr. Herbert Pryme.

CHAPTER XVII.

AN UNLUCKY LOVE-LETTER.

Heaven first taught letters for some wretch's aid,
Some banished lover, or some captive maid.

POPE, "Eloisa and Abelard."

To ascertain rightly how Mr. Pryme and Miss Miller came to be found in the parish of Tripton at nine o'clock in the morning, standing together under a wet hedge-row, it will be necessary to take a slight retrospect of what had taken place in the history of these two people since the time when the young barrister had spent that memorable week at Shadonake.

The visit had come to an end uneventfully for either of them; but two days after his departure from the house Mr. Pryme had been guilty of a gross piece of indiscretion. He had forgotten to observe a golden rule which should be strongly impressed upon every man and woman. The maxim should be inculcated upon the young with at least as much earnestness as the Catechism or the Ten Commandments. In homely language, it runs something in this fashion: "Say what you like, but never commit yourself to paper."

Mr. Pryme had observed the first portion of this maxim religiously, but he had failed to pay equal regard to the latter. He *had* committed himself to paper in the shape of a very bulky and very passionate love-letter, which was duly delivered by the morning postman and laid at the side of Miss Miller's plate upon the breakfast-table.

Now, Miss Miller, as it happened on that particular morning, had a very heavy influenza cold, and had stayed in bed for breakfast. When, therefore, Mrs. Miller prepared to send a small tray up to her daughter's bedroom with her breakfast, she took up her letters also from the table to put upon it with her tea and toast. The very thick envelope of one of them first attracted her notice; then the masculine nature of the handwriting; and when, upon turning it over, she furthermore perceived a very large-sized monogram of the letters "H. P." upon the envelope, her mind underwent a sudden revolution as to the sending of her daughter's correspondence upstairs.

"There, that will do," she said to the lady's maid, "you can take up the tray; I will bring Miss Miller's letters up to her myself after breakfast."

After which, without more ado, she walked to the window and opened the letter. Some people might have had scruples as to such a strong measure. Mrs. Miller had none at all. Her children, she argued, were her own property and under her own care; as long as they lived under her roof, they had no right over anything that they possessed independently of their mother.

Under ordinary circumstances she would not have opened a letter addressed to any of her children; but if there was anything of a suspicious nature in their correspondence, she certainly reserved to herself the perfect right of dealing with it as she thought fit.

She opened the letter and read the first line; it ran thus:—

"My dearest darling Beatrice." She then turned to the end of it and read the last; it was this: "Your own most devoted and loving Herbert."

That was quite enough for Mrs. Miller; she did not want to read any more of it. She slipped the letter into her pocket, and went back to the breakfast-table and poured out the tea and coffee for her husband and her sons.

But when the family meal was over, it was with a very angry aspect that Mrs. Miller went upstairs and stood by her eldest daughter's bedside.

"Beatrice, here is a letter which has come for you this morning, of which I must ask you an explanation."

"You have read it, mamma!" flushing angrily, as she took it from her mother's hand.

"I have read the first line and the last. I certainly should not take the trouble to wade all through such contemptible trash!" Which was an unprovoked insult to poor Beatrice's feelings.

She snatched the letter from her mother's hand, and crumpled it jealously under her pillow.

"How can you call it trash, then, if you have not read it?"

It was hard, certainly; to have her letter opened was bad enough, but to have it called names was worse still. The letter, which to Beatrice would be so full of sacred charm and delight—such a poem on love and its sweetness—was nothing more to her mother than "contemptible trash!"

But where in the whole world has a love-letter been indited, however delightful and perfect it may be to the writer and the receiver of it, that is nothing but an object of ridicule or contempt to the whole world beside? Love is divine as Heaven itself to the two people who are concerned in its ever new delights; but to us lookers-on its murmurs are but fooleries, its sighs are ludicrous, and its written words absolute imbecilities; and never a memory of our own lost lives can make the spectacle of it in others anything but an irritating and idiotic exhibition.

"I have read quite enough," continued Mrs. Miller, sternly, "to understand the nature of it. It is from Mr. Pryme, I imagine?"

"Yes, mamma."

"And by what right, may I ask, does Mr. Pryme commence a letter to you in the warm terms of affection which I have had the pleasure of reading?"

"By the right which I myself have given him," she answered, boldly.

Regardless of her cold, she sat upright in her bed; a flush of defiance in her face, her short dark hair flung back from her brow in wild confusion. She understood at once that all had been discovered, and she was going to do battle for her lover.

"Do you mean to tell me, Beatrice, that you have engaged yourself to this Mr. Pryme?"

"Certainly I have."

"You know very well that your father and I will never consent to it."

"Never is a long day, mamma."

"Don't take up my words like that. I consider, Beatrice, that you have deceived me shamefully. You persuaded me to ask that young man to the house because you said that Sophy Macpherson was fond of him."

"So she is."

"Beatrice, how can you be so wicked and tell such lies in the face of that letter to yourself?"

"I never said he was fond of her," she answered, with just the vestige of a twinkle in her eyes.

"If I had known, I would never have asked him to come," continued her mother.

"No; I am sure you would not. But I did not tell you, mamma."

"I have other views for you. You must write to this young man and tell him you will give him up."

"I certainly shall not do that."

"I shall not give my consent to your engagement."

"I never imagined that you would, mamma, and that is why I did not ask for it."

And then Mrs. Miller got very angry indeed.

"What on earth do you intend to do, you ungrateful, disobedient, rebellious child?"

"I mean to marry Herbert some day because I love him," answered her daughter, coolly; "but I will not run away with him unless you force me to it; and I hope, by-and-by, when Geraldine is grown up and can take my place, that you will give us your consent and your blessing. I am quite willing to wait a reasonable time for the chance of it."

"Is it likely that I shall give my consent to your marrying a young man picked up nobody knows where—out of the gutter, most likely? Who are his people, I should like to know?"

"I daresay his father is as well connected as mine," answered Beatrice, who knew all about her mother's having married a *parvenu*.

"Beatrice, I am ashamed of you, sneering at your own father!"

"I beg your pardon, mamma; I did not mean to sneer, but you say very trying things; and Mr. Pryme is a gentleman, and every bit as good as we are!"

"And where is the money to be found for this precious marriage, I should like to know? Do you suppose Mr. Pryme can support you?"

"Oh dear, no; but I know papa will not let me starve."

And Mrs. Miller knew it too. However angry she might be, and however unsuitably Beatrice might choose to marry, Mr. Miller would never allow his daughter to be insufficiently provided for. Beatrice's marriage portion would be a small fortune to a poor young man.

"It is your money he is after!" she said, angrily.

"I don't think so, mamma; and of course of that I am the best judge."

"He shall never set foot here again. I shall write to him myself and forbid him the house."

"That, of course, you may do as you like about, mamma; I cannot prevent your doing so, but it will not make me give him up, because I shall never marry any one else."

And there Mrs. Miller was, perforce, obliged to let the matter rest. She went her way angry and vexed beyond measure, and somewhat baffled too. How is a mother to deal with a daughter who is so determined and so defiant as was Beatrice Miller? There is no known method in civilized life of reducing a young lady of twenty to submission in matters of the heart. She could not whip her, or put her on bread and water, nor could she shut her up in a dark cupboard, as she might have done had she been ten years old.

All she could do was to write a very indignant letter to Mr. Pryme, forbidding him ever to enter her doors, or address himself in any way to her daughter again. Having sent this to the post, she was at the end of her resources. She did, indeed, confide the situation with very strong and one-sided colouring to her husband; but Mr. Miller had not the strong instincts of caste which were inherent in his wife. She could not make him see what dreadful deed of iniquity Herbert Pryme and his daughter had perpetrated between them.

"What's wrong with the young fellow?" he asked, looking up from the pile of parliamentary blue-books on the library table before him.

"Nothing is wrong, Andrew; but he isn't a suitable husband for Beatrice."

"Why? you asked him here, Caroline. I suppose, if he was good enough to stay in the house, he is no different to the boys, or anybody else who was here."

"It is one thing to stay here, and quite another thing to want to marry your daughter."

"Well, if he's an honest man, and the girl loves him, I don't see the good of making a fuss about it; she had better do as she likes."

"But, Andrew, the man hasn't a penny; he has made nothing at the bar yet." It was no use appealing to his exclusiveness, for he had none; it was a better move to make him look at the money-point of the question.

"Oh, well, he will get on some day, I daresay, and meanwhile I shall give Beatrice quite enough for them both when she marries."

"You don't understand, Andrew."

"No, my dear," very humbly, "perhaps I don't; but there, do as you think best, of course; I am sure I don't wish to interfere about the children; you always manage all these kind of things; and if you wouldn't mind, my dear, I am so very busy just now. You know there is to be this attack upon the Government as soon as the House meets, and I have the whole of the papers upon the Patagonian and Bolivian question to look up, and most fraudulent misstatements of the truth I believe them to be; although, as far as I've gone, I haven't been able to make it quite out yet, but I shall come to it—no doubt I shall come to it. I am going to speak upon this question, my dear, and I mean to tell the House that a grosser misrepresentation of facts was never yet promulgated from the Ministerial benches, nor flaunted in the faces of an all too leniently credulous Opposition; that will warm 'em up a bit, I flatter myself; those fellows in office will hang their heads in shame at the word Patagonia for weeks after."

"But who cares about Patagonia?"

"Oh, nobody much, I suppose. But there's bound to be an agitation against the Government, and that does as well as anything else. We can't afford to neglect a single chance of kicking them out. I have planned my speech pretty well right through; it will be very effective—withering, I fancy—but it's just these plaguy blue-books that won't quite tally with what I've got to say. I must go through them again though——"

"You had better have read the papers first, and settled your speech afterwards," suggested his wife.

"Oh dear, no! that wouldn't do at all; after all, you know, between you and me, the facts don't go for much; all we want is, to denounce them; any line of argument, if it is ingenious enough, will do; lay on the big words thickly— that's what your constituents like. Law bless you! *they* don't read the blue books; they'll take my word for granted if I say they are full of lies; it would be a comfort, however, if I could find a few. Of course, my dear, this is only between you and me."

A man is not always heroic to the wife of his bosom. Mrs. Miller went her way and left him to his righteous struggle among the Patagonian blue-books. After all, she said to herself, it had been her duty to inform him of his daughter's conduct, but it was needless to discuss the question further with him. He was incapable of approaching it from her own point of view. It would be better for her now to go her own way independently of him. She had always been accustomed to manage things her own way. It was nothing new to her.

Later in the day she attempted to wrest a promise from Beatrice that she would hold no further communication with the prohibited lover. But Beatrice would give no such promise.

"Is it likely that I should promise such a thing?" she asked her mother, indignantly.

"You would do so if you knew what your duty to your mother was."

"I have other duties besides those to you, mamma; when one has promised to marry a man, one is surely bound to consider him a little. If I have the chance of meeting him, I shall certainly take it."

"I shall take very good care that you have no such chances, Beatrice."

"Very well, mamma; you will, of course, do as you think best."

It was in consequence of these and sundry subsequent stormy conversations that Mr. Herbert Pryme suddenly discovered that he had a very high regard and affection for Mr. Albert Gisburne, the vicar of Tripton, the same to whom once Vera's relations had wished to unite her.

The connection between Mr. Gisburne and Herbert Pryme was a slender one; he had been at college with an elder brother of his, who had died in his (Herbert's) childhood. He did not indeed very clearly recollect what this elder brother had been like; but having suddenly called to mind that, during the course of his short visit to Shadonake, he had discovered the fact of the college friendship, of which, indeed, Mr. Gisburne had informed him, he now was unaccountably inflamed by a desire to cultivate the acquaintance of the valued companion of his deceased brother's youth.

He opened negotiations by the gift of a barrel of oysters, sent down from Wilton's, with an appropriate and graceful accompanying note. Mr. Gisburne was surprised, but not naturally otherwise than pleased by the attention. Next came a box of cigars, which again were shortly followed by two brace of pheasants purporting to be of Herbert's own shooting, but which, as a matter of fact, he had purchased in Vigo Street.

This munificent succession of gifts reaped at length the harvest for which they had been sown. In his third letter of grateful acknowledgment for his young friend's kind remembrance of him, Mr. Gisburne, with some diffidence, for Tripton Rectory was neither lively nor remarkably commodious, suggested how great the pleasure would be were his friend to run down to him for a couple of days or so; he had nothing, in truth, to offer him but a bachelor's quarters and a hearty welcome; there was next to no attraction beyond a pretty rural village and a choral daily service; but still, if he cared to come, Mr. Gisburne need not say how delighted he would be, etc., etc.

It is not too much to say that the friend jumped at it. On the shortest possible notice he arrived, bag and baggage, professing himself charmed with the bachelor's quarters; and, burning with an insatiable desire to behold the rurality of the village, to listen to the beauty and the harmony of the daily choral performances, he took up his abode in the clergyman's establishment; and the very next morning he sent a rural villager over to Shadonake with a half-crown for himself and a note to be given to Miss Miller the very first time she walked or rode out alone. This note was duly delivered, and that same afternoon Beatrice met her lover by appointment in an empty lime-kiln up among the chalk hills. This romantic rendezvous was, however, discontinued shortly, owing to the fact of Mrs. Miller having become suspicious of her daughter's frequent and solitary walks, and insisting on sending out Geraldine and her governess with her.

A few mornings later a golden chance presented itself. Mr. and Mrs. Miller went away for the night to dine and sleep at a distant country house. Beatrice had not been invited to go with them. She did not venture to ask her lover to the house he had been forbidden to enter, but she ordered the carriage for herself, caught the early train to Tripton, met Herbert, by appointment, outside the station, and stood talking to him in the fog by the wayside, where Vera suddenly burst upon their astonished gaze.

There was nothing for it but to take Vera into their confidence; and they were so much engrossed in their affairs that they entirely failed to notice how mechanically she answered, and how apathetically she appeared for the first few minutes to listen to their story. Presently, however, she roused herself into a semblance of interest. She promised not to betray the fact of the stolen interview, all the more readily because it did not strike either of them to inquire what she herself was doing in the Tripton road.

In the end Vera walked on slowly by herself, and the Shadonake carriage, ordered to go along at a foot's pace from Sutton station towards Tripton, picked both girls up and conveyed them safely, each to their respective homes.

"You will never tell of me, will you, Vera?" said Beatrice to her, for the twentieth time, ere they parted.

"Of course not; indeed, I would gladly help you if I could," she answered, heartily.

"You will certainly be able to help us both very materially some day," said Beatrice, who had visions of being asked to stay at Kynaston, to meet Herbert.

"I am afraid not," answered Vera, with a sigh. Already there was regret in her mind for the good things of life which she had elected to relinquish. "Put me down at this corner, Beatrice; I don't want to drive up to the vicarage. Good-bye."

"Good-bye, Vera—and—and you won't mind my saying it—but I like you so much."

Vera smiled, and, with a kiss, the girls parted; and Mrs. Daintree never heard after all the story of her sister's early visit to Tripton, for she returned so soon that she had not yet been missed. The vicar and his family had but just gathered round the breakfast-table, when, after having divested herself of her walking garments, she came in quietly and took her vacant place amongst them unnoticed and unquestioned.

CHAPTER XVIII.

LADY KYNASTON'S PLANS.

Swift as a shadow, short as any dream,
Brief as the lightning in the collied night.

And ere a man hath power to say, "Behold!
"The jaws of darkness do devour it up:
So quick bright things come to confusion.

"Midsummer Night's Dream."

Sir John Kynaston sat alone in his old-bachelor rooms in London. They were dark, dingy rooms, such as are to be found in countless numbers among the narrow streets that encompass St. James's Street. They were cheerless and comfortless, and, withal, high-rented, and possessed of no other known advantage than that of their undeniably central situation. They were not rooms that one would suppose any man would care to linger in in broad daylight; and yet Sir John remained in them now a days almost from morning till night.

He sat for the most part as he is sitting now—in a shabby, leathern arm-chair, stooping a little forward, and doing nothing. Sometimes he wrote a few necessary letters, sometimes he made a feint of reading the paper; but oftenest he did nothing, only sat still, staring before him with a hopeless misery in his face.

For in these days Sir John Kynaston was a very unhappy man. He had received a blow such as strikes at the very root and spring of a man's life—a blow which a younger man often battles through and is none the worse in the end for, but under which a man of his age is apt to be crushed and to succumb. Within a week of his wedding-day Vera Nevill had broken her engagement to him. It had been a nine days' wonder in Meadowshire—the county had rung with the news—everybody had marvelled and speculated, but no one had got any nearer to the truth than that Vera was supposed to have "mistaken her feelings." The women had cried shame upon her for such capriciousness, and had voted her a fool into the bargain for throwing over such a match; and if a male voice, somewhat less timid than the rest, had here and there uplifted itself in her defence and had ventured to hint that she might have had sufficient and praiseworthy motives for her conduct, a chorus of feminine indignation had smothered the kindly suggestion in a whole whirl-wind of abuse and reviling.

As to Sir John, he blamed her not, and yet he knew no more about it than any of them; he, too, could only have told you that Vera had mistaken her feelings—he knew no more than that—for it was but half the truth that she had told him. But it had been more than enough to convince him that she was perfectly right. When, after telling him plainly that she found she did not love him enough, that there had been other and extraneous reasons that had blinded her to the fact at the time she had accepted him, but that she had found it out later on; when, after saying this she had asked him plainly whether he would wish to have a wife who valued his name, and his wealth, and his fine old house at least as much as he did himself, Sir John had been able to give her but one answer. No, he would not have a wife who loved him in such a fashion. And he had thought well of her for telling him the truth beforehand instead of leaving him to find it out for himself later. If there had been a little, a very little, falling of his idol from the high pillar upon which he had set her up, in that she should at any time have been guided by mercenary and worldly motives; there had been at the same time a very great amount of respect for her brave and straightforward confession of her error at a time when most women would have found themselves unequal to the task of drawing back from the false position into which they had drifted. No, he could not blame her in any way.

But, all the same, it was hard to bear. He said to himself that he was a doomed and fated man; twice had love and joy and domestic peace been within his grasp, and twice they had been wrested from his arms; these things, it was plain, were not for him. He was too old, he told himself, ever to make a further effort. No, there was nothing before him now but to live out his loveless life alone, to sink into a peevish, selfish old bachelor, and to make a will in Maurice's favour, and get himself out of the world that wanted him not with as much expedition as might be.

And he loved Vera still. She was still to him the most pure and perfect of women—good as she was beautiful. Her loveliness haunted him by day and by night, till the bitter thought of what might have been and the contrast of the miserable reality drove him half wild with longings which he did not know how to repress. He sat at home in his rooms and moped; there were more streaks of white in his hair than of old, and there were new lines of care upon his brow—he looked almost an old man now. He sat indoors and did nothing. It was April by this time, and the London season was beginning; invitations of all kinds poured in upon him, but he refused them all; he would go nowhere. Now and then his mother came to see him and attempted to cheer and to rouse him; she had even asked him to come down to Walpole Lodge, but he had declined her request almost ungraciously.

He never had much in common with his mother, and he felt no desire now for her sympathy; besides, the first time she had come she had been angry, and had called Vera a jilt, and that had offended him bitterly; he had rebuked her sternly, and she had been too wise to repeat the offence; but he had not forgotten it. Maurice, indeed, he would have been glad to see, but Maurice did not come near him. His regiment had lately moved to Manchester, and either he could not or would not get leave; and yet he had been idle enough at one time, and glad to run up to town upon the smallest pretext. Now he never came. It added a little to his irritation, but scarcely to his misery. On this particular afternoon, as he sat as usual brooding over the past, there came the sudden clatter of carriage wheels over the flagged roadway of the little back street, followed by a sharp ring at his door. It was his mother, of course; no other woman came to see him; he heard the rustle of her soft silken skirts up the narrow staircase, and her pleasant little chatter to the fat old landlady who was ushering her up, and presently the door opened and she came in.

"Good morning, John. Dear me, how hot and stuffy this room is," holding up her soft old face to her son.

He just touched her cheek. "I am sorry you find it so—shall I open the window?"

"Oh!" sinking down in a chair, and throwing back her cloak; "how can you stand a fire in the room, it is quite mild and spring-like out. Have you not been out, John? it would do you good to get a little fresh air."

"I shall go round to the club presently, I daresay," he answered, abstractedly, sitting down in his arm-chair again; all the pleasant flutter that the bright old lady brought with her, the atmosphere of life and variety that surrounded her, only vexed and wearied him, and jarred upon his nerves. She was always telling him to go somewhere or to do something; why couldn't she let him alone? he thought, irritably.

"To your club? No further than that? Why, you might as well stay at home. Really, my dear, it's a great pity you don't go about and see some of your old friends; you can't mean to shut yourself up like a dormouse for ever, I suppose!"

"I haven't the least idea what I mean to do," he answered, not graciously; she was his mother, and so he could not very well put her out at the door, but that was what he would have liked to do.

"I don't see," continued Lady Kynaston, with unwonted courage, "I don't at all see why you should let this unfortunate affair weigh on you for ever; there is really no reason why you should not console yourself and marry some nice girl; there is Lady Mary Hendrie and plenty more only too ready to have you if you will only take that trouble——"

"Mother, I wish you would not talk to me like that," he said, interrupting suddenly the easy flow of her consoling suggestions, and there was a look of real pain upon his face that smote her somewhat. "Never speak to me of marrying again. I shall never marry any one." He looked away from her, stern and angry, stooping again over the red ashes in the grate; if he had only given her one plea for her pity—if he had only added, "I have suffered too much, I love her still"—all her mother's heart must have gone out to him who, though he was not her favourite, was her first born after all; but he did not want her pity, he only wanted her to go away.

"It is a great pity," she answered, stiffly, "because of Kynaston."

"I shall never set foot at Kynaston again."

Her colour rose a little—after all, she was a cunning little old lady. The little fox-terrier lay on the rug between them; she stooped down and patted it. "Good dog, good little Vic," she said, a little nervously; then, with a sudden courage, she looked up at her son again. "John, it is a sad thing that Kynaston must be left empty to go to rack and ruin; though I have never cared to live there myself, I have always hoped that you would. It would have grieved your poor father sadly to have thought that the old place was always to lie empty."

"I cannot help it," he answered, moodily, wishing more than ever that she would go.

"John;" she fidgeted with her bonnet strings, and her voice trembled a little; "John, if you are quite sure you will never live there yourself, why should not Maurice have it?"

"Maurice! Has he told you to ask for it?" He sat bolt upright in his chair; he was attentive enough now; the idea that Maurice had commissioned his mother to ask for something he had not ventured to ask for himself was not pleasant to him. "Is it Maurice who has sent you?"

"No, no, my dear John; certainly not; why, I haven't seen Maurice for weeks and weeks; he never comes to town now. But I'll tell you why the idea came to me. I called just now in Princes Gate; poor old Mr. Harlowe has had a stroke—it is certain he cannot live long now, after the severe attack he had of bronchitis, too, two months ago. I just saw Helen for a minute, she reported him to be unconscious. If he dies, he must surely leave Helen something; it may not be all, but it will be at least a competency; and I was thinking, John, that if you did not want Kynaston, and would let them live there, the marriage might come off at last; they have been attached to each other a long time, and to live rent free would be a great thing."

"How are they to keep it up? Kynaston is an expensive place."

"Well, I thought, John, perhaps, if Maurice looks after the property, you might consider him as your agent, and allow him something, and that and her money——"

"Yes, yes, I understand; well, I will see; wait, at all events, till Mr. Harlowe is dead. I will think it over. No, I don't see any reason why they should not live there if they like;" he sighed, wearily, and his mother went away, feeling that she had reason to be satisfied with her morning's work.

She was in such a hurry to install her darling there—to see him viceroy in the place where now it was certain he must eventually be king. Why should he be doomed to wait till Kynaston came to him in the course of nature; why should he not enter upon his kingdom at once, since Sir John, by his own confession, would never marry or live there himself?

Lady Kynaston was very far from wishing evil to her eldest son, but for years she had hoped that he would remain unmarried; for a short time she had been forced to lay her dreams aside, and she had striven to forget them and to throw herself with interest into her eldest son's engagement; but now that the marriage was broken off, all her old schemes and plans came back to her again. She was working and planning again for Maurice's happiness and aggrandisement. She wanted to see him in his father's house, "Kynaston of Kynaston," before she died, and to know that his future was safe. To see him married to Helen and living at Kynaston appeared to her to be the very best that she could desire for him. In time, of course, the title and the money would be his too; meanwhile, with old Mr. Harlowe's fortune, an ample allowance from his brother, and all the prestige of his old name and his old house, she should live to see him take his own rightful place among the magnates of his native county. That would be far better than to be a captain in a line regiment, barely able to live upon his income. That was all she coveted for him, and she said to herself that her ambition was not unreasonable, and that it would be hard indeed if it might not be gratified.

As she drove homewards to Walpole Lodge she felt that her schemes were in a fair way for success. She was not going to let Maurice know of them too soon; by-and-by, when all was settled, she would tell him; she would keep it till then as a pleasant surprise.

All the same, she had been unable to refrain from telling Helen Romer something of what was in her mind.

"If John does not marry, he might perhaps make Maurice his agent and let him live at Kynaston," she had said to her a few days ago when they had been speaking of old Mr. Harlowe's illness.

"How would Maurice like to leave the army?" Helen had asked.

"If he marries, he must do so," his mother had replied, significantly; and Helen's heart had beat high with hope and triumph.

Again to-day, on her way to her eldest son's rooms, she had stopped at Princes Gate and had alluded to it.

"I am on my way to see Sir John; I shall sound him about his intentions with regard to Kynaston, but, of course, I must go to work cautiously;" and Helen had perfectly understood that she herself had entered into the old lady's scheme for her younger son's future.

Sitting alone in the hushed house, where the doctors are coming and going in the darkened room above, Helen feels that at last the reward of all her long waiting may be at hand. Love and wealth at last seemed to beckon to her. Her grandfather dead; his fortune hers; and this offer of a home at Kynaston, which Maurice himself would be sure to like so much—everything good seemed coming to her at last.

And there was something about the idea of living at Kynaston that gratified her particularly. Helen had not forgotten the week at Shadonake. Too surely had her woman's instinct told her that Maurice and Vera had been drawn to each other by a strong and mutual attraction. The wildest jealousy and hatred against Vera burnt fiercely in her lawless, untutored heart. She hated her, for she knew that Maurice loved her. To live thus under her very eyes as Maurice's wife, in the very house her rival herself had once been on the point of inhabiting, was a notion that commended itself to her with all the sweetness of gratified revenge, with all the charm of flaunting her success and triumph in the face of the other woman's failure which is dear to such a nature as Helen's.

She alone, of all those who had heard of Vera's broken engagement, had divined its true cause. She loved Maurice—that was plain to Helen; that was why she had thrown over Sir John, and at her heart Helen despised her for it. A woman must be a fool indeed to wreck herself at the last moment for a merely sentimental reason. There was much, however, that was incomprehensible to Helen Romer in the situation of things, which she only half understood.

If Maurice loved Vera, why was it that he was in Manchester whilst she was still in Meadowshire? that was what Helen could not understand. A sure instinct told her that Maurice must know better than any one why his brother's marriage had been broken off. But, if so, then why were he and Vera apart? It did not strike her that his honour to his brother and his promises to herself were what kept him away. Helen said to herself, scornfully, that they were both of them timid and cowardly, and did not half know how to play out life's game.

"In her place, with her cards in my hand, I would have married him by this," she said to herself, as she sat alone in her grandfather's drawing-room, while her busy fingers ran swiftly through the meshes of her knitting, and the doctor and the hired nurse paced about the room overhead. "But she has not the pluck for it; his heart may be hers, but, for all that, I shall win him; and how bitterly she will repent that she ever interfered with him when she sees him daily there—my husband! And in time he will forget her and learn to love me; Maurice will never be false to a woman when once she is his wife; I am not afraid of that. How dared she meddle with him?—*my* Maurice!"

The door softly opened, and one of the doctors stepped in on tip-toe. Helen rose and composed her face into a decorous expression of mournful anxiety.

"I am happy to tell you, Mrs. Romer," began the doctor. Helen's heart sank down chill and cold within her.

"Is he better?" she faltered, striving to conceal the dismay which she felt.

"He has rallied. Consciousness has returned, and partial use of the limbs. We may be able to pull your grandfather through this time, I trust."

Put off again! How wretched and how guilty she felt herself to be! It was almost a crime to wish for any one's death so much.

She sank down again pale and spiritless upon her chair as the doctor left the room.

"Never mind," she said to herself, presently; "it can't last for ever. It must be soon now, and I shall be Maurice's wife in the end."

But all this time she had forgotten Monsieur Le Vicomte D'Arblet, whom she had not seen again since the night she had driven him home from Walpole Lodge.

He had left England, she knew. Helen privately hoped he had left this earth. Any way, he had not troubled her, and she had forgotten him.

CHAPTER XIX.

WHAT SHE WAITED FOR.

Go, forget me; why should sorrow
O'er that brow a shadow fling?
Go, forget me, and to-morrow
Brightly smile and sweetly sing.
Smile—though I shall not be near thee;
Sing—though I shall never hear thee.

CHAS. WOLFE.

All this time what of Vera? Would any one of them at the vicarage ever forget that morning when she had come in after her walk with Sir John Kynaston, and had stood before them all and, pale as a ghost, had said to them,

"I am not going to be married; I have broken it off."

It had been a great blow to them, but neither the prayers of her weeping sister, nor the angry indignation of old Mrs. Daintree, nor even the gentle remonstrances of her brother-in-law could serve to alter her determination, nor would she enter into any explanation concerning her conduct.

It was not pleasant, of course, to be reviled and scolded, to be questioned and marvelled at, to be treated like a naughty child in disgrace; and then, whenever she went out, to feel herself tabooed by her acquaintances as a young woman who had behaved very disgracefully; or else to be stared at as a natural curiosity by persons whom she hardly knew.

But she lived through all this bravely. There was a certain amount of unnatural excitement which kept up her courage and enabled her to face it. It was no more than what she had expected. The glow of her love and her impulse of self-sacrifice were still upon her; her nerves had been strung to the uttermost, and she felt strong in the knowledge of the justice and the right of her own conduct.

But by-and-by all this died away. Sir John left the neighbourhood; people got tired of talking about her broken-off marriage; there was no longer any occasion for her to be brave and steadfast. Life began to resume for her its normal aspect, the aspect which it had worn in the old days before Sir John had ever come down to Kynaston, or ever found her day-dreaming in the churchyard upon Farmer Crupps' family sarcophagus. The tongue of the sour-tempered old lady, snapping and snarling at her with more than the bitterness of old, and the suppressed sighs and mournful demeanour of her sister, whose sympathy and companionship she had now completely forfeited, and who went about the house with a face of resigned woe and the censure of an ever implied rebuke in her voice and manner.

Only the vicar took her part somewhat. "Let her alone," he said, sometimes, to his wife and mother; "she must have had a better reason than we any of us know of; the girl is suffering quite enough—leave her alone."

And she was suffering. The life that she had doomed herself to was almost unbearable to her. The everlasting round of parish work and parish talk, the poor people and the coal-clubs—it was what she had come back to. She had been lifted for a short time out of it all, and a new life, congenial to her tastes and to her nature, had opened out before her; and yet with her own hands she had shut the door upon this brighter prospect, and had left herself out in the darkness, to go back to that life of dull monotony which she hated.

And what had she gained by it? What single advantage had she reaped out of her sacrificed life? Was Maurice any nearer to her—was he not hopelessly divided from her—helplessly out of her reach? She knew nothing of him, no word concerning him reached her ears: a great blank was before her. When she went over the past again and again in her mind, she could not well see what good thing could ever come to her from what she had done. There were moments indeed when the whole story of her broken engagement seemed to her like the wild delusion of madness. She had had no intention of acknowledging her love to Maurice when she had gone up to the station to see him off; she had only meant to see him once more, to hold his hand for one instant, to speak a few kind words; to wish him God speed. She asked herself now what had possessed her that she had not been able to preserve the self-control of affectionate friendship when the unfortunate accident of her being taken on in the train with him had left her entirely alone in his society. She did not go the length of regretting what she had done for his sake; but she did acknowledge to herself that she had been led away by the magnetism of his presence and by the strange and unexpected chance which had thus left her alone with him into saying and doing things which in a calmer moment she would not have been betrayed into.

For a few kisses—for the joy of telling him that his love was returned—for a short moment of delirious and transient happiness, and alas! for nothing more—she had thrown away her life!

She had behaved hardly and cruelly to a good man who loved her, and whose heart she had half broken, and she had lost a great many very excellent and satisfactory things.

And Maurice was no nearer to her. With his own lips he had told her that he could not marry her. There had been mention, indeed, of that problematical term of five years, in which he had bound himself to await Mrs. Romer's pleasure—but, even had Mrs. Romer not existed, it was plain that Maurice was the last man in the world to take advantage of a woman's weakness in order to supplant his brother in her heart.

Instinctively Vera felt that Maurice must be no less miserable than herself; that his regret for what had happened between them must be as great as her own, and his remorse far greater. They were, indeed, neither of them blameless in the matter; for, if it was Maurice who had first spoken of his love to his brother's promised wife, it was Vera who had made that irrevocable step along the road of her destiny from which no going back was now possible.

It was a time of utter misery to her. If she sat indoors there was the persecution of Mrs. Daintree's ill-natured remarks, and Marion's depression of spirits and half-uttered regrets; and there was also the scaffolding rising round the chancel walls to be seen from the windows, and the sound of the sawing of the masonry in the churchyard, as a perpetual, reproachful reminder of the friend whose kindness and affection she had so ill requited. If she went out, she could not go up the lane without passing the gates of Kynaston, or towards the village without catching sight of the venerable old house among its terraced gardens, which, so lately, she had thought would be her home. Sometimes she met her old friend, Mrs. Eccles, in her wanderings, but she did not venture to speak to her; the cold disapproval in the housekeeper's passing salutation made her shrink, like a guilty creature, in her presence; and she would hurry by with scarcely an answering sign, with downcast eyes and heightened colour.

Somehow, it came to pass in these days that Vera drifted into a degree of intimacy with Beatrice Miller that would, possibly, never have come about had the circumstances of her life been different. Ever since her accidental meeting with the lovers outside Tripton station Vera had, perforce, become a confidant of their hopes and fears; and Beatrice was glad enough to have found a friend to whom she could talk about her lover, for where is the woman who can completely hold her tongue concerning her own secrets?

Against all the long category of female virtues, as advantageously displayed in contradistinction to masculine vices, there is still this one peculiarity which, of itself, marks out the woman as the inferior animal.

A man, to be worthy of the name, holds his tongue and keeps the secret of his heart to himself, enjoying it and delighting in it the more, possibly, for his reticence. A woman may occasionally—very occasionally—be silent respecting her neighbour, but concerning herself she is bound to have at least one confidant to whom she will rashly tell the long story of her loves and her sorrows; and not a consideration either of prudence or of worldly wisdom will suffice to restrain her too ready tongue.

Beatrice Miller was a clever girl, with a fair knowledge of the world; yet she was in no way dismayed that Vera should have discovered her secret; on the contrary, she was overjoyed that she had now found some one to talk to about it.

Vera became her friend, but Beatrice was not Vera's friend—the confidences were not mutual. Over and over again Beatrice was on the point of questioning her concerning the story that had been on every one's lips for a time; of asking her what, indeed, was the truth about her broken engagement; but always the proud, still face restrained her curiosity, and the words died away unspoken upon her lips.

Vera's story, indeed, was not one that could be easily revealed. There was too much of bitter regret, too great an element of burning shame at her heart, for its secrets to be laid bare to a stranger's eye.

Nevertheless, Beatrice's society amused and distracted her mind, and kept her from brooding over her own troubles. She was glad enough to go over to Shadonake; even to sit alone with Beatrice and her mother was better than the eternal monotony of the vicarage, where she felt like a prisoner waiting for his sentence.

Yes, she was waiting. Waiting for some sign from the man she loved. Sooner or later, whether it was for good or for evil, she knew it must come to her; some token that he remembered her existence; some indication as to what he would have her do with the life that she had laid at his feet. For, after all, when a woman loves a man, she virtually makes him the ruler of her destiny; she leaves the responsibility of her fate in his hands. For the nonce, Maurice Kynaston held the skein of Vera's life in his grasp; it was for him to do what he pleased with it. Some day, doubtless, he would tell her what she had to do: meanwhile, she waited.

What else, indeed, can a woman do but wait? To sit still with folded hands and bated breath, to possess her soul in patience as best she may, to still the wild beatings of her all too eager spirit—that is what a woman has to do, and does often enough. God help her, all too badly.

It is so easy when one is old, and the pulses are sluggish, and the hot passions of youth are quelled, it is so easy then to learn that lesson of waiting; but when we are young, and our best days slipping away, and life's hopes all before us, and life's burdens well-nigh unbearable; then it is that it is hard, that waiting in itself becomes terrible—more terrible almost than the worst of our woes.

So wearily, feverishly, impatiently enough, Vera waited.

Winter died away into spring. The rough wind of March, worn out with its own boisterous passions, sobbed itself to rest like a tired child, and little green buds came cropping up sparsely and timidly out of the brown bosom of the earth; and, presently, all the glory of the golden crocuses unfolded itself in long golden lines in the vicarage garden; and there were twittering of birds and flutterings of soft breezes among the tree-tops, and a voice seemed to go forth over the face of the earth. The winter is over, and summer is nigh at hand.

And then it came to her at last. An envelope by the side of her plate at breakfast; a few scrawled words in a handwriting she had never seen before, and yet identified with an unfailing instinct, ere even she broke the seal. One minute of wild hope, to be followed by a sick, chill numbness, and the story of her love and its longings shrank away into the despair of impossibility.

How small a thing to make so great a misery! What a few words to make a wilderness of a human life!

"Her grandfather is dead, and she has claimed me. Good-bye; forget me and forgive me."

That was all; nothing more. No passionate regrets, no unavailing self-pity; nothing to tell her what it cost him to resign her; no word to comfort her for the hopelessness of his desertion; nothing but those two lines.

There was a chattering going on at the table around her. Tommy was clamouring for bread and butter; the vicar was reading out the telegrams from the seat of war; Marion was complaining that the butter was not good; the maid-servant was bringing in the hot bacon and eggs—it all went on like a dream around her; presently, like a voice out of a fog, somebody spoke to her:

"Vera, are you not feeling well? You look as if you were going to faint."

And then she crunched the letter in her hand and recalled herself to life.

"I am quite well, thanks," and busied herself with attending to the wants of the children.

The vicar glanced up over his spectacles. "No bad news, I hope, my dear."

Oh! why could they not let her alone? But somehow she sat through the breakfast, and answered all their questions, and bore herself bravely; and when it was over and she was free to go away by herself with her trouble, then by that time the worst of it was over.

There are some people whom sorrow softens and touches, but Vera was not one of them. Her whole soul revolted and rebelled against her fate. She said to herself that for once she had let her heart guide her; she had cast aside the crust of worldliness and self-indulgence in which she had been brought up.

She had listened to the softer whisperings of the better nature within her—she had been true to herself—and lo! what had come of it?

But now she had learnt her lesson; there were to be no more dreams of pure and unsullied happiness for her,—no more cravings after what was good and true and lovely; henceforth she would go back to the teachings of her youth, to the experience which had told her that a handsome woman can always command her life as she pleases, and that wealth, which is a tangible reality, is better worth striving after than the vain shadow called love, which all talk about and so few make any practical sacrifices for. Well, she, Vera Nevill, had tried it, and had made her sacrifices; and what remained to her? Only the fixed determination to crush it down again within her as if it had never been, and to carve out her fortunes afresh. Only that she started again at a disadvantage—for now she knew to her cost that she possessed the fatal power of loving—the knowledge of good and evil, of which she had eaten the poisoned fruit.

There were no tears in Vera's eyes as she wandered slowly up and down the garden paths between the straight yellow lines of the crocus heads.

Her lover had forsaken her. Well, let him go. She told herself that, had he loved her truly, no power on earth would have been great enough to keep him from her. She said to herself scornfully—she, Vera Nevill, who was prepared to sell herself to the highest bidder—that it was Mrs. Romer's money that kept him from her. Well, let him go to her, then? but for herself life must begin afresh.

And then she set to work to think about what she could do. To remain here at Sutton any longer was impossible. It was absolutely necessary that she should get away from it all, from the family upon whose hands she was nothing now but a beautiful, helpless burden, and still more from the haunting memories of Kynaston and all the unfortunate things that had happened to her here.

Suddenly, out of the memories of her girlhood, she recollected the existence of a woman who had been her friend once in the old happy days, when she had lived with her sister Theodora. It was one of those passing friendships which come and go for a month or two in one's life.

A pretty, spoilt girl, married four, perhaps five, years ago to a rich man, a banker; who had taken a fancy to Vera, and had pleased herself by decking her out in a quaint costume to figure at a carnival party; who had kissed her rapturously at parting, swearing eternal friendship, giving her her address in London, and making her promise never to be in England without going to see her. And then she had gone her way, and had never come back again the next winter, as she had promised to do; a letter or two had passed between them, and afterwards Vera had forgotten her. But somewhere upstairs she must have got her direction still.

It was to this friend she would go; and, turning her back for a time at least upon Meadowshire and its memories, she would see whether, in the whirl of London life, she could not crush out the pain at her heart, and live down the fatal weakness that had led her astray from all the traditions of her youth, and from that cold and prudent wisdom which had stood her in good stead for so many years.

CHAPTER XX.

A MORNING WALK.

And e'en while fashion's brightest arts decoy,
The heart, distrusting, asks if this be joy.

GOLDSMITH.

A bright May morning, cold, it is true, and with a biting wind from the east—
as indeed our English May mornings generally are—but sunny and cloudless
as the heart can desire. On such a morning people do their best to pretend
that it is summer. Crowds turn out into the park, and sit about recklessly on
the iron chairs, or lounge idly by the railings; and the women-folk, with that
fine disregard of what is, when it is antagonistic of what they wish it to be,
don their white cottons and muslins, and put up their parasols against the
sun's rays, and, shivering inwardly, poor things, openly brave the terrors of
rheumatism and lumbago, and make up their minds that it *shall* be summer.

The sunblinds are drawn all along the front windows of a house in Park Lane,
and though the gay geraniums and calceolarias in the flower-boxes, which
were planted only yesterday, look already nipped and shrivelled up with the
cold, the house, nevertheless, presents from the exterior a bright and well-
cared-for appearance.

Within the drawing-room are two ladies. One, the mistress of the house, is
seated at the writing-table with her back to the room, scribbling off
invitations for dear life, cards for an afternoon "at-home," at the rate of six
per minute; the other sits idle in a low basket-chair doing nothing.

There is no sound but the scratching of the quill pen as it flies over the paper,
and the chirping of a bullfinch in a cage in the bow-window.

"What time is it, Vera?"

"A quarter to twelve."

"Almost time to dress; I've only ten more cards to fill up. What are you going
to wear—white?"

Vera shivers. "Look how the dust is flying—it must be dreadfully cold out—
I should like to put on a fur jacket."

"*Do*," says the elder lady, energetically. "It will be original, and attract
attention. Not that you could well be more stared at than you are."

Vera smiles, and does not answer.

Mrs. Hazeldine goes on with her task.

"There! that's done!" she cries, at last, getting up from the table, and piling her notes up in a heap on one side of it. "Now, I am at your orders."

She comes forward into the room—a pretty, dark-eyed, oval-faced woman, with a figure in which her dressmaker has understood how to supplement all that nature has but imperfectly carried out. A woman with restless movements and an ever-ready tongue—a thorough daughter of the London world she lives in.

Vera leans her head back in her chair, and looks at her. "Cissy," she says, "I must really go home, I have been with you a month to-day."

"Go home! certainly not, my dear. Don't you know that I have sworn to find you a husband before the season is out? I must really get you married, Vera. I have half a mind," she adds, reflectively, as she smooths down her shining brown hair at the glass, and contemplates, not ill satisfied, her image there— "I have really half a mind to let you have the boy if I could manage to spare him."

"Do you think he would make a devoted husband?" asks Vera, with a lazy smile.

"My dear child, don't be a fool. What is the use of devotion in a husband? All one wants is a good fellow, who will let one alone. After all, the boy might not answer. I am afraid, Vera," turning round suddenly upon her, "I am very much afraid that boy is in love with you; it's horrid of you to take him from me, because he is so useful, and I really can't well do without him. I am going to pay him out to-night though: he is to sit opposite you at dinner; he will only be able to gaze at you."

"That is hard upon us both."

"Pooh! don't waste your time upon him. I shall do better than that for you; he is an eldest son, it is true, but Sir Charles looks as young as his son, and is quite as likely to live as long. It is only married women who can afford the luxury of ineligibles. Go and dress, child."

Half-an-hour later Mrs. Hazeldine and Miss Nevill are to be found upon two chairs on the broad and shady side of the Row, where a small crowd of men is already gathered around them.

Vera, coming up a stranger, and self-invited to the house of her old acquaintance a few weeks ago, had already created a sensation in London. Her rare beauty, the strange charm of her quiet, listless manner, the shade of melancholy which had of late imperceptibly crept over her, aroused a keen admiration and interest in her, even in that city, which more than all others is satiated with its manifold types of beautiful women.

There was a rush to get introduced to her; a *furore* to see her. As she went through a crowd people whispered her name and made way for her to pass, staring at her after a fashion which is totally modern and detestably ill-bred; and yet which, sad token of the *decadence* of things in these later days, is not beneath the dignity or the manners of persons whose breeding is supposed to be beyond dispute.

Already the "new beauty" had been favourably contrasted with the well-known reigning favourites; and it was the loudly expressed opinion of more than one-half of the *jeunesse dorée* of the day that not one of the others could "hold a candle to her, by Jove!"

Mrs. Hazeldine was delighted. It was she to whom belonged the honour of bringing this new star into notice; the credit of launching her upon London society was her own. She found herself courted and flattered and made up to in a wholly new and delightful manner. The men besieged her for invitations to her house; the women pressed her to come to theirs. It was all for Miss Nevill's sake, of course, but, even so, it was very pleasant, and Mrs. Hazeldine dearly loved the importance of her position.

It came to pass that, whereas she had been somewhat put out at the letter of her old Roman acquaintance, offering to come and stay with her, and had been disposed to resent the advent of her self-invited guest as an infliction, which a few needlessly gushing words in the past had brought upon herself, she had, in a very short time, discovered that she could not possibly exist without her darling Vera, and that she would not and could not let her go back again to her country vicarage.

It was, possibly, what Vera had counted upon. It was pretty certain to have been either one thing or the other. Either her beauty would arouse Mrs. Hazeldine's jealousy, and she would be glad to be rid of her as quickly as possible, or else she would be proud of her, and wish to retain her as an attraction to her house. Fortunately for Vera, Cissy Hazeldine, worldly, frivolous, pleasure-loving as she was, was, nevertheless, utterly devoid of the mean and petty spitefulness which goes far to disfigure many a better woman's character. She was not jealous of Vera; on the contrary, she was as unfeignedly proud of her as though she had created her. Besides, as she said to herself, "Our style is so different, we are not likely to clash."

When she found that in a month's time Vera's beauty had made her house the most popular one in London, and that people struggled for her invitation-cards and prayed to be introduced to her, Mrs. Hazeldine was at the zenith of her delight and self-importance. If only Vera herself had been a little more practicable!

"I don't despair of getting you introduced to royalty before the season is out," she would say, triumphantly.

"I don't want to be introduced to royalty," Vera would answer indifferently.

"Oh! Vera, how can you be so disloyal? And it's quite wicked too; almost against Scripture. Honour the King, you know it says somewhere; of course that means the Prince of Wales too."

"I can honour him very well without being introduced to him," said Vera, who, however, let me assure you, was filled with feelings of profound loyalty towards the reigning family.

"But only think what a triumph it would be over those other horrid women who think themselves at the top of the tree!" Mrs. Hazeldine would urge, with a curious conglomeration of ideas, sacred and profane.

But Vera was indifferent to the honour of becoming acquainted with his Royal Highness.

Another of Mrs. Hazeldine's troubles was that she absolutely refused to be photographed.

"Your portrait might be in every shop window if you chose!" Mrs. Hazeldine would exclaim, despairingly.

"I may be very depraved, Cissy," Vera would answer, indignantly, "but I have not yet sunk so low as to desire that every draper's assistant may have the privilege of buying my likeness for a shilling to stick up on his mantelshelf, with a tight-rope dancer on one side, and a burlesque actress on the other!"

"My dear, it is done by every one; and women who are beautiful as you are ought not to mind being admired."

"But I prefer being admired by my friends only, and by those of my own class. I have no ambition to expose myself, even in effigy, in a shop window for the edification of street boys and city clerks."

"Well, you can't help your name having been in *Vanity Fair* this week!"

"No, and I only wish I could get hold of the man who put it there!" cried Miss Nevill, viciously; and it is certain that unfortunate literary person would not have relished the interview.

A "beauty" with such strange and unnatural views was, it must be confessed, as much of a trial as a triumph to an anxious chaperon.

There was a certain amount of fashionable routine, the daily treadmill of pleasure, to which, however, Vera submitted readily enough, and even extracted a good deal of enjoyment out of it. There was the morning saunter into the Row, the afternoons spent at garden parties or "at-homes," the evenings filled up with dinner parties, to be followed almost invariably by balls lasting late into the night. All these things repeat themselves year after year: they are utter weariness to some of us, but to her they were still new, and Vera entered into the daily whirl of the London season with an amount of zest which was almost a surprise to herself.

Just at first there had been a daily terror upon her, that of meeting Sir John Kynaston or his brother; but London is a large place, and you may go out to different houses for many nights running without ever coming across the friend or the foe whom you desire or dread most to encounter.

After a little while, she forgot to glance hurriedly and fearfully around her every time she entered a ball-room, or to look up shudderingly each time the door was opened and a fresh guest announced at a dinner-party. She never met either of them, nor did the name of Kynaston ever strike upon her ear.

She told herself that she had forgotten the two brothers, whose fate had seemed at one time so intimately bound up with her own—the one as well as the other. They were nothing more to her now—they had passed away out of her life. Henceforth she had entered upon a new course, in which her beauty and her mother wit were to exact their full value, but in which her heart was to count for nothing more. It was to be smothered up within her. That, together with all the best, and sweetest, and truest part of her, once awakened for a brief space by the magic touch of love, was now to be extinguished within her as though they had never been.

Meanwhile Vera enjoys herself.

She looks happy enough now as she sits by her friend's side in the park, with a little knot of admirers about her; not taking very much trouble to talk to them, indeed, but smiling serenely from one to the other, letting herself be talked to and amused, with just a word here and there, to show them she is listening to what they say. It is, perhaps, the secret of her success that she is so thoroughly indifferent to it all. It matters so little to her whether they come or go; there is so little eagerness about her, so perfect an *insouciance* of manner. Other women lay themselves out to attract and to be admired; Vera only sits still, and waits with a certain queenliness of manner for the worship that is laid at her feet, and which she receives as her due.

Behind her, with his hand on the back of her chair, stands a young fellow of about two or three and twenty; he does not speak to her much, nor join in the merry, empty chatter that is going on around her; but it is easy to see by the way he looks down at her, by the fashion in which he watches her slightest movement, that Vera exercises no ordinary influence over him.

He is a tall, slight-figured boy, with very fair yellow hair and delicate features; his blue eyes are frank and pleasant, but his mouth is a trifle weak and vacillating, and the lips are too sensitively cut for strength of character, whilst his chest is too narrow for strength of body. He is carefully dressed, and wears a white, heavy-scented flower in his coat, a flower which, five minutes ago, he had ineffectually attempted to transfer to Miss Nevill's dress; but Vera had only gently pushed back his hand. "My dear boy, pray keep your gardenia; a flower in one's dress is such a nuisance, it is always tumbling out."

Denis Wilde, "the boy," as Mrs. Hazeldine called him with a flush on his fair face, had put it back quietly in his button-hole, too well bred to show the pain he felt by flinging it, as he would have liked to do, over the railing, to be trampled under the feet of the horses.

The little group kept its place for some time, the two well-dressed and good-looking women sitting down, the two or three idlers who stood in front of them gossiping about nothing at all—last night's ball, to-day's plans, a little bit of scandal about one passer-by, somebody's rumoured engagement, somebody else's reported elopement. Denis Wilde stood behind Vera's chair and listened to it all, the well-known familiar chatter of a knot of London idlers. There was nothing new or interesting or entertaining about it. Only a string of names, some of which were strange to him, but most of which were familiar; and always some little story, ill-natured or harmless as the case might be, about each name that was mentioned. And Vera listened, smiling, assenting, but only half attentive, with her eyes dreamily fixed upon the long procession of riders passing ever ceaselessly to and fro along the ride.

Suddenly Denis Wilde felt a sudden movement of the chair beneath his hand. Vera had started violently.

"Here comes Sir John Kynaston," the man before her was saying to his companion. "What a time it is since he has shown himself; he looks as if he had had a bad illness."

"Some woman jilted him, I've heard," answered the other man: "some girl down in the country. People say, Miss Nevill, he is going to die of that old-fashioned complaint, which you certainly will not believe in, a broken heart! Poor old boy, he looks as if he had been buried, and had come up again for a breath of air!"

Vera followed the direction of their eyes. Sir John was walking slowly towards them; he was thin and careworn; he looked aged beyond all belief. He walked slowly, as though it were an effort to him, with his eyes upon the ground. He had not seen her yet; in another minute he would be within a couple of yards of her. It was next to impossible that he could avoid seeing her, the centre, as she was, of that noisy, chattering group.

A sort of despair seized her. How was she to meet him—this man whom she had so cruelly treated? She could *not* meet him; she felt that it was an impossibility. Like an imprisoned bird that seeks to escape, she looked about instinctively from side to side. What possible excuse could she frame? In what direction could she fly to avoid the glance of reproach that would smite her to the heart.

Suddenly Denis Wilde bent down over her.

"Miss Nevill, there goes a *Dachshund*, exactly like the one you wanted; come quickly, and we shall catch him up. He ran away down here."

She sprang up and turned after him; a path leading away from the crowded Row, towards the comparatively empty park at the back, opened out immediately behind her chair.

Young Wilde strode rapidly along it before her, and Vera followed him blindly and thankfully.

After a few minutes he stopped and turned round.

"Where is—the dog—wasn't it a dog, you said? Where is it?" She was white and trembling.

"There is no dog," he answered, not looking at her. "I—I saw you wanted to get away for a minute. You will forgive me, won't you?"

Vera looked at him with a sudden earnestness. The watchfulness which had seen her distress, the ready tact which had guessed at her desire to escape, and had so promptly suggested the manner of it, touched her suddenly. She put forth her hand gently and almost timidly.

"Thank you," she said, simply. "I did not imagine you were so clever—or so kind."

The boy blushed deeply with pleasure. He did not know her trouble, but the keen eye of love had guessed at its existence. It had been easy for him who watched her every look, who knew every shade and every line of her face, to tell that she was in distress, to interpret her pallor and her trembling terror aright.

"You don't want to go back?" he asked.

"Oh, no, I cannot go back! Besides, I am tired; it is time to go home."

"Stay here, then, and I will call Mrs. Hazeldine."

He left her standing alone upon the grass, and went back to the crowded path. Presently he returned with her friend.

"My dear Vera, what is the matter? The boy says you have such a headache! I am so sorry, and I wouldn't let any of those chattering fools come back to lunch. Why, you look quite pale, child! Will it be too much for you to have the boy, because we will send him away, too, if you like?"

But Vera turned round and smiled upon the boy.

"Oh, no, let him come, certainly; but let us go home, all three of us at once, if you don't mind."

The thoughtfulness that had kept her secret for her, even from the eyes of the woman who was supposed to be her intimate friend, surely deserved its reward.

They walked home slowly together across the park, and, when Vera came down to luncheon, a white gardenia had somehow or other found its way to the bosom of her dress.

That was Denis Wilde's reward.

CHAPTER XXI.

MAURICE'S INTERCESSION.

Youth is a blunder; manhood a struggle; old age a regret.

B. DISRAELI, "Coningsby."

Two or three days later the east wind was still blowing, and the chilled sunshine still feebly shining down upon the nipped lilac and laburnum blossoms. The garden at Walpole Lodge was shorn of half its customary beauty, yet to Helen Romer, pacing slowly up and down its gravel walks, it had never possibly presented a fairer appearance. For Mrs. Romer had won her battle. All that she had waited for so long and striven for so hard was at length within her grasp. Her grandfather was dead, his money had been all left to her, her engagement to Captain Kynaston was an acknowledged fact, and she herself was staying as an honoured and welcome guest in her future mother-in-law's house. Everything in the present and the future seemed to smile upon her, and yet there were drawbacks—as are there not in most earthly delights?—to the full enjoyment of her happiness.

For instance, there was that unreasonable and unaccountable codicil to her grandfather's will, of which no one had been able to discern either the sense or the meaning, and which stated that, should his beloved grand-daughter, Helen Romer, be still unmarried within two months of the date of his death, the whole of the previous bequests and legacies were to be revoked and cancelled, and, with the exception of five thousand pounds which she would retain, the whole bulk of his fortune was to devolve upon the Crown, for the special use of the pensioners of Greenwich and Chelsea Hospitals.

Why such an extraordinary clause had been added to the old man's will it was difficult to say. Possibly he feared that his grand-daughter might be tempted to remain unmarried, in order that she might the more freely squander her newly-acquired fortune in selfish pleasures; possibly he desired to ensure her future by the speedy shelter and support of a husband's name and authority, or perhaps he only hoped at his heart that she would be unable to fulfil his condition; and, whilst his memory would be left free from blame towards his daughter's orphaned child, his money might go away from her by her own fault, and enrich the institutions of his country at the expense of the grand-daughter, whom he had always disliked.

Be that as it may, it was sufficient to place Helen in a very awkward and uncomfortable position. She had not only to claim Maurice's promised troth to her, but she had also to urge on him an almost immediate marriage; the task was a thankless and most unpleasant one.

Besides that, there was the existence of a certain little French vicomte which caused Mrs. Romer not a little anxiety. Now, if ever, was the time when she had reason to dread his re-appearance with those fatal letters with which he had once threatened to spoil her life should she ever attempt to marry again.

But her grandfather had died and had left her his money, and her engagement and approaching marriage to another man was no secret, yet still Monsieur Le Vicomte D'Arblet made no sign, and gave forth no token of his promised vengeance.

Helen dared not flatter herself that he was dead, but she did hope, and hoped rightly, that he was not in England, and had not heard of the change in her fortunes. She had been afraid to make any inquiries concerning him; such a step might only excite suspicion, and defeat her own object of remaining hidden from him. If only she could be safely married before he heard of her again—all, she thought, might yet be well with her. Of what use, then, would be his vengeance? for she did not think it likely he could be so cruel as to wreak an idle and profitless revenge upon her after she herself and her fortune were beyond his power.

Perhaps, had she known that her enemy had been on a distant journey to Constantinople, from which he was now returning, and that every hour she lived brought him nearer and nearer to her, she would have been less easy in her mind concerning him. As it was, she consoled herself by thinking in how short a time her marriage would put her out of his power, and hoped, for the rest, that things would all turn out right for her. Nevertheless, strive how she would, she could not quite put away the dread of it out of her mind—it was an anxiety.

And then there was Maurice himself. She had known, of course, for long, how slight was her hold upon her lover's heart, but never had he appeared so cold, so unloving, so full of apathetic indifference towards her as he had seemed to be during the few days since he had arrived at his mother's house. His every word and look, the very change in his voice when he turned from his mother to her, told her, as plainly as though he had spoken it, that she was forcing him into a marriage that was hateful and repulsive to him, and which duty alone made him submit to. However little pride a woman may retain, such a position must always bring a certain amount of bitterness with it.

To Helen it was gall and wormwood, yet she was all the more determined upon keeping him. She said to herself that she had toiled, and waited, and striven for him for too long to relinquish him now that the victory was hers at length.

Poor Helen, with all her good looks, and all her many attractions, she had been so unfortunate with this one man whom she loved! She had always gone the wrong way to work with him.

Even now she could not let him alone; she was foolishly jealous and suspicious.

He had come to her, all smarting and bleeding still with the sacrifice he had made of his heart to his duty. He had shut the woman he loved determinedly out of his thoughts, and had set his face resolutely to do his duty to the woman whom he seemed destined to marry. Even now a little softness, a little womanly gentleness and sympathy, and, above all, a wise forbearance from probing into his still open wounds, might have won a certain amount of gratitude and affection from him. But Helen was unequal to this. She only drove him wild with causeless and senseless jealousy, and goaded him almost to madness by endless suspicions and irritating cross-questioning.

It is difficult to know what she expected more of him. He slept under the same roof with her, he dined at his mother's table, and spent the evenings religiously in her society. She could not well expect to keep him also at her side all day long; and yet his daily visits to town, amounting usually to between three and four hours of absence, were a constant source of annoyance and disquiet to her. Where did he go? What did he do with himself? Whom did he see in these diurnal expeditions into London? She wore herself into a fever with her perpetual effort to fathom these things.

Even now she is fretting and fuming because he has promised to be home to luncheon, and he is twenty minutes late.

She paces impatiently up and down the garden. Lady Kynaston opens the French window and calls to her from the house:

"Come, my dear, lunch is on the table; are you not coming in?"

"I had rather wait for Maurice, please; do sit down without me," she answers, with the irritation of a spoilt child. Lady Kynaston closes the window. "Oh, these lovers!" she groans to herself, somewhat impatiently, as she sits down alone to the well-furnished luncheon-table; but she bears it pretty composedly because Helen has her grandfather's money, and is to bring her son wealth as well as love, and Lady Kynaston is not at all above being glad of it. One can stand little faults of manner and temper from a daughter-in-law, who is an heiress, which one would be justly indignant at were she a pauper.

A sound of wheels turning in at the lodge-gates—it is Maurice's hansom.

Helen hurries forward to meet him in the hall; Captain Kynaston is handing a lady out of the hansom; Helen peers at her suspiciously.

"I am bringing you ladies a friend to lunch," says Maurice, gaily, and Mrs. Romer's face clears when she sees that it is Beatrice Miller.

"Oh, Beatrice, it is you! I am delighted to see you! Go in to the dining-room, you will find Lady Kynaston. Maurice," drawing him back a minute, "how late you are again! What have you been doing?"

"I waited whilst Miss Miller put her bonnet on."

"Why, where did you meet her?"

"I met her at her mother's, where I went to call. Have you any objection?" He looked at her almost defiantly as he answered her questions; it was intolerable to him that she should put him through such a catechism.

"You can't have been there all the morning," she continued, suspiciously; unable or unwilling, perhaps, to notice his rising displeasure. "Where did you go first?"

Maurice bit his lip, but controlled himself with an effort.

"My dear child," he said, lightly, "one can't sell out of the army, or prepare for the holy estate of matrimony, without a certain amount of business on one's hands. Suppose now we go in to lunch." She stepped aside and let him pass her into the dining-room.

"He is shuffling again," she said to herself, angrily; "that was no answer to my question. Is it possible that he sees *her*? But no, what folly; if she is at Sutton, how can he get at her?"

"Oh, Helen," cried out Beatrice to her from the table as she entered, "you and Lady Kynaston are positively out of the world this season. You know none of the gossip."

"I go nowhere, of course, now; my grandfather's death is so recent. I have so many preparations to make just now; and dear Lady Kynaston is good enough to shut herself up on my account."

"Exactly; you are a couple of recluses," cried Beatrice. "Now, I daresay you will never guess who is the new beauty whom all the world is talking about; no other than our friend Vera Nevill. She is creating a perfect sensation!"

"Indeed!" politely, but with frigid unconcern, from Lady Kynaston.

"Yes; I assure you there is a regular rage about her. Oh, how stupid I am! Perhaps I ought not to have mentioned her, Lady Kynaston, for of course she did not behave very well to Sir John, as we all know; but now that is all over, isn't it? and everybody is wild about her beauty."

"I am glad to hear that Miss Nevill is prospering in any way," said her ladyship, stiffly. "I owe her no ill-will, poor girl."

Helen Romer is looking at Maurice Kynaston; he has not said one single word, nor has he raised his eyes once from his plate; but a deep flush has overspread his handsome face at the sound of Vera's name.

"*That* is where he goes," said Helen, to herself. "I knew it; he has seen her, and he loves her still."

The conversation drifted on to other matters. Beatrice passed all the gossip and scandal of the town under review for Lady Kynaston's benefit; presently Maurice roused himself, and joined in the talk. But Mrs. Romer uttered not a word; she sat in her place with a thunder-cloud upon her brow until the luncheon was over; then, as they rose from the table, she called her lover to her side.

"I want to speak to you," she said, and detained him until the others had left the room.

"You knew that Vera Nevill was in town, and you have seen her!" she burst forth impetuously.

"If I had seen her, I do not know that it would signify, would it?" he answered, calmly.

"Not signify? when you knew that it was for *your* sake that she threw over John, because——"

"Be silent, Helen, you have no right to say that, and no authority for such a statement," he said, interrupting her hotly.

"Do you suppose you can deceive me? Did not everybody see that she could not keep her eyes off you? What is the use of denying it? You have seen her probably; you have been with her to-day."

"As it happens, I have *not* been with her either to-day or any day; nor did I know she was in town until Beatrice Miller told us so just now."

"You have not seen her?"

"No, I have not."

"I don't believe you!" she answered, angrily. Now, no man likes to be given the lie direct even by a lady; and Maurice was a man who was scrupulously truthful, and proud of his veracity; he lost his temper fairly.

"I have never told you a lie yet," he began furiously; "and if you think so, it is time——"

"Maurice! Maurice!" she cried, frantically, stopping the outspoken words upon his lips, and seeing in one minute that she had gone too far. "My darling, forgive me; I did not mean to say it. Yes, of course, I believe you; don't say anything unkind to me, for pity's sake. You know how much I love you; kiss me, darling. No, Maurice, I won't let you go till you kiss me, and say you forgive your foolish, jealous little Helen!"

It was the old story over again; angry reproaches—bitter words—insults upon her side; to be succeeded, the minute he turned round upon her, by wild cries of regret and entreaties for forgiveness, and by the pleading of that love which he valued so little.

She drove him wild with anger and indignation; but she never would let him go—no, never, however much he might strain against the chain by which she held him.

The quarrel was patched up again; he stooped and kissed her. A man must kiss a lady when she asks him. How, indeed, is he to refuse to do so? A woman's kisses are the roses of life—altogether sweet, and lovely, and precious. No man can say he dislikes a rose, nor refuse so harmless and charming a gift when it is freely offered to him without absolute churlishness. Maurice could not well deny her the embrace for which her upturned lips had pleaded. He kissed her, indeed; but it will be easily understood that there was very little spontaneity of affection in that kiss.

"Now let me go," he said, putting her from him gently but coldly; "I want to speak to my mother."

The two younger ladies wandered out into the garden, whilst Maurice sought his mother's room.

"Mother, I have been to see John this morning. I am afraid he is really very ill," he said, gravely.

Lady Kynaston shrugged her shoulders. "He is like a baby over that foolish affair," she said, impatiently. "He does not seem able to get over it; why does he shut himself up in his rooms? If he were to go out a little more———"

"He has been out; it is that that has made him ill. He went out a few mornings ago—the wind was very cold; he says it is that which gave him a chill. But, from what he says, I fancy he saw, or he thinks he saw, Miss Nevill."

Lady Kynaston sat at her davenport with all the litter of her daily correspondence before her; her son stood up by the mantelpiece, leaning his back against it, and looked away out of window at the figures of Beatrice and his future wife sauntering up and down the garden walks. She could not well see his face as he spoke these last words.

"Tiresome woman!" cried Lady Kynaston, angrily; "there is no end to the trouble she causes. John ought to be thankful he is well rid of her. Did you hear what Beatrice Miller said at lunch about her? I call it shocking bad taste, her coming up to town and flirting and flaunting about under poor John's nose—heartless coquette! Creating 'a sensation,' indeed! That is one of those horrible American expressions that are the fashion just now!"

"It is no wonder she is admired," said Maurice, dreamily: "she is very beautiful."

"I wish to goodness she would keep out of John's way. Where did he see her?"

"It was in the Row, I think, and, from what he said, he only fancied he saw her back, walking away. I told him, of course, it could not be her, because I thought she was down at Sutton; but, after what Beatrice told us at lunch, I make no doubt that it was her, and that John really did see her."

"I should have thought that your brother would have had more spirit than to sit down and whine over a woman in that way," said her ladyship, sharply; "it is really contemptible."

"But if he is ill in body as well as in mind, poor fellow?"

"Pooh! fiddlesticks! I am quite sure, if Helen jilted you, you would bear it a great deal better—losing the money and all—than he does."

Maurice smiled.

"That is very possible; but a man can't help his disposition, and John has been utterly shattered by it."

"Well, I am sorry for him, of course; but I confess that I don't see that anybody can do anything for him."

And then Maurice was silent for a minute. God only knew what passed through his soul at that minute—what agonies of self-renunciation, what martyrdom of all that makes life pleasant and dear to a man! It is certain his mother did not know it.

"I think," he said, after a minute, and only a slight harshness in his voice marked the internal struggle that the words were to cost him—"I think, mother, *you* might do a great deal for him. Miss Nevill is in town. Could you not see her?"

"I see her! What on earth for?"

"If you were to tell her how ill John is, how desperately he feels her treatment of him—how———"

"Stop, stop, my dear! You cannot possibly suppose that I am going down upon my knees to entreat Miss Nevill to marry my son after she has thrown him over!"

"It is no question of going on your knees, mother. A few words would suffice to show her the misery she is causing to John, and if those few words would restore his lost happiness——"

"How can I tell that anything I can say would influence her? I suppose she had good reasons for throwing him over. She cared for some one else, I suppose, or, at all events, she did not care for him."

"I am quite certain, on the contrary, that she had a very sincere affection for my brother; and, as to the some one else, I do not think that will prevent her returning to him. Oh, mother!" he cried, with a sudden passion, "the world is full of miserable misunderstandings and mistakes. For God's sake, let us try to put some of its blunders right! Do not let any poor, mean feelings of false pride stand in our way if we can make one single life happy!"

She looked up at him, wondering a little at his earnestness. It did not strike her at the minute that his interest in Vera was unusual, but only that his affection for his brother was stronger than she imagined it to be. "You know," she said, "I do not want things to come right in that way. I do not want John to marry. I want the old place to come to you and your children; and now that John has agreed to let you and Helen live there——"

He waved his hand impatiently. "And you know, mother dear, that such desires are unlawful. John is the eldest, and I will never move a step to take his birthright from him. To stand in the way of his marriage for such a cause would be a crime. Is it not better that I should speak plainly to you, dear? As to my living at Kynaston, I think it highly unlikely that I should do so in any case, much as you and Helen seem to wish it. But that has nothing to do with John's affairs. Promise me, little mother, that you will try and set that right by seeing Miss Nevill?"

"I do not suppose I should do any good," she answered, with visible reluctance.

"Never mind; you can but try."

"You can't expect me to go and call upon her for such a purpose, nor speak to her, without John's authority."

"You might ask her to come here, or go to some house where you will meet her naturally in public."

"Yes, that would be best; perhaps she will be at Lady Cloverdale's ball next week."

"It is easy, at all events, to ensure her an invitation to it; ask Beatrice Miller to get her one."

"Oh, yes; that is easy enough. Oh, dear me, Maurice, you always manage to get your own way with me; but you have given me a dreadfully hard task this time."

"As if a woman of your known tact and *savoir faire* was not capable of any hard and impossible task!" answered her son, smiling, as he bent and kissed her soft white face.

The gentle flattery pleased her. The old lady sat smiling happily to herself, with her hands idle before her, for some minutes after he had left her.

How dear he was to her, how good, how upright, how thoroughly generous too, and unselfish to think so much of his brother's troubles just now, in the midst of all his own happiness.

She got up and went to the window, and watched him as he strolled across the garden to join the ladies, smiling and kissing her hand to him when he looked back and saw her.

"Dear fellow, I hope he will be happy!" she said to herself, turning away with a half sigh. And then suddenly something brought back the ball at Shadonake to her recollection. There flashed back into her memory a certain scene in a cool, dimly-lit conservatory: two people whispering together under a high-swung Chinese lamp, and a background of dark-leaved shrubs behind them.

She had been puzzled that night. There had been something going on that she had not quite understood. And now again that feeling of unsatisfied comprehension came back to her. For the first time it struck her painfully that the son whom she idolized so much—whose life and character had been her one study and her one delight ever since the day of his birth—was nevertheless a riddle to her. That the secret of his inner self was as much hidden from her—his mother—as though she had been the merest stranger; that the life she had striven so closely to entwine with her own was nothing after all but a separate existence, in the story of whose soul she herself had no part. He was a man struggling single-handed in all the heat and turmoil of the battle of life, and she, nothing but a poor, weak old woman, standing feebly aside, powerless to help or even to understand the creature to whom she had given birth.

There fell a tear or two down upon her wrinkled little hands as she thought of it. She could not understand him; there was something in his life she could not fathom. Oh, what did it all mean?

Alas, sooner or later, is not that what comes to every mother concerning the child she loves best?

CHAPTER XXII

MR. PRYME'S VISITORS.

For courage mounteth with occasion.

SHAKESPEARE, "King John."

Mr. Herbert Pryme stood by a much ink-stained and littered table in his chambers in the Temple, with his hands in his trousers pockets, whistling a slow and melancholy tune.

It was Mr. Pryme's habit to whistle when he was dejected or perplexed; and the whistling generally partook of the mournful condition of his feelings. Indeed, everything that this young man did was of a ponderous and solemn nature; there was always the inner consciousness of the dignity of the Bar vested in his own person, to be discerned in his outer bearing. Even in the strictest seclusion of the, alas! seldom invaded privacy of his chambers Mr. Pryme never forgot that he was a barrister-at-law.

But when this young gentleman was ill at ease within himself he was in the habit of whistling. He also was given to the thrusting of his hands into his pockets. The more unhappy he was, the more he whistled, and the deeper he stuffed in his hands.

Just now, to all appearances, he was very unhappy indeed.

The air he had selected for his musical self-refreshment was the lively and slightly vulgar one of "Tommy make Room for your Uncle;" but let anybody just try to whistle that same vivacious tune to the time of the Dead March in "Saul," and with a lingering and plaintive emphasis upon each note, with "linked sweetness long drawn out," and then say whether the gloomiest of dirges would not be festive indeed in comparison.

Thus did Herbert Pryme whistle it as he looked down upon the piles of legal documents heaped up together upon his table.

All of them meant work, but none of them meant money. For Herbert was fain to accept the humble position of "devil" to a great legal light who occupied the floor below him, and who considered, and perhaps rightly, that he was doing the young man above him, who had been sent up from the country with a letter of introduction to him from a second cousin, a sufficient and inestimable benefit in allowing him to do his dirty work gratis.

It was all very useful to him, doubtless, but it was not remunerative; and Herbert wanted money badly.

"Oh, if I could only reckon upon a couple of hundred a year," he sighed, half aloud to himself, "I might have a chance of winning her! It seems hard that heaps of these fellows can make hundreds a week by a short speech, or a few strokes of the pen, that cost them no labour and little forethought, whilst I, with all my hard work, can make nothing! What uphill work it is! Not that the Bar is not a fine profession; quite the finest there is," for not even to himself would Herbert Pryme decry the legal muse whom he worshipped; "but, I suppose, like every other profession, it is overstocked; there are too many struggling for the same prizes. The fact is, that England is over-populated. Now, if a law were to be passed compelling one-half of the adult males in this country to remain in a state of celibacy for the space of fifteen years——" but here he stopped short in his soliloquy and smiled; for was not the one desire of his life at present to marry Beatrice Miller immediately? And how was the extra population to be stayed if every one of the doomed quota of marriageable males were of the same mind as himself?

Presently Mr. Pryme sauntered idly to the window, and stood looking drearily out of it, still whistling, of course.

The prospect was not a lively one. His chambers looked out upon a little square, stone-flagged court, with a melancholy-looking pump in the centre of it. There was an arched passage leading away to one side, down which a distant footstep echoed drearily now and then, and a side glimpse of the empty road at the other end, beyond the corner of the opposite houses. Now and then some member of the learned profession passed rapidly across the small open space with the pre-occupied air of a man who has not a minute to spare, or a clerk, bearing the official red bag, ran hastily along the passage; for the rest, the London sparrows had it pretty much to themselves. As things were, Mr. Pryme envied the sparrows, who were ready clothed by Providence, and had no rates and taxes to pay, as well as the clerks, who, at all events, had plenty to do and no time to soliloquize upon the hardness and hollowness of life. To have plenty of brains, and an indefinite amount of spare time to use them in; to desire ardently to hasten along the road towards fortune and happiness, and to be forced to sit idly by whilst others, duller-witted, perchance, and with less capacity for work, are amassing wealth under your very nose—when this is achieved by sheer luck, or good interest, or any other of those inadequate causes which get people on in life independent of talent and industry—that is what makes a radical of a man. This is what causes him to dream unwholesome dreams about equality and liberty, about a republic, where there shall be no more principalities and powers, where plutocracy, as well as aristocracy, shall be unregarded, and where every good man and true shall rise on his own merits, and on none other.

Oh, happy and impossible Arcadia! You must wait for the millennium, my friend, before your aspirations shall come to pass. Wait till jealousy, and selfishness, and snobbism—that last and unconquerable dragon—shall be destroyed out of the British heart, then, and only then, when jobbery, and interest, and mammon-worship shall be abolished; then will men be honoured for what they are, and not for what they seem to be.

Something of all this passed through our friend's jaundiced mind as he contemplated those homely and familiar little birds, born and bred and smoke-dried in all the turmoil of the City's heart, who ruffled their feathers and plumed their wings with contented chirpings upon the dusty flags of the little courtyard.

Things were exceptionally bad with Herbert Pryme just now. His exchequer was low—had never been lower—and his sweetheart was far removed out of his reach. Beatrice had duly come up with her parents to the family mansion in Eaton Square for the London season, but although he had, it is true, the satisfaction, such as it was, of breathing the same air as she did, she was far more out of his reach in town than she had been in the country. As long as she was at Shadonake Mr. Pryme had always been able to run down to his excellent friend, the parson of Tripton, and once there, it had been easy to negotiate a surreptitious meeting with Beatrice. The fields and the lanes are everybody's property. If Tom and Maria are caught love-making at the stile out of the wood, and they both swear that the meeting was purely accidental, I don't see how any one is to prove that it was premeditated; nor can any parents, now that it is no longer the fashion to keep grown women under lock and key, prevent their daughters from going out in the country occasionally unattended, nor forbid strange young men from walking along the Queen's highway in the same direction.

But remove your daughter to London, and the case is altered at once. To keep a girl who goes out a great deal in the whirl of London society out of the way of a man who goes out very little, who is not in the inner circle of town life, and is not in the same set as herself, is the easiest thing in the world.

So Mrs. Miller found it. She kept Beatrice hard at work at the routine of dissipation. Not an hour of her time was unoccupied, not a minute of her day unaccounted for; and, of course, she was never alone—it is not yet the fashion for young girls to dance about London by themselves—her mother, as a matter of course, was always with her.

As a natural sequence, the lovers had a hard time of it. Beatrice had been six weeks in London, and Herbert, beyond catching sight of her once or twice as she was driven past in her mother's carriage down Bond Street, or through the crowd in the Park, had never seen her at all.

Mrs. Miller was congratulating herself upon the success of her tactics; she flattered herself that her daughter was completely getting over that unlucky fancy for the penniless and briefless barrister. Beatrice gave no sign; she appeared perfectly satisfied and contented, and seemed to be enjoying herself thoroughly, and to be troubled by no love-sick hankerings after her absent swain.

"She has forgotten him," said Mrs. Miller, to herself.

But the mother did not take into account that indomitable spirit and stubborn determination in her own character which had served to carry out successfully all the schemes of her life, and which she had probably transmitted to her child.

In Beatrice's head, under its short thick thatch of dark rough hair, and in her sturdily-built little frame, there lurked the tenacity of a bulldog. Once she had taken an idea firmly into her mind, Beatrice Miller would never relinquish it until she had got her own way. Herbert, in the dingy solitude of his untempting chambers, might despair and look upon life and its aims as a hopeless enigma. Beatrice did not despair at all. She only bided her time.

One day, if she waited for it patiently, the opportunity would come to her, and when it came she would not be slow to make use of it. It came to her in the shape of a morning visit from Captain Maurice Kynaston.

"Come down and see my mother," Maurice had said to her; "she has not seen you for a long while. I am just going back to Walpole Lodge to lunch."

"I should like to come very much. You have no objection, I suppose, mamma?"

No; Mrs. Miller could have no possible objection. Lady Kynaston was amongst her oldest and most respected friends; under whose house could Beatrice be safer? And even Maurice, as an escort, engaged to be married so shortly as he was known to be, was perfectly unobjectionable.

Beatrice went, and, as we have seen, lunched at Walpole Lodge. She had told her mother not to expect her till late in the afternoon, as, in all probability, Lady Kynaston would drive her into town and would drop her in Eaton Square at the end of her drive. Mrs. Miller, to whose watchful maternal mind the Temple and Kew appeared to be in such totally different directions that they presented no connecting suggestions, agreed, unsuspiciously, not to expect her daughter back until after six o'clock.

In this way Beatrice secured the whole afternoon to herself to do what she liked with it. She was not slow to make use of it. There was all the pluck of the Esterworths in her veins, together with all the determination and energy which had raised her father's family from a race of shopkeepers to take their place amongst gentlemen.

As soon as Captain Kynaston joined the two ladies in the garden at Walpole Lodge after luncheon Beatrice requested him to order a hansom to be fetched for her.

"Why should you hurry away?" said Maurice, politely. "My mother will take you back to town in the carriage if you will wait."

Helen was stooping over the flower-beds, gathering some violets. Beatrice stepped closer to Maurice.

"Don't say a word, there's a good fellow, but get me the hansom—and—and—please don't mention it at home."

Then Maurice, who was no tyro in such matters, understood that it was expected of him that he should ask no questions, but do what he was told and hold his tongue.

The sequence of which proceedings was, that a hansom cab drew up at the far corner of the little stone-flagged court in the Temple between four and five that afternoon.

Mr. Pryme was no longer by the window when it did so, so that he was totally unprepared for the visitor, whose trembling and twice-repeated tap at his door he answered somewhat impatiently—

"Come in, and be d——d to you, and don't stand rapping at that door all day."

The people, as a rule, who solicited admittance to his chambers were either the boy from the legal light below, who came to ask whether the papers were ready that had been sent up this morning, or else they were smiling and sleek-faced tradesmen who washed their hands insinuatingly whilst they requested that Mr. Pryme would be kind enough to settle that little outstanding account.

Either of these visitors were equally unwelcome, which must be some excuse for the roughness of Mr. Pryme's language.

The door was softly pushed ajar.

"Now, then—come in, can't you; who the deuce are you—*Beatrice!*"

Enter Miss Miller, smiling.

"Oh, fie, Herbert! what naughty words, sir."

"Beatrice, is it possible that it is you! Where is your mother? Are you alone?" looking nervously round at the door, whilst he caught her outstretched hand.

"Yes, I am quite alone; don't be very shocked. I know I am a horrid, bold girl to come all by myself to a man's chambers; it's dreadful, isn't it! Oh, what would people say of it if they knew—why, even *you* look horrified! But oh,

Herbert, I did want to see you so. I was determined to get at you somehow— and now I am here for a whole hour; I have managed it beautifully—no one will ever find out where I have been. Mamma thinks I am driving with Lady Kynaston!"

And then she sat down and took off her veil, and told him all about it.

She had got at her lover, and she felt perfectly happy and secure, sitting there with his arm round her waist and her hand in his. Not so Herbert. He was pleased, of course, to see her, and called her by a thousand fond names, and he admired her courage and her spirit for breaking through the conventional trammels of her life in order to come to him; but he was horribly nervous all the same. Supposing that boy were to come in from below, or the smiling tradesman, or, still worse, if the great Q.C. were to catch a glimpse of her as she went out, and recognize her from having met her in society, where would Miss Miller's reputation be then?

"It is very imprudent of you—most rash and foolish," he kept on repeating; but he was glad to see her all the same, and kissed her between every other word.

"Now, don't waste any more time spooning," says Beatrice, with decision, drawing herself a little farther from him on the hard leather sofa. "An hour soon goes, and I have plenty to say to you. Herbert," with great solemnity, "*I mean to elope with you!*"

Herbert gives an irrepressible start.

"*Now!* this minute?" he exclaims, in some dismay, and reflects swiftly that, just now he possesses exactly three pounds seven and sixpence in ready money.

"No; don't be a goose; not now, because I haven't any clothes." Herbert breathes more freely. "But some day, very soon, before the end of the season."

"But, my pet, you are not of age," objects her lover; whilst sundry clauses in the laws concerning the marriages of minors without the consent of their parents pass hurriedly through his brain.

"What do I care about my age?" says Beatrice, with the recklessness of an impetuous woman bent upon having her own way. "Of course, I don't wish to do anything disreputable, or to make a scandal, but mamma is driving me to it by never allowing me to see you, and forbidding you to come to the house, and by encouraging all sorts of men whom she wants me to marry."

"Ah! And these men, do they make love to you?" The instinct of the lover rises instantly superior to the instinct of legal prudence within him. "That is hard for me to bear."

"Now, Herbert, don't be a fool!" cries Beatrice, jumping up and making a grimace at herself in the dusty glass over his mantelpiece. "Do I look like a girl whom men would make love to? Am I not too positively hideous? Oh, you needn't shake your head and look indignant. Of course I am ugly, everybody but you thinks so. Of course it's not me, myself, but because papa is rich, and they think I shall have money. Oh, what a curse this money is!"

"I think the want of it a far greater one," says Herbert, ruefully.

"At any rate," continues Beatrice, "I am determined to put an end to this state of things; we must take the law into our own hands."

"Am I to wait for you in a carriage and pair at the corner of Eaton Square in the middle of the night?" inquires Herbert, grimly.

"No; don't be foolish; people don't do things now-a-days in the way our grandmothers did. I shall go to morning service one day at some out of-the-way church, where you will meet me with a licence in your pocket; it will be the simplest thing in the world."

"And afterwards?"

"Afterwards I shall go home to lunch."

"And what am I to do?"

"Oh! you will come back here, I suppose."

"I don't think that will be very amusing," objects the bridegroom elect, dubiously.

"No; but then we shall be really married, and when we know that no one can part us, we shan't mind waiting; and then, some day, after about six months or so, I shall confess to papa, and there will be a terrible scene, ending in tears on my part, and in forgiveness on the part of my parents. Once the deed is done, you see, they will be forced to make the best of it; and, of course, they will not allow us to starve. I think it is a very ingenious plan. What do you think of it, Herbert? You don't look very much delighted at the idea."

"I don't think that I should play a very noble part in such a scheme as that. Dearly as I love you, Beatrice, I do not think I could consent to steal you away in such a pitiful and cowardly manner."

"Pooh! you would have nothing to do with it; it is all my doing, of course. Hush! is not that somebody coming up the stairs?"

They were silent for half a minute, listening to the sound of advancing steps upon the wooden staircase.

"It is nothing—only somebody to see the man above me. By Jove, though, it *is* for me!" as somebody suddenly stopped outside and knocked at the door. "Wait one minute, sir! Good heavens, Beatrice, what am I to do with you?"

Herbert looked frightened out of his life. Beatrice, on the contrary, could hardly smother her laughter.

"I must hide!" she said, in a choked whisper. "Oh, Herbert, it is like a scene out of a naughty French play! I shall die of laughter!"

Without a moment's thought, she fled into the inner room, the door of which stood ajar, and which was none other than Mr. Pryme's bed-chamber! There was no time to think of any better expedient. Beatrice turned the key upon herself, and Herbert called out "Come in!" to the intruder. Neither of them had noticed that Beatrice's little white lace sunshade lay upon the table with her gloves and veil beside it.

If Mr. Pryme had been alarmed at the bare fact of an unknown and possibly unimportant visitor, it may be left to the imagination to describe the state of his feelings when the door, upon being opened, disclosed the Member for North Meadowshire standing without!

———

CHAPTER XXIII.

A WHITE SUNSHADE.

For ever, Fortune, wilt thou prove
An unrelenting foe to love,
And when we meet a mutual heart,
Come in between, and bid us part?

"Well, Mr. Pryme, how d'ye do?" said Mr. Miller, in his rough, hearty voice, holding out his hand. "I dare say you are surprised to see me here. I haven't met you since you were staying down with us at Christmas time. Well, and how goes the world with you, young man?"

Herbert, who at first had thought nothing less than that Mr. Miller had tracked his daughter to his rooms, and that he was about to have the righteous wrath of an infuriated and exasperated parent to deal with, by this time began to perceive that, to whatever extraordinary cause his visit was owing, Beatrice, at all events, had nothing to do with it. He recovered himself sufficiently to murmur, in answer to his visitor's greeting, that the world went pretty well with him, and to request his guest to be seated.

And then, as he pushed an arm-chair forward for him, his eye fell upon Beatrice's things upon the table, and his heart literally stood still within him. What was he to do? They lay so close to the father's elbow that, to move them without attracting attention was impossible, and to attract attention to them was to risk their being recognized.

Meanwhile Mr. Miller had put on his spectacles, and was drawing some voluminous papers out of his breast coat-pocket.

"Now, I dare say, young man, you are wondering what brings me to see you? Well, the fact is, there is a little matter about which I am going to law. I'm going to bring an action for libel against a newspaper; it is that rascally paper the *Cat o' Nine Tails*. They had an infamous paragraph three weeks ago concerning my early life, which, let me tell you, sir, was highly respectable in every way, sir—in every way."

"I am quite sure of that, Mr. Miller."

"I've brought the paragraph with me. Oh, here it is. Well, I've had a good deal of correspondence with the editor, and he refuses to publish an apology, and so I'm tired of the whole matter, and have placed it in the hands of my solicitors. I'm going to prosecute them, sir, and I don't care what it costs me to do it; and I'll expose the whole system of these trumped-up fabrications, that contain, as a rule, one grain of truth to a hundredweight of lies. Well, now, Mr. Pryme, I want a clever barrister to take up this case, and I have instructed Messrs. Grainge, my solicitors, to retain you."

"I am sure, sir, you are very kind; I hardly know how to thank you," faltered poor Herbert. Never in the whole course of his life had he felt so overcome with shame and confusion! Here was this man come to do him a really great and substantial benefit, whilst his own daughter was hidden away in a shameful fashion in the next room! Herbert would sooner that Mr. Miller had pointed a pistol at his head and threatened to shoot him. The deception that he was practising towards this kind-hearted and excellent gentleman struck him to the heart with a sense of guilty remorse.

But what on earth was he to do? He could not reveal the truth to the unconscious father, nor open the door and disclose Beatrice hiding in his bedroom, without absolutely risking the reputation of the girl he loved. There was nothing for it but to go on with the serio-comedy as best he could, and to try and get Mr. Miller off the premises as speedily as possible.

He made an effort to decline the proffered employment.

"It is most kind, most generous of you to have thought of me, but I must tell you that there are many better men, even amongst the juniors, who would do your case more justice than I should."

"Oh! I believe you have plenty of talent, Mr. Pryme. I've been making inquiries about you. You only want an opportunity, and I like giving a young fellow a chance. One must hold out a helping hand to the young ones now and then."

"Of course, sir, I would do my very best for you, but I really think you are risking your own case by giving it to me."

"Nonsense—take it and do what you can for me; if you fail, I shall not blame you;" and here suddenly Mr. Miller's eyes rested upon the sunshade and the gloves upon the table half-a-yard behind his arm. Now, had it been Miss Miller's mother who, in the place of her father, had been seated in Herbert's wooden arm-chair, the secret of her proximity would have been revealed the very instant the maternal eyes had been set upon that sunshade and those gloves. Mrs. Miller could have sworn to that little white lace, ivory-handled toy, with its coquettish pink ribbon bows, had she seen it amongst a hundred others, nor would it have been easy to have deceived the mother's eyes in the matter of the gray *peau de suède* gloves and the dainty little veil, such as her daughter was in the habit of wearing. But a father's perceptions in these matters are not accurate. Mr. Miller had not the remotest idea what his child's sunshade was like, nor, indeed, whether she had any sunshade at all. Nevertheless, as his eyes alighted upon these indications of a feminine presence which lay upon the young barrister's table, they remained fixed there with distinct disapproval. These obnoxious articles of female attire of course conveyed clearly to the elder man's perceptions, in a broad and general sense, the fatal word "woman," and woman in this case meant "vice."

Mr. Miller strove to re-direct his attention to his case and the papers in his hand. Herbert made a faint and ineffectual attempt to remove the offending objects from the table. Mr. Miller only looked back at them with an ever-increasing gloom upon his face, and Herbert's hand, morally paralyzed by the glance, sank powerlessly down by his side. He imagined, of course, that the father had recognized his daughter's property.

"Well, to continue the subject," said Mr. Miller, looking away with an effort, and turning over the papers he had brought with him; "there are several points in the case I should like to mention to you." He paused for a minute, apparently to collect his thoughts, and to Herbert's sensitive ears there was a sudden coldness and constraint in his voice and manner. "You will, of course, take instructions in the main from Grainge and Co.; but what I wished to point out to you was—ahem———" here his voice unaccountably faltered, and his eyes, as though drawn by a magnet, returned once more with ominous displeasure to that little heap of feminine finery that lay between them. Mr. Miller flung down his papers, and turning round in his chair, rested both elbows upon the table.

"Mr. Pryme," he said, with decision, "I think it is best that I should be frank with you!" He looked the young barrister full in the face.

"Certainly, certainly, if you please, Mr. Miller," said Herbert, not quite knowing what he had to fear, and turning hot and cold alternately under his visitor's scrutinizing gaze.

"Well, then, let me tell you fairly that I came to seek you to-day with the friendliest motives."

"I am sure you did, and you are most kind to me, sir," murmured Herbert, playing nervously with an ivory paper-cutter that lay on the table.

Mr. Miller waved his hand, as though to dispense with his grateful acknowledgments.

"The fact is," he continued, "I had understood from Mrs. Miller that you were a suitor for my daughter's hand. Well, sir, Mrs. Miller, as you know, disapproves of your suit. My daughter will be well off, Mr. Pryme, and you, I understand, have no income at all. You have no other resource than a profession, at which, as yet, you have made nothing. There is some reason in Mrs. Miller's objection to you. Nor should I be willing to let my daughter marry an idle man who will live upon her money. Then, on the other hand, Mr. Pryme, I find that my girl is fond of you, and, if this is the case, I am unwilling to make her unhappy. I said to myself that I would give you an opening in this case of mine, and if you will work hard and make yourself known and respected in your profession, I should not object, in the course of time, to your being engaged to her, and I would endeavour to induce her mother to agree to it. I came here to-day, Mr. Pryme, to give you a fair chance of winning her."

"You are too good, Mr. Miller," cried Herbert, with effusion, stretching forth his hand. "I do not know how to thank you enough, nor how to assure you of my grateful acceptance of your terms."

But Mr. Miller drew back from the young man's proffered hand.

"Wait, there is no occasion to thank me;" and again his eyes fell sternly upon that unlucky little heap of lace and ribbon. "I am sorry to tell you that, since I have come here, my friendly and pleasant intentions towards you have undergone a complete change."

"Sir!"

"Yes, Mr. Pryme; I came here prepared to treat you—well, I may as well confess it—as a son, under the belief that you were an upright and honourable man, and were sincerely and honestly attached to my daughter."

"Mr. Miller, is it possible that you can doubt it?"

The elder man pointed with contemptuous significance to the sunshade before him.

"I find upon your table, young man, the evidences of the recent presence of some wretched woman in your rooms, and your confusion of manner shows me too plainly that you are not the kind of husband to which a man may safely entrust his daughter's happiness."

"Mr. Miller, I assure you you are mistaken; it is not so."

"Every man in this country has a right to justify himself when he is accused. If I am mistaken, Mr. Pryme, explain to me the meaning of *that*," and the heavy forefinger was again levelled at the offending objects before him.

Not one single word could Herbert utter. In vain ingenious fabrications concerning imaginary sisters, maiden aunts, or aged lady clients rushed rapidly through his brain; the natural answer on Mr. Miller's part to all such inventions would have been, "Then, where is she?"

Mr. Miller must know as well as he did himself that the lady, whoever she might be, must still be in his rooms, else why should her belongings be left on his table; and if in the rooms, then, as there was no other egress on the staircase than the one by which he had entered, clearly, she must be secreted in his bedroom. Mr. Miller was not a young man, and his perceptions in matters of intrigue and adventure might no longer be very acute, but it was plain to Herbert that he probably knew quite as well as he did himself that the owner of the gloves and sunshade was in the adjoining room.

"Have you any satisfactory explanation to give me?" asked Mr. Miller, once more, after a solemn silence, during which he glared in a stern and inquisitorial manner over his spectacles at the young man.

"I have nothing to say," was the answer, given in a low and dejected voice.

Mr. Miller sprang to his feet and hurriedly gathered up his papers.

"Then, sir," he said, furiously, "I shall wish you good afternoon; and let me assure you, most emphatically, that you must relinquish all claim to my daughter's hand. I will never consent to her union with a man whose private life will not bear investigation; and should she disobey me in this matter, she shall never have one single shilling of my money."

There was a moment's silence. Mr. Miller was buttoning-up his coat with the air of a man who buttons up his heart within it at the same time. He regarded the young man fiercely, and yet there was a lingering wistfulness, too, in his gaze. He would have given a good deal to hear, from his lips, a satisfactory explanation of the circumstances which told so suspiciously against him. He liked the young barrister personally, and he was fond enough of his daughter to wish that she might be happy in her own way. He spoke one word more to the young man.

"Have you nothing to say; Mr. Pryme?"

Herbert shook his head, with his eyes gloomily downcast.

"I can only tell you, sir, that you are mistaken in what you imagine. If you will not believe my word, I can say nothing more."

"And what of *these*, Mr. Pryme—what of *these*?" pointing furiously downwards to Beatrice's property.

"I cannot explain it any further to you, Mr. Miller. I can only ask you to believe me."

"Then, I do not believe you, sir—I do not believe you. Would any man in his senses believe that you haven't got a woman hidden in the next room? Do you suppose I'm a fool? I have the honour of wishing you good day, sir, and I am sorry I ever took the trouble of calling upon you. It is, of course, unnecessary for you to trouble yourself concerning my case, in these altered circumstances, Mr. Pryme; I beg to decline the benefit of your legal assistance. Good afternoon."

The door closed upon him, and the sound of his retreating footsteps echoed noisily down the stairs. Herbert sank into a chair and covered his face with his hands. So lately hope and fortune seemed to have smiled upon him for one short, blissful moment, only to withdraw the sunshine of their faces again from him more completely, and to leave him more utterly in the dark than ever. Was ever man so unfortunate, and so unlucky?

But for the *contretemps* concerning that wretched sunshade, he would now have been a hopeful, and almost a triumphant, lover. Now life was all altered for him!

The door between the two rooms opened softly, and Beatrice, no longer brave, and defiant, and laughing as she had been when she went in, but white, and scared, and trembling, crept hesitatingly forth, and knelt down by her lover's side.

"Oh, Herbert! what has happened? It was papa—I heard his voice; but I could not hear what you talked about, only I heard that he was angry at the last, when he went away. Oh! tell me, dearest, what has happened?"

Herbert pointed bitterly to her belongings on the table.

"What fatality made me overlook those wretched things?" he cried, miserably; "they have ruined us!"

Beatrice uttered an exclamation of dismay.

"Papa saw them—he recognized them!"

"Not as *yours*, thank God!"

"What then?"

"He thinks me unworthy of you," answered the lover, in a low voice, and Beatrice understood. "He has forbidden me ever to think of you now; and he will leave you penniless if you disobey him; it is a terrible misfortune, my darling; but still, thank God that your good name is safe!"

"Yes, at the expense of yours, Herbert!" cried the girl, frantically; "I see it all now, and, if I dared, I would confess to papa the truth."

"Do not think of it!"

"I dare not; but, Herbert, don't despair; I see now how wicked and how foolish I was to come here to-day, and what a terrible risk I have run, for if papa knew that it was I who was in the next room, he would never forgive me; we can do nothing now but wait until brighter and happier days; believe me, Herbert, if you will be true to me, I will be true to you, and I will wait for you till I am old and grey."

He strained her passionately to his heart.

"I will never forget what you have done for me to-day, never!" said the girl, as she clung to his neck.

And then she put on her gloves and veil, and took up the sunshade that had been the cause of such a direful ending to her escapade, and went her way. And after she was gone, Mr. Pryme, with his hands in his pockets, began once more to whistle, as though the events of the afternoon had never taken place.

CHAPTER XXIV.

HER SON'S SECRET.

But love is such a mystery,I cannot find it out,For when I think I'm best resolved,I then am most in doubt."

SIR J. SUCKLING.

Lady Kynaston sat alone in her little morning-room; as far as she knew, she was alone in the house; Mrs. Romer had driven into London, on the cares of her trousseau intent, and she believed that Maurice had gone with her; at all events, she had heard him state his intention of going, and the departing carriage had, some time since, driven away from the door.

The morning-room looked on to the garden side of the house, and the windows were wide open; the east wind had departed, and summer had set in at last. Real summer, coming in with a rush when it did come, with warm whiffs of flower-scented wind, with flutterings of lime blossoms from the trees along the high brick wall, with brown bees and saffron butterflies hovering over the reviving flower-borders, and dragon-flies darting out of the shadows into the hot blinding sunshine. Summer at last; and oh, how welcome when it comes upon our rain-drenched and winter-pinched land.

The gardener was bedding out the geraniums along the straight ribbon border. Lady Kynaston went out once to superintend his operations, holding up a newspaper in her hand to shield her head from the rays of the sun. But it was hot, and old McCloud, the Scotch gardener, was intelligent enough to be safely left to his own devices, so she did not stop out long.

She came in again, and sat down in a low basket-chair by the window, and thought how wise she had been to settle herself down in the old house with its velvet lawns and its wide shadowy trees, instead of in the heat and turmoil of a London home.

She looked a little anxious and worried to-day—she was not happy about her eldest son—somebody had told her last night that he was talking about going to Australia, and turning sheep farmer. Lady Kynaston was annoyed at the report; it did not strike her as seemly or right that the head of the Kynaston family should become a sheep farmer. Moreover, she knew very well that he only wanted to get himself away out of the country where no one would know of his story, or remind him of his trouble again. The man's heart was broken. He did not want to farm sheep, or to take to any other rational or healthful employment; he only wanted, like a sick animal, to creep away and hide his hurt. Little as Lady Kynaston had in common with her eldest son, she was sorry for him. She would have done what she could to help him had she known how. She had written to him only yesterday, begging him to come to her, but he had not replied to her letter.

The Cloverdales' ball had come and gone, and Lady Kynaston had taken pains to ensure that an invitation might be sent to Mrs. Hazeldine and Miss Nevill. She had also put herself to some inconvenience in order to be present at it herself, but all to no purpose—Vera was not there. Perhaps she had had another engagement that evening.

The old lady's promise to her youngest son was still unfulfilled. She half repented now that she had given him any such promise. What good was she to do by interceding between her son and Miss Nevill? and why was she to lay herself open to the chance of a rebuff from that young lady? It had been a senseless and quixotic idea on Maurice's part altogether. Young women do not take back a jilted lover because the man's mother advises them to do so; nor is a broken-off marriage likely to get itself re-settled in consequence of the interference of a third person.

The old lady had taken out her fancy-work, a piece of crewel work such as is the fashion of the day. But she was not fond of work; the leaves of muddy-shaded greens grew but slowly under her fingers, and, truth to say, the occupation bored her. It was artistic, certainly, and it was fashionable; but Lady Kynaston would have been happier over a pair of cross-stitch slippers for her son, or a knitted woollen petticoat for the old woman at her lodge gate. All the same, she took out her crewels and put in a few stitches; but the afternoon was warm, there was a humming of insects in the summer air, a click-clicking from the gardener as he dropped one empty red flower-pot into the other along the edge of the ribbon border, a cawing of rooks from the elms over the wall, a very harmony of soft soothing sounds, just enough to lull worry to rest, not enough to scare drowsiness from one's brain.

By degrees, it all became mixed up in a delicious confusion. The rooks, and the bees, and the gardener made one continuous murmur to her, like the swishing of summer waves upon a sandy shore, or the moaning of soft winds in the tree tops.

Then the crewel work slipped off her lap, and Lady Kynaston slept.

How long she was asleep she could not rightly have said: it might have been an hour, it might have been but twenty minutes; but suddenly she awoke with a start.

The rustle of a woman's dress was beside her, and somebody spoke her name.

"Lady Kynaston! Oh, I am so sorry I have disturbed you; I did not see you were asleep."

The old lady opened her eyes wide, and came back suddenly from dreamland. Vera Nevill stood before her.

"Vera, is it *you*? Good gracious! how did you get in? I never even heard the door open."

"I came in by the front-door quite correctly," said Vera, smiling and reaching out her hand for a chair, "and was duly announced by the footman; but I had no idea you were asleep."

"Only dozing. Sit down, my dear, sit down; I am glad to see you." And, somehow, all the awkwardness of the meeting between the two vanished. It was as though they had parted only yesterday on the most friendly terms. In Vera's absence, Lady Kynaston had thought hard things of her, and had spoken condemning words concerning her; but in her presence all this seemed to be altered.

There was something so unspeakably refreshing and soothing about Vera; there was a certain quiet dignity in her movements, a calm serenity in her manner, which made it difficult to associate blame and displeasure with her. Faults she might have, but they could never be mean or ignoble ones; there was nothing base or contemptible about her. The pure, proud profile, the broad grave brow, the eyes that, if a trifle cold, were as true withal as the soul that looked out, sometimes earnestly, sometimes wistfully, from their shadowy depths; everything about her bade one judge her, not so much by her actions, which were sometimes incomprehensible, but by a certain standard that she herself created in the minds of all who knew her.

Lady Kynaston had called her a jilt and a heartless coquette; she had made no secret of saying, right and left, how badly she had behaved: what shameful and discreditable deductions might be drawn from her conduct towards Sir John. Yet, the very instant she set eyes upon her, she felt sorry for the hard things she had said of her, and ashamed of herself that she should have spoken them.

Vera drew forward a chair, and sat down near her. The dress she wore was white, of some clear and delicate material, softened with creamy lace; it had been one of kind-hearted Cissy Hazeldine's many presents to her. Looking at her, Lady Kynaston thought what a lovely vision of youth and beauty she made in the sombre quiet of the little room.

"They tell me half the men in London have gone mad over you," were her first words following the train of her own thoughts, and she liked her visitor none the less, that world-loving little old woman, because she could not but acknowledge the reasonableness of the madness of which she accused her of being the object.

"I care very little for the men in London, Lady Kynaston," answered Vera, quietly.

"My dear, what *do* you care for?" asked her ladyship, with earnestness, and Vera understood that she was expected to state her business.

"Lady Kynaston, I have come to ask you about your son," she answered, simply.

"About John?"

"Of course, it is Sir John I mean," she said, quickly, a hot flush rising for one instant to her face, and dying away rapidly again, to leave her a trifle paler than before. "I know," she continued, with a little hesitation—"I know that I have no right to inquire—but I cannot forget all that is past—all his goodness and generosity to me. I shall never forget it; and oh, I hear such dreadful things of him, that he is ill—that he is talking of going to Australia. Oh, Lady Kynaston, is it all true?"

She had clasped her hands together, and bent a little forward towards the old lady in her earnestness; she looked at her piteously, almost entreatingly.

"Does she love him after all?" thought Lady Kynaston, as she watched her; and the meaning of the whole story of her son's love seemed more unfathomable than ever.

"John is neither well nor happy," she said, aloud. "I think, Vera, you must know the reason of it better than any of us."

"It is my fault—my doing," cried the girl, with a ring of deep regret in her voice. "Yes," she added, looking away sadly out of the open window; "that is why I have come. Do you know that I saw him once? I don't think he saw me—it was in the Park one morning. He looked so aged, so saddened, I realized then what I had done—his face haunts me."

"Vera, you could alter all that if you chose," said the old lady, earnestly.

A sudden flush sprang to her face; she looked startled.

"You don't suppose I came here to say *that*, Lady Kynaston?"

"No, my dear; but I have decided to say it to you. Vera, I entreat you to tell me the truth. What is it that stands between you and John?"

She was silent, looking down upon her hands that lay crossed one over the other upon her knee.

"I cannot tell you, Lady Kynaston," she answered, at length, in a low voice.

Lady Kynaston sighed; she was a little disappointed.

"And you cannot, marry him?"

Vera shook her head.

"No, it would not be right."

The old lady bent forward and laid her hand upon her visitor's arm.

"Forgive me for asking you. Do you love some one else? is it that?"

She bent her head silently.

"Have you any hopes of marrying the man you love?"

"Oh no, none—not the slightest," she said, hurriedly; "I shall never marry."

"Then, Vera, will you listen to an old woman's advice?"

"Yes, dear Lady Kynaston."

"My dear, if you cannot marry the man you love, put him out of your mind."

"I must do that in any case," she said, wearily.

"Listen to me, my dear. Don't sacrifice your own life and the life of a man who is good and loves you dearly to a caprice of your heart. Hush! don't interrupt me; I dare say you don't think it a caprice; you think it is to last for ever. But there is no 'for ever' in these matters; the thing comes to us like an ordinary disease; some of us take it strongly, and it half kills us; some of us are only a very little ill; but we all get over it. There is a pain that goes right through one's heart: it is worse to bear than any physical suffering: but, thank God, that pain always wears itself out. My dear, I, who speak to you, have felt it, and I tell you that no man is worth it. You can cure yourself of it if you will; and the remedy is work and change of the conditions of your life. You don't think I look very much like a blighted being, do you? and yet I did not marry the man I loved. I could not; he was poor, and my parents would not allow it. I thought I should die, but you see I did not. I took up my life bravely, and I married a most estimable man; I lived an active and healthy life, so that by degrees it became a happy one. Now, Vera, why should you not do the same? Your people have a right to expect that you should marry; they cannot afford to support you for always. Because you are disappointed in one thing, why are you not to make the best you can of your life?"

"I do mean to marry—in time," said Vera, brokenly, with tears in her eyes.

"Then why not marry John?"

There was a minute's silence. Was it possible that Lady Kynaston did not know? Vera asked herself. Was it possible that she could, in cold blood, advise her to marry one son whilst the other one loved her! That was what was so terrible to her mind. To marry was simple enough, but to marry Sir

John Kynaston! She thought of what such an action might bring upon them all. The daily meetings, the struggles with temptation, the awful tampering with deadly sin. Could any one so constituted as she was walk deliberately and with open eyes into such a situation?

She shuddered.

"I cannot do it," she said, wringing her hands together; "don't ask me; I cannot do it!"

Lady Kynaston got up, and went and stood by her chair.

"Vera, I entreat you not to let any false pride stand in the way of this. Do not imagine that I ask you to do anything that would wound your vanity, or humble you in your own eyes. It would be so easy for me to arrange a meeting between you and John; it shall all come about simply and naturally. As soon as he sees you again, he will speak to you."

"It is not that, it is not that!" she murmured, distractedly; but Lady Kynaston went on as if she had not heard her.

"You must know that I should not plead like this with you if I were not deeply concerned. For myself, I had sooner that John remained unmarried. I had sooner that Maurice's children came into Kynaston. It is wrong, I know, but it is the case, because Maurice is my favourite. But when we hear of John shutting himself up, of his refusing to see any of his friends, and of his talking of going to Australia, why, then we all feel that it is you only who can help us; that is why I have promised Maurice to plead with you."

She looked up quickly.

"You promised Maurice! It is *Maurice* who wants me to marry his brother." She turned very pale.

"Certainly he does. You don't suppose Maurice likes to see his brother so unhappy."

The darkened room, the spindle-legged furniture, Lady Kynaston's little figure, in her black dress and soft white tulle cap, the bright garden outside, the belt of trees beyond the lawn, all swam together before her eyes.

She drew a long breath; then she rose slowly from her place, a little unsteadily, perhaps, and walked across the Persian rug to the empty fireplace. She stood there half a minute leaning with both hands upon the mantelshelf, her head bent forwards.

Maurice wished it! To him, then, there were no fears, and no dangers. He could look forward calmly to meeting her constantly as his brother's wife; it would be nothing to him, that temptation that she dreaded so much; nothing that an abyss which death itself could never bridge over would be between them to all eternity!

And then the woman's pride, without which, God help us, so many of us would break our hearts and die, came to her aid.

Very well, then, if he was strong, she would learn to be strong too; if the danger to him was so slight that he could contemplate it with calmness and with indifference, then she, too, would show him that it was nothing to her. Only, then, what a poor thing was this love of his! And surely the man she had loved so fatally was not Maurice Kynaston at all, but only some creature of her own imagination, whom she had invested with things that the man himself had not lost because he had never possessed them.

If this was so, then why, indeed, listen to the voice of her heart when everything urged her to stifle it? Why not make Sir John Kynaston happy and herself prosperous and rich, as everybody round her seemed to consider it her duty to do?

It passed rapidly through her mind what a fine place Kynaston was; how dear everything that wealth can bring had always been to her, what a wise and prudent match it was in every way for her, and what a good indulgent husband Sir John would be.

Who in the wide world would blame her for going back to him? Would not everybody, on the contrary, praise her for reconsidering her folly, and for becoming Lady Kynaston, of Kynaston? The errors of the successful in this world's race are leniently treated; it is only when we are unfortunate and our lives become failures that our friends turn their backs upon our misdeeds in righteous condemnation.

"So long as thou doest well unto thyself men will speak good of thee."

Surely, surely, it was the best and the wisest thing she could do. And yet even at that moment Eustace Daintree's pale, earnest face came for one instant before her. What side in all this would he take—he of the pure heart, of the stainless life? If he knew all, what would he say?

Pooh! he was a dreamer—an idealist, a man of impossible aims; his theories, indeed, were beautiful, but impracticable. Vera knew that he expected better things of her; but she had striven to be what he would have desired, and if she had failed, was it her fault? was it not rather the fault of the world and the generation in which her life had been cast?

She had struggled, and she had failed; henceforth let her life be as fate should ordain for her.

"What is it you wish me to say, Lady Kynaston?" she asked, turning suddenly towards Maurice's mother.

"My dear child, I only want you to say that if John asks you again to be his wife, you will consent, or say only, if you like it better, that you will agree to meet him here. There shall be nothing unpleasant for you; I will write to him and settle everything."

"If you write to him, I will come," she said, briefly, and then Lady Kynaston came up to her and kissed her, taking her hands within her own, and drawing her to her with motherly tenderness. "My dear, everybody will think well of you for this."

And the words ran so nearly in the current of her own bitter thoughts that Vera laughed, shortly and disdainfully, a low laugh of scorn at the world, whose mandates she was prepared to obey, even though she despised herself for doing so.

"You will be glad by-and-by that you were so sensible and so reasonable," said Lady Kynaston.

"Yes—I dare say I shall be glad by-and-by; and now I am going, dear Lady Kynaston; I have a hansom waiting all this time, and Mrs. Hazeldine will be wondering what has become of me."

At this moment they both heard the sound of a carriage driving up to the door.

"It must be some visitors," said Lady Kynaston; "wait a minute, or you will meet them in the hall. Oh, stay, go through this door into the dining-room, and you can get through the dining-room window by the garden round to the front of the house; I dare say you would rather not meet anybody—you might know them."

"Thank you—yes, I should much prefer to get away quickly and quietly—I will go through the dining-room; do not come with me, I can easily find my way."

She gathered up her gloves and her veil and opened the door which communicated between the morning-room and the dining-room. She heard the chatter of women's voices and the fluttering of women's garments in the hall; it seemed as though they were about to be ushered into the room she was leaving.

She did not want to be seen; besides, she wanted to get away quickly and return to London. She closed the morning-room door behind her, and took a couple of steps across the dining-room towards the windows.

Then she stopped suddenly short; Maurice sat before her at the table. He lifted his eyes and looked at her; he did not seem surprised to see her, but there was a whole world of grief and despair in his face. It was as though he had lived through half a lifetime since she had last seen him.

Pride, anger, wounded affection, all died away within her—only the woman was left, the woman who loved him. Little by little she saw him only through the blinding mist of her own tears.

Not one single word was spoken between them. What was there that they could say to each other? Then suddenly she turned away, and went swiftly back into the room she had just left, closing the door behind her.

It was empty. Lady Kynaston was gone. Vera stooped over the writing-table, and, taking up a sheet of paper, she wrote in pencil:—

"Do not write to Sir John—it is beyond my strength—forgive me and forget me. VERA." And then she went out through the other door, and got herself away from the place in her hansom.

Twenty minutes later, when her bevy of chattering visitors had left her, Lady Kynaston came back into her morning-room and found the little pencil note left upon her writing-table. Wondering, perplexed and puzzled beyond measure, she turned it over and over in her fingers.

What had happened? Why had Vera so suddenly altered her mind again? What had influenced her? Half by accident, half, perhaps, with an instinct of what was the truth, she softly opened the door of communication between the morning-room and the dining-room, opened it for one instant, and then drew back again, scared and shocked, closing it quickly and noiselessly. What she had seen in the room was this—

Maurice, half stretched across the table, his face downwards upon his arm, whilst those tearless, voiceless sobs, which are so terrible to witness in a man, sobs which are the gasps of a despairing heart, shook the strong broad shoulders and the down-bent head that was hidden from her sight.

And then the mother knew at last the secret of her son's heart. It was Vera whom Maurice loved.

CHAPTER XXV.

ST. PAUL'S, KNIGHTSBRIDGE.

Hide in thy bosom, poor unfortunate,
That love which is thy torture and thy crime,
Or cry aloud to those departed hosts
Of ghostly lovers! can they be more deaf
To thy disaster than the living world?
Who, with a careless smile, will note the pain
Caused by thy foolish, self-inflicted wound.

VIOLET FANE, "Denzil Place."

Upon the steps of the Charing Cross Hotel stood, one morning in June, a little French gentleman buttoning his lavender gloves. He wore a glossy new hat, a frock-coat, and a flower in his button-hole; he had altogether a smart and jaunty appearance.

He hailed a passing hansom and jumped into it, taking care as he did so to avoid brushing against the muddy wheel, lest he should tarnish the glories of his light-coloured trousers. Monsieur D'Arblet was more than usually particular about his appearance this morning. He said to himself, with a chuckle, as he was driven west-ward, that he was on his way to win a bride, and a rich bride, too. It behoved him to be careful of his outer man on such an occasion.

He had heard of Mr. Harlowe's death and of his grand-daughter's good fortune when he was at Constantinople, for he had friends in London who kept him *au courant* with the gossip of society, and he had straightway made his preparations to return to England. He had not hurried himself, however, for what he had not heard of was that clause in the old man's will which made his grand-daughter's marriage within two months the *sine quâ non* of her inheriting his fortune. Such an idea as that had never come into Monsieur D'Arblet's head; he had no conception but that he should be in plenty of time.

When he got to the house in Princes Gate he found it shut up. This, however, did not disconcert him, it was no more than he expected. After a considerable amount of ringing at both bells, there was a grating sound within as of the unfastening of bolts and chains, and an elderly woman, evidently fresh from her labours over the scouring of the kitchen grate, appeared at the door, opening it just a couple of inches, as though she dreaded the invasion of a gang of housebreakers.

"Will you please tell me where Mrs. Romer is now living?"

The woman grinned. "She has been living at Walpole Lodge, at Kew—Lady Kynaston's, sir."

"Oh, thank you;" and he was preparing to re-enter his hansom.

"But I don't think you will see her to-day, sir."

"Why not?" turning half-round again.

"It is Mrs. Romer's wedding-day."

"*What?*"

That elderly female, who had been at one time a housemaid in Mr. Harlowe's household, confided afterwards to her intimate friend, the kitchenmaid next door, that she was so frightened at the way that foreign-looking gentleman shouted at her, that she felt as if she should have dropped. "Indeed, my dear, I was forced to go down and get a drop of whisky the very instant he was gone, I felt so fluttered, like."

Monsieur Le Vicomte turned round to her, with his foot midway between the pavement and the step of the hansom, and shouted at her again.

"*What* did you say it was, woman?"

"Why, Mrs. Romer's wedding-day, to be sure, sir; and no such wonder after all, I should say; and a lovely morning for the wedding it be, too."

Lucien D'Arblet put his hand vaguely up to his head, as though he had received a blow; she had escaped him, then, after all.

"So soon after the old man's death," he murmured, half aloud; "who could have expected it?"

"Well, sir, and soon it is, as you say," replied the ancient ex-housemaid, who had caught the remark; "but people do say as how Mr. Harlowe, my late master, wished it so, and of course Mrs. Romer, she were quite ready, so to speak, for the Captain had been a-courting her for ever so long, as we who lived in the house could have told."

The vicomte was fumbling at his breast-coat pocket, his face was as yellow as the rose in his button-hole.

"Where was the wedding to be? At Kew?"

"No, sir; at Saint Paul's church, in Wilton Crescent. Mrs. Romer would have it so, because that's the place of worship she used to go to when she lived here. You'd be in time to see them married now, sir, if you was to look sharp; it was to be at half-past eleven, and it's not that yet; my niece and a young friend has just started a-foot to go there. I let her go, because she'd never seen a grand wedding. I'd like to have gone myself, but, in course, we couldn't both be out of the house——"

The gentleman was listening no longer; he had sprung into his hansom.

"Drive to Saint Paul's, Knightsbridge, as fast as your horse can go," he called out to the cabman. "I might even now be in time; it would be a *coup d'état*," he muttered.

Round the door of Saint Paul's church a crowd had gathered, waiting to see the bridal party come out; there was a strip of red cloth across the pavement, and a great many carriages were standing down the street; big footmen were lounging about, chatting amicably together; a knot of decently-dressed women were pressing up as close to the porch as the official personage, with a red collar on his coat and gold lace on his hat, would allow them to go; and an indiscriminate collection of those chance passers-by who never seem to be in any hurry, or to have anything better to do than to stand and stare at any excitement, great or small, that they may meet on their road, were blocking up the pavement on either side of the red cloth carpeting.

Two ladies came walking along from the direction of the Park.

"There's a wedding going on; do let us go in and see it, Vera."

"My dear Cissy, I detest looking at people being married; it always makes me low-spirited."

"And I love it. I always get such hints for dresses from a wedding. I'd go anywhere to see anybody married. I've been to the Jewish synagogue, to Spurgeon's tabernacle, and to the pro-cathedral, all in one week, before now just to see weddings."

"There must be a sameness about the performances. Don't you get sick of them?"

"Never. I wonder whose wedding it is; there must be thirty carriages waiting. I'll ask one of these big footmen. Whose wedding is it?"

"Captain Kynaston's, ma'am."

"Oh, I used to know him once; he is such a handsome fellow. Come along, Vera."

"Cissy, I *cannot* come."

"Nonsense, Vera; don't be so foolish; make haste, or we shan't get in."

Somebody just then dashed up in a hansom, and came hurrying up behind them. Somehow or other, what with Mrs. Hazeldine dragging her by the arm, and an excited-looking gentleman pushing his way through the crowd behind her, Vera got swept on into the church.

"You are very late, ladies," whispered the pew-opener, who supposed them to belong to the wedding guests; "it is nearly over. You had better take these seats in this pew; you will see them come out well from here." And she evidently considered them to be all one party, for she ushered them all three into a pew; first, Mrs. Hazeldine, then Vera, and next to her the little foreign-looking gentleman who had bustled up so hurriedly.

It was an awful thing to have happened to Vera that she should have been thus entrapped by a mere accident into being present at Maurice's wedding; and yet, when she was once inside the church, she felt not altogether sorry for it.

"I can at least see the last of him, and pray that he may be happy," she said to herself, as she sank on her knees in the shelter of the pew, and buried her face in her hands.

The church was crowded, and yet the wedding itself was not a particularly attractive one, for, owing to the fact that the bride was a widow, there was, of course, no bevy of bridesmaids in attendance in diaphanous raiment. Instead of these, however, there was a great concourse of the best-dressed women in London, all standing in rows round the upper end of the nave; and there was a little old lady, in brown satin and point lace, who stood out conspicuously detached from the other groups, who bent her head solemnly over the great bouquet of exotics in her hands, and prayed within herself, with a passionate fervour such as no other soul present could pray, save only the pale, beautiful girl on her knees, far away down at the further end of the church. Surely, if God ever gave happiness to one of his creatures because another prayed for it, Maurice Kynaston, with the prayers of those two women being offered up for him, would have been a happy man.

And the mother, by this time, knew that it was all a mistake—a mistake, alas, which she, in her blindness, had fostered.

No wonder that she trembled as she prayed.

The service, that portion of it which makes two people man and wife, was over; the clergyman was reading the final exhortation to the newly-married pair.

They stood together close to the altar rails. The bride was in a pale lavender satin, covered with lace, which spread far away behind her across the tesselated pavement. The bridegroom stood by her side, erect and handsome, but pale and stern, and with a far-away look in his eyes that would have made any one fancy, had any one been near enough or attentive enough to remark it, that he was only an indifferent spectator of the scene, in no way interested in what was going on. He looked as if he were thinking of something else.

He was thinking of something else. He was thinking of a railway carriage, of a train rushing onwards through a fog-blotted landscape, and of two arms, warm and soft, cast up round his neck, and a trembling, passionate voice, ever crying in his ears—

"While you live I will never marry another man."

That was what the bridegroom was thinking about.

As to the bride, she was debating to herself whether she should have the body of her wedding-dress cut V or square when she left it with her dressmaker to be altered into a dinner-dress.

Meanwhile the clergyman, who mumbled his words slightly, and whose glasses kept on tumbling off his nose, waded through the several duties of husbands towards their wives, and of wives towards their husbands, as expounded by Scripture, in a monotonous undertone, until, to the great relief of the weary guests, the ceremony at last came to an end.

Then the best man, Sir John, who stood behind his brother, looking, if possible, more like a mute at a funeral even than the bridegroom himself, stepped forward out of the shadow. The new-married couple went into the vestry, followed by Sir John, his mother, and a select few, upon which the door was closed. All the rest of the company then began to chatter in audible whispers together; they fidgeted backwards and forwards, from one pew to the other. There were jokes, and smiles, and nods, and hand-shakings between the different members of the wedding party. All in a low and decorous undertone, of course, but still there was a distinct impression upon every one that all the religious part of the business being well got over, they were free to be jolly about it now, and to enjoy themselves as much as circumstances would admit of.

All at once there was a sudden hush, everybody scuffled back into their places. The best man put his nose out of the vestry door, and the "Wedding March" struck up. Then came a procession of chorister boys down the church, each bearing a small bouquet of fern and white flowers. They ranged themselves on either side of the porch, and the bride and bridegroom came down the aisle alone.

Then it was that Monsieur D'Arblet, leaning forward with the rest to see them pass, caught sight of the face of the girl who stood by his side.

She was pale as death; a look as of the horror of despair was in her eyes, her teeth were set, her hands were clenched together as one who has to impose a terrible and dreadful task upon herself. Nobody in all that gaily-dressed chattering crowd noticed her, for were not all eyes fixed upon the bride, the queen of the day? Nobody save the man who stood by her side. Only he saw that fixed white look of despair, only he heard the long shuddering sigh that burst from her pale lips as the bridegroom went by. Monsieur D'Arblet said, to himself:

"This woman loves Monsieur le Capitaine! *Bon!* Two are better than one; we will avenge ourselves together, my beautiful incognita."

And then he looked sharply at her companion, and found that her face was familiar to him. Surely he had dined at that woman's house once. Oh, yes! to be sure, it was that insufferable little chatterbox, Mrs. Hazeldine. He remembered all about her now.

There was a good deal of pushing and cramming at the doorway. By the time Vera could get out of the stifling heat of the crowded church most of the wedding party had driven off, and the rest were clamouring wildly for their carriages; she herself had got separated from her companion, and when she could rejoin her in the little gravelled yard outside, she found her shaking hands with effusion with the foreign-looking gentleman who had sat next her in the church, but whom, truth to say, she had hardly noticed.

"Let me present to you my friend," said Cissy. "Miss Nevill, Monsieur D'Arblet—you will walk with us as far as the park, won't you?"

"I shall be enchanted, Mrs. Hazeldine."

"And wasn't it a pretty wedding," continued Mrs. Hazeldine, rapturously, as they all three walked away together down the shady side of the street; "so remarkably pretty considering that there were no bridesmaids; but Mrs. Romer is so graceful, and dresses so well. I don't visit her myself, you know; but of course I know her by sight. One knows everybody by sight in London; it's rather embarrassing sometimes, because one is tempted to bow to people one doesn't visit, or else one fancies one ought not to bow to somebody one does. I've made some dreadfully stupid mistakes myself sometimes. Did you notice the rose point on that old lady's brown satin, Vera?"

"That was Lady Kynaston."

"Oh, was it? By the way, of course, you must know some of the Kynastons, as they come from your part of the world. I wonder they didn't ask you to the wedding."

Vera murmured something unintelligible. Monsieur D'Arblet looked at her sharply. He saw that she had in no way recovered her agitation yet, and that she could hardly bear her companion's brainless chatter over this wedding.

"That has been no ordinary love affair," said this astute Frenchman to himself. "I must decidedly cultivate this young lady's acquaintance, for I mean to pay you out well yet, ma belle Hélène."

"How fortunate it was we happened to be passing just as it was going on. I wouldn't have missed seeing that lovely lavender satin the bride wore for worlds; did you notice the cut of the jacket front, Vera; it was something new; she looked as happy as possible too. I daresay her first marriage was a *coup manqué*; they generally are when women marry again."

"Suppose we take these three chairs in the shade," suggested Monsieur D'Arblet, cutting short, unceremoniously the string of her remarks, which apparently were no more soothing to himself than to Miss Nevill.

They sat down, and for the space of half an hour Monsieur D'Arblet proceeded to make himself politely agreeable to Miss Nevill, and he succeeded so well in amusing her by his conversation, that by the time they all got up to go the natural bloom had returned to her cheeks, and she was talking to him quite easily and pleasantly, as though no catastrophe in her life had happened but an hour ago.

"You will come back with us to lunch, Monsieur D'Arblet?"

"I shall be delighted, madame."

"If you will excuse me, Cissy, I am not going to lunch with you to-day," said Vera.

"My dear! where are you going, then?"

"I have a visit to pay—an engagement, I mean—in—in Cadogan Place. I will be home very soon, in time for your drive, if you don't mind my leaving you."

"Oh, of course, do as you like, dear."

Lucien D'Arblet was annoyed at her defection, but, of course, having accepted Mrs. Hazeldine's invitation, there was nothing for it but to go on with her; so he swallowed his discomfiture as best he could, and proceeded to make himself agreeable to his hostess.

As to Vera, she turned away and retraced her steps slowly towards St. Paul's Church. It was a foolish romantic fancy, she could not tell what impelled her to it, but she felt as though she must go back there once more.

The church was not closed. She pushed open the swing-door and went in. It was all hushed and silent and empty. Where so lately the gay throng of well-dressed men and women had passed in and out, chattering, smiling, nodding—displaying their radiant toilettes one against the other, there were only now the dark, empty rows of pews, and the bent figure of one shabbily-dressed old woman gathering together the prayer-books and hymn-books that had been tumbled out of their places in the scuffle, and picking up morsels of torn finery that had dropped about along the nave.

Vera passed by her and went up into the chancel. She stood where Maurice had stood by the altar rails. A soft, subdued light came streaming in through the coloured glass window; a bird was chirping high up somewhere among the oak rafters of the roof, the roar of the street without was muffled and deadened; the old woman slammed-to the door of a pew, the echo rang with a hollow sound through the empty building, and her departing footsteps shuffled away down the aisle into silence.

Vera lifted her eyes; great tears welled down slowly, one by one, over her cheeks—burning, blistering tears, such as, thank God, one sheds but once or twice in a lifetime—that seem to rend our very hearts as they rise.

Presently she sank down upon her knees and prayed—prayed for him, that he might be happy and forget her, but most of all for herself, that she might school her rebellious heart to patience, and her wild passion of misery into peace and submission.

And by degrees the tempest within her was hushed. Then, ere she rose from her knees, something lying on the ground, within a yard of where she knelt, caught her eye. It was a little Russia-leather letter-case. She recognized it instantly; she had often seen Maurice take it out of his pocket.

She caught at it hungrily and eagerly, as a miser clutches a treasure-trove, pressing it wildly to her bosom, and covering it with passionate kisses. Dear little shabby case, that had been so near his heart; that his hand, perchance, only on hour ago had touched. Could anything on earth be more priceless to her than this worn and faded object!

It seemed to be quite empty. It had fallen evidently from his pocket during the service. If he ever missed it, there was nothing in it to lose; and now it was hers, hers by every right; she would never part with it, never. It was all she had of him; the one single thing he had touched which she possessed.

She rose hurriedly. She was in haste now to be gone with her treasure, lest any one should wrest it from her. She carried it down the church with a guilty delight, kissing it more than once as she went. And then, as she opened the church door, some one ran up the steps outside, and she stood face to face with Sir John Kynaston.

CHAPTER XXVI.

THE RUSSIA-LEATHER CASE.

"Never again," so speaketh one forsaken,
In the blank desolate passion of despair:
Never again shall the bright dream I cherished
Delude my heart, for bitter truth is there:
The Angel Hope shall still my cruel pain;
Never again, my heart—never again!

A. PROCTER.

"Vera!"

Sir John Kynaston fell back a step or two and turned very white.

"How do you do?" said Vera, quietly, and put out her hand.

They stood in the open air. There was a carriage passing, some idle cabmen on the stand with nothing to do but to stare at them, a gaping nursery-maid and her charges at the gate. Whatever people may feel on suddenly running against each other after a deadly quarrel, or a heart-rending separation, or after a long interval of heart-burnings and misunderstandings, there are always the externals of life to be observed. It is difficult to rush into the tragedy of one's existence at a gulp; it is safer to shake hands and say, "How do you do?"

That is what Vera felt, and that was what these two people did. Sir John took her proffered hand, and responded to her stereotyped greeting. By the time he had done so he had recovered his presence of mind.

"What an odd thing to meet you at the door of this church," he said, rather nervously. "Do you know that my brother was married here this morning?"

"Yes; I was in the church."

"Were you? How glad I am I did not know it," almost involuntarily.

There was a little pause; then Vera asked him if he was going to Walpole Lodge.

"Eventually; but I have come back here to look for something. My brother has lost a little Russia-leather case; he thinks he may have dropped it in the church; there were two ten-pound notes in it. I am going in to look for it. Why, what is that in your hand? I believe that is the very thing."

"I—I—just picked it up," stammered Vera. She began searching in the pockets of the case. "I did not think there was anything in it. Yes, here are the notes, quite safe."

She took them out and gave them to him. He held out his hand mechanically for the case also.

"Thank you; you have saved me the trouble of looking for it. I will take it back to him at once."

But she could not part with her treasure; it was all she had got of him.

"The letter-case is very shabby," she said, crimsoning with a painful confusion. "I do not think he can want it at all; it is quite worn out."

Sir John looked at her with a slight surprise.

"It can be very little use to him. One likes sometimes to have a little remembrance of those—of people—one has known; he would not mind my keeping it, I think. Tell him—tell him I asked for it." The tears were very near her voice; she could scarcely keep them back out of her eyes.

John Kynaston dropped his hand, and Vera slipped the little case quickly into her pocket.

"Would you mind walking a little way with me, Vera?" he said, gently and very gravely.

She drew down her veil, and went with him in silence. They had walked half-way down Wilton Crescent before he spoke to her again; then he turned towards her, and looked at her earnestly and sadly.

"Why did you go back again into the church, Vera?"

"I wanted to think quietly a little," she murmured. There was another pause.

"So *that* is what parted us!" he exclaimed, with a sudden bitterness, at length.

She looked up, startled and pale.

"What do you mean?" she stammered.

"Oh, child! I see it all now. How blind I have been. Ah, why did you not trust me, love? Why did you fear to tell me your secret? Do you not think that I, who would have laid down my life for you to make you happy, do you not suppose I would have striven to make your path smooth for you?"

She could not answer him; the kind words, the tender voice, were too much for her. Her tears fell fast and silently.

"Tell me," he said, turning to her almost roughly, "tell me the truth. Has he ill-treated you, this brother of mine, who stole you from me, and then has left you desolate?"

"No, no; do not say that; it was never his fault at all, only mine; and he was always bound to her. He has been everything that is good and loyal and true to you and to her; it has been only a miserable mistake, and now it is over. Yes, thank God, it is over; never speak of it again. He was never false to you; only I was false. But it is ended."

They were walking round Belgrave Square by this time, not near the houses, but round the square garden in the middle. All recollection of his brother's marriage, of the wedding breakfast at Walpole Lodge, of the speech the best man would be expected to make, had gone clean out of his head; he thought of nothing but Vera and of the revelation concerning her that had just come to him. It was the quiet hour of the day; there were very few people about; everybody was indoors eating heavy luncheons, with sunblinds drawn down to keep out the heat. They were almost as much alone as in a country lane in Meadowshire.

"What are you going to do with yourself?" he said to her, presently. "What use are you going to make of your life?"

"I don't know," she answered, drearily; "I suppose I shall go back to Sutton. Perhaps I shall marry."

"But not me?"

She looked up at him piteously.

"Listen, child," he said, eagerly. "If I were to go away for a year, and then come back to you, how would it be? Oh, my darling! I love you so deeply that I could even be content to do with but half your heart, so that I could win your sweet self. I would exact nothing from you, love, no more than what you could give me freely. But I would love you so well, and make your life so sweet and pleasant to you, that in time, perhaps, you would forget the old sorrow, and learn to be happy, with a quiet kind of happiness, with me; I would ask for no more. Look, child, I have grieved sorely for you; I have sat down and wept, and mourned for you as though I had no strength or life left in me. But now I am ashamed of my weakness, for it is unworthy of *you*. I am going away abroad, across the world, I care not where, so long as I can be up and doing, and forget the pain at my heart. Vera, tell me that I may come back to you in a year. Think with what fresh life and courage I should go if I had but that hope before my eyes. In a year's time your pain will be less; you will have forgotten many things; you will be content, perhaps, to come to me, knowing that I will never reproach you with the past, nor expect more than you can give me in the future. Vera, let me come back and claim you in a year!"

How strange it was that the chance of marrying this man was perpetually being presented to her. Never, perhaps, had the temptation been stronger to her than it was now. He had divined her secret; there would be no concealment between them; he would ask her for no love it was not in her power to give; he would be content with her as she was, and he would love her, and worship her, and surround her with everything that could make her life pleasant and easy for her. Could a man offer more? Oh! why could she not take him at his word, and give him the hope he craved for?

Alas! for Vera; she had eaten too deeply of the knowledge of good and evil— that worldly wisdom in whose strength she had started in life's race, and in the possession of which she had once deemed herself so strong—so absolutely invulnerable to the things that pierce and wound weaker woman— this was gone from her. The baser part of her nature, wherewith she would so gladly have been content, was uppermost no longer; her heart had triumphed over her head, and, with a woman of strong character, this is generally only done at the expense of her happiness.

To marry Sir John Kynaston, to be lapped in luxury, to receive all the good things of this world at his hands, and all the while to love his brother with a guilty love, this was no longer possible to Vera Nevill.

"I cannot do it; do not ask me," she said, distractedly. "Your goodness to me half breaks my heart; but it cannot be."

"Why not, child? In a year so much may be altered."

"I shall not alter."

"No; but, even so, you might learn to be happy with me."

"It is not that; you do not understand. I daresay I could be happy enough; that is not why I cannot marry you."

"Why not, then?"

"*I dare not*," she said, in a low voice.

He drew in his breath. "Ah!" he said, between his teeth, "is it so bad with you as that?"

She bent her head in silent assent.

"That is hard," he said, almost to himself, looking gloomily before him. Presently he spoke again. "Thank you, Vera," he said, rather brokenly. "You are a brave woman and a true one. Many would have taken my all, and given me back only deception and falseness. But you are incapable of that, and—and you fear your own strength; is that it?"

"Whilst he lives," she said, with a sudden burst of passion, "I can know no safety. Never to see his face again can be my only safeguard, and with you I could never be safe. Why, even to bear your name would be to scorch my heart every time I was addressed by it. Forgive me, John," turning to him with a sudden penitence, "I should not have pained you by saying these things; you who have been so infinitely good to me. Go your way across the world, and forget me. Ah! have I not been a curse to every one who bears the name of Kynaston?"

He was silent from very pity. Vera was no longer to him the goddess of his imagination; the one pure and peerless woman, above all other women, such as he had once fancied her to be. But surely she was dearer to him now, in all her weakness and her suffering, than she had ever been on that lofty pedestal of perfection upon which he had once lifted her.

He pitied her so much, and yet he could not help her; her malady was past remedy. And, as she had told him, it was no one's fault—it was only a miserable mistake. He had never had her heart—he saw it plainly now. Many little things in the past, which he had scarcely remembered at the time, came back to his memory—little details of that week at Shadonake, when Maurice had lived in the same house with her, whilst he had only gone over daily to see her. Always, in those days, Maurice had been by her side, and Vera had been dreamily happy, with that fixed look of content with which the presence of the man she loves best beautifies and poetises a woman's face. Sir John was not a very observant man; but now, after it was all over, these things came back to him. The night of the ball, Mrs. Romer's mysterious hints, and his own vague disquietude at her words; later on Maurice's reasonless refusal to be present at his wedding, and Vera's startled face of dismay when he had asked her to go and plead with him to stay for it.

They had struggled against their hearts, it was clear, these poor lovers, whose lives were both tied up and bound before ever they had met each other. But nature had been too strong for them; and the woman, at least, had torn herself free from the chains that had become insupportable to her.

They walked on silently, side by side, round the square. Some girls were playing at lawn-tennis within the garden. There was an occasional shout or a ringing laugh from their fresh young voices. A footman was walking along the pavement opposite, with two fat pugs and a white Spitz in the last stage of obesity in tow, which it was his melancholy duty to parade daily up and down for their mid-day airing. An occasional hansom dashing quickly by broke the stillness of the "empty" hour. Years and years afterwards every detail of the scene came back to his memory with the distinctness of a photograph when he passed once more through the square.

"You have been no curse to me, Vera," he said, presently, breaking the silence. "Do not reproach yourself; it is I who was a madman to deem that I could win your love. Child, we are both sufferers; but time heals most things, and we must learn to wait and be patient. Will you ever marry, Vera?"

"I don't know. Perhaps I may be obliged to. It might be better for me. I cannot say. Don't speak of it. Why, is there nothing else for a woman to do but to marry? John, it must be late. Ought you not to go back—to—to your mother's?"

Insensibly, she resumed a lighter manner. On that other subject there was nothing left to be said. She had had her last chance of becoming John Kynaston's wife. After what she had said to him, she knew he would never ask her again. That chapter in her life was closed for ever.

They parted, unromantically enough, in front of St. George's Hospital. He called a hansom for her, and stood holding her hand, one moment longer, possibly, than was strictly necessary, looking intently into her face as he did so.

"Will you think of me sometimes?"

"Yes, surely."

"Good-bye, Vera."

"Good-bye, John. God bless you wherever you may go."

She got into her hansom, and he told the cabman where to drive her; then he lifted his hat to her with grave politeness, and walked away in the opposite direction. It was a common-place enough parting, and yet these two never saw each other's faces again in this world.

So it is with our lives. Some one or other who has been a part of our very existence for a space goes his way one day, and we see him no more. For a little while our hearts ache, and we shed tears in secret for him who is gone, but by-and-by we get to understand that he is part of our past, never, to be recalled, and after a while we get used to his absence; we think of him less and less, and the death of him, who was once bound up in our very lives, strikes us only with a mild surprise, hardly even tinged with a passing melancholy.

"Poor old so-and-so, he is dead," we say. "What a time it is since we met," and then we go our way and think of him no more.

But Vera knew that, in all human probability, she would never see him again, this man, who had once so nearly been her husband. It was another link of her past life severed. It saddened her, but she knew it was inevitable.

The little letter-case, at all events, was safely hers; and for many a night Vera slept with it under her pillow.

CHAPTER XXVII.

DINNER AT RANELAGH.

Here is the whole set, a character dead at every word.

SHERIDAN.

It was the fag end of the London season; people were talking about Goodwood and the Ryde week, about grouse and about salmon-fishing. Members of Parliament went about, like martyrs at the stake, groaning over the interminable nature of every debate, and shaking their heads over the prospect of getting away. Women in society knew all their own and their neighbours' dresses by heart, and were dead sick of them all; and even the very gossip and scandal that is always afloat to keep up the spirits of the idlers and the chatterers had lost all the zest, all the charm of novelty that gave flavour and piquancy to every *canard* that was started two months ago.

It was all stale, flat, and unprofitable.

What was the use of constantly asserting, on the very best authority, that Lady So-and-so was on the eve of running away with that handsome young actor, whose eyes had taken the female population by storm, when Lady So-and-so persisted in walking about arm-in-arm with her husband day after day, with a child on either side of them, in the most provoking way, as though to prove the utter fallacy of the report, and her own incontestable domestic felicity? Or, what merit had a man any longer who had stated in May that the heiress *par excellence* of the season was about to sell herself and her gold to that debauched and drunken marquis, who had evidently not six months of life left in him in which to enjoy his bargain, when the heiress herself gave the lie to the *on dit* in July by talking calmly about going to Norway with her papa for a month's retirement and rest after the fatigues of the season?

What a number of lies are there not propounded during the months of May and June by the inventive Londoner, and how many of them are there not proved to be so during the latter end of July!

Heaven only knows how and where the voice of scandal is first raised. Is it at the five o'clock tea-tables? Or, is it in the smoking-rooms of the clubs that things are first spoken of, and the noxious breath of slander started upon its career? Or, are there evil-minded persons, both men and women, prowling about, like unclean animals, at the skirts of that society into whose inner recesses they would fain gain admittance, picking up greedily, here and there, in their eaves-dropping career, some scrap or morsel of truth out of which they weave a well-varnished tale wherewith to delight the ears of the vulgar and the coarse-minded? There are such men and such women; God forgive them for their wickedness!

Do any of these scandal-mongers ever call to mind, I wonder, an ancient and, seemingly, a well-nigh forgotten injunction?

"Thou shalt not bear false witness," said the same Voice who has also said, "Thou shalt do no murder."

And which is the worst—to kill a man's body, or to slay a man's honour, or a woman's reputation?

In truth, there seems to me to be but little difference between the two; and the man or the woman who will do the one might very possibly be guilty of the other—but for the hanging!

We should all do a great many more wicked things than we do if there were no consequences.

It is a very trite observation, which is, nevertheless, never spoken with more justice or more truth than at or about Hyde Park Corner between May and July, that the world we live in is a very wicked one.

Well, the season, as I have said, was well-nigh over, and all the scandal had run dry, and the gossip, for the most part, been proved to be incorrect, and there was nobody in all London who excited so much irritation among the talkers as the new beauty, Vera Nevill.

For Vera was Miss Nevill still, and there was every prospect of her remaining so. What on earth possessed the girl that she would not marry? Had not men dangled at her elbow all the season? Could she not have had such and such elder sons, or such and such wealthy commoner? What was she waiting for? A girl without a penny, who came nobody knew from where, ushered in under Mrs. Hazeldine's wings, with not a decent connection in the world to her name! What did she want—this girl who had only her beauty to depend upon? and everybody knows how fleeting *that* is!

And then, presently, the women who were envious of her began to whisper amongst themselves. There was something against her; she was not what she seemed to be. The men flirted, of course—men will always flirt! but they were careful not to commit themselves! And even that mysterious word "adventuress," which has an ugly sound, but of which no one exactly knows the precise meaning, began to be bruited about.

"There was an unpleasant story about her, somebody told me once," said one prettily-dressed nonentity to another, as they wandered slowly up and down the velvet lawns at Ranelagh. "She was mixed up in some way with the

Kynaston family. Sir John was to have married her, and then something dreadful came out, and he threw her over."

"Oh, I thought she jilted him."

"I daresay it was one or the other; at all events, there was some fracas or other. I believe her mother was—hum, hum—you understand—she couldn't be swallowed by the Kynastons at any price; they must have been thankful to get out of it."

"It looks very bad, her not marrying any one, with all the fuss there has been made over her."

"Yes; even Cissy Hazeldine told me, in confidence, yesterday, she could not try her again next season. It wouldn't do, you know; it would look too much as if she had some object of her own in getting her married. Cissy must find something else for another year. Of course, with a husband, she could sail her own course and make her own way; but a girl can't go on attracting attention with impunity—she gets herself talked about—it is only we married women can do as we like."

"Exactly. Do you suppose *that* will come to anything?" casting a glance towards the further end of the lawn, where Vera Nevill sat in a low basket-chair, under the shadow of a spreading tulip-tree, whilst a slight boyish figure, stretched at her feet, alternately chewed blades of grass and looked up worshippingly into her face.

"*That!*" following the direction of her companion's eyes. "Oh dear, no! Denis Wilde is too wideawake to be caught, though he is such a boy! They say she is crazy to get him; everybody else has slipped through her fingers, you see, and he would be better than nothing. Now we are in the last week in July, I daresay she is getting desperate; but young Wilde knows pretty well what he is about, I expect!"

"He seems to admire her."

"Oh, yes, I daresay; those large kind of women do get admired; men look upon them as fine animals. *I* should not care to be admired in that way, would you?"

"No, indeed! it is disgusting," replied the other, who was fain to conceal the bony corners of her angular figure with a multiplicity of lace ruchings and puffings.

"As to Miss Nevill, she is nothing else. A most material type; why, her waist must be twenty-two inches round!"

"Quite that, dear," with sweetness, from the owner of a nineteen-inch article, which two maids struggled with daily in order to reduce it to the required measurement.

"Well, I never could—between you and me—see much to admire in her."

"Neither could I, although, of course, it has been the fashion to rave over her."

And, with that, these two amiable young women fell at it tooth and nail, and proceeded to cry down their victim's personal appearance in the most unmeasured and sweeping terms.

After the taking away of a fellow-woman's character, comes as a natural sequence the condemnation of her face and figure, and it is doubtful which indictment is the most grave in eyes feminine. Meanwhile the object of all this animadversion sat tranquilly unconscious under her tulip-tree, whilst Denis Wilde, that astute young gentleman, whom they had declared to be too well aware of what he was about to be entrapped into matrimony, was engaged in proposing to her for the fourth time.

"I thought we had settled this subject long ago, Mr. Wilde," says Vera, tranquilly unfolding her large, black, feather fan—for it is hot—and slowly folding it up again.

"It will never be settled for me, Vera; never, so long as you are unmarried."

"What a dreadful mistake life is!" sighs Vera, wearily, more to herself than to the boy at her feet. Was anybody ever happy in this world? she began to wonder.

"I know very well," resumed Denis Wilde, "that I am not good enough for you; but, then, who is? My prospects, such as they are, are very distant, and your friends, I daresay, expect you to marry well."

"How often must I tell you that that has nothing to do with it," cries Vera, impatiently. "If I loved a beggar, I should marry him."

Young Wilde plucked at the grass again, and chewed a daisy up almost viciously. There was a supreme selfishness in the way she had of perpetually harping upon her lack of love for him.

"There is always some fellow or other hanging about you," grumbles the young man, irritably; "you are an inveterate flirt!"

"No woman is worthy of the name who is not!" retorts Vera, laughing.

"I *hate* a flirt," angrily.

"This is very amusing when you know that your flirtation with Mrs. Hazeldine is a chronic disease of two years' standing!"

"Pooh!—mere child's play on both sides, and you know it is! You are very different; you lead a fellow on till he doesn't know whether his very soul is his own, and then you turn round and snap your fingers in his face and send him to the devil."

"What an awful accusation! Pray give me an instance of a victim to this shocking conduct."

"Why, there's that wretched little Frenchman whom you are playing the same game with that you have already done with me; he follows you like a shadow."

"Poor Monsieur D'Arblet!" laughed Vera, and then grew suddenly serious. "But do you know, Mr. Wilde, it is a very singular thing about that man—I can't think why he follows me about so."

"*Can't* you!" very grimly.

"I assure you the man is in no more love with me than—than——"

"*I* am! I suppose you will say next."

"Oh dear, no, you are utterly incorrigible and quite in earnest; but Monsieur D'Arblet is *pretending* to be in love with me."

"He makes a very good pretence of it, at all events. Here he comes, confound him! If I had known Mrs. Hazeldine had asked *him*, I would never have come."

At which Vera, who had heard these outbursts of indignant jealousy before, and knew how little poor Denis meant the terrible threats he uttered, only laughed with the pitiless amusement of a woman who knows her own power.

Lucien D'Arblet came towards her smiling, and sank down into a vacant basket-chair by her side with the air of a man who knows himself to be welcome.

He had been paying a great deal of attention latterly to the beautiful Miss Nevill; he had followed her about everywhere, and had made it patent in every public place where he had met her that she alone was the sole aim and object of his thoughts. And yet, with it all, Monsieur Le Vicomte was only playing a part, and not only that, but he was pretty certain that she knew it to be so. He gazed rapturously into her beautiful face, he lowered his voice tenderly in speaking to her, he pressed her hand when she gave it to him, and even on occasions he raised it furtively to his lips; but, with all this, he knew perfectly well that she was not one whit deceived by him. She no more believed him to be in love with her than he believed it of himself. She was clever and beautiful, and he admired and even liked her, but in the beginning of their acquaintance Monsieur D'Arblet had had no thought of making her the object of any sentimental attentions. He had been driven to it by a discovery that he had made concerning her character.

Miss Nevill had a good heart. She was no enraged, injured woman, thirsting for revenge upon the woman who had stolen her lover from her—such as he had desired to find in her; she was only a true-hearted and unhappy girl, who was not in any case likely to develop into the instrument of vengeance which he sought for.

It was a disappointment to him, but he was not completely disheartened. It was through her that he desired to punish Helen for daring to brave him, and he swore to himself that he would do it still; only he must now set about it in a different way, so he began to make love to Miss Nevill.

And Vera was shrewd enough to perceive that he was only playing a part. Nevertheless, there were times when she felt so completely puzzled by his persistent adoration, that she could hardly tell what to make of it. Was he trying to make some other woman jealous? It even came into her head, once or twice, to suspect that Cissy Hazeldine was the real object of his devotion, so utterly incomprehensible did his conduct appear to her.

If she had been told that Lucien D'Arblet's real quest was not love, but revenge, she would have laughed. An Englishman does not spend his time nor his energies in plotting a desperate retaliation on a lady who has disregarded his threats and evaded his persecution; it is not in the nature of any Briton, however irascible, to do so; but a Frenchman is differently constituted. There is something delightfully refreshing to him in an atmosphere of plotting and intrigue. There is the same instinct of the chase in both nationalities, but it is more amusing to the Frenchman to hunt down his fellow-creatures than to pursue unhappy little beasts of the field; and he understands himself in the pursuit of the larger game infinitely better.

Nevertheless, Monsieur D'Arblet had no intention of getting himself into trouble, nor of risking the just fury of an indignant British husband, who stood six feet in his stockings, nor did he desire, by any anonymous libel, to bring himself in any way under the arm of the law. All he meant to do was to dig his trench and to lay his mine, to place the fuse in Vera Nevill's hands—leave her to set fire to it—and then retire himself, covered with satisfaction at his cleverness, to his own side of the Channel.

Who could possibly grudge him so harmless an entertainment?

Monsieur D'Arblet, as he sat down by her side under the tulip-tree, began by paying Miss Nevill a prettily turned compliment upon her fresh white toilette; as he did so Vera smiled and bent her head; she had seen him before to-day.

"Fine evening, Mr. Wilde," said the Frenchman, turning civilly, but with no evident *empressement*, towards the gentleman he addressed.

Denis only answered by a sulky grunt.

Then began that process between the two men which is known in polite society as the endeavour to sit each other out.

Monsieur D'Arblet discoursed upon the weather and the beauty of the gardens, with long and expressive pauses between each insignificant remark, and the air of a man who wishes to say, "I could talk about much more interesting things if that other fellow was out of the way."

Denis Wilde simply reversed himself, that is to say, he lay on his back instead of his face, stared up at the sky, and chewed grass perseveringly. He had evidently no intention of being driven off the field.

"I had something of great importance to say to you this evening," murmured Monsieur D'Arblet, at length, looking fixedly at his enemy's upturned face.

"All right, go ahead, don't mind me," says the young gentleman, amiably. "I'm never in the way, am I, Miss Nevill?"

"Never, Mr. Wilde," answers Vera, sweetly. Like a true woman, she quite appreciates the fun of the situation, and thoroughly enjoys it; "pray tell me what you have to say, monsieur."

"Ah! Ces choses-là ne se disent qu'à deux!" murmurs he Frenchman, with a sentimental sigh.

"It is no use your saying it in French," says Denis, with a chuckle, twisting himself round again upon his chest, "because I have the good fortune, D'Arblet, to understand your charming language like a native, absolutely like a native."

"You have a useful proverb in English, which says, that two is company, and three is none," retorts D'Arblet, with a smile.

"I'm awfully sorry, old fellow; but I am so exceedingly comfortable, I really can't get up; if I could oblige you in any other way, I certainly would."

"Come to dinner!" cries out Mrs. Hazeldine, coming towards them from the garden side of the lawn; "we are all here now."

The two men sprang simultaneously to their feet. This is, of course, the moment that they have both been waiting for. Each offers an arm to Miss Nevill; Monsieur D'Arblet bends blandly and smilingly forward; Denis Wilde has a thunder-cloud upon his face, and holds out his arm as though he were ready to knock somebody down with it.

"What am I to do?" cries Vera, laughing, and looking with feigned indecision from one to the other.

"Make haste and decide, my dear," says Mrs. Hazeldine; "for whichever of you two gentlemen does *not* take in Miss Nevill must go and take that eldest Miss Frampton for me."

The eldest Miss Frampton is thirty-five if she is a day; she is large and bony, much given to beads and bangles, and to talking about the military men she has known, and whom she usually calls by their surnames alone, like a man. She goes familiarly amongst her acquaintance by the name of the Dragoon.

A cold shiver passes visibly down Mr. Wilde's back; unfortunately Miss Nevill perceives it, and makes up her mind instantly.

"I would not deprive you of so charming a companion," she says, smiling sweetly at him, and passes her arm through that of the French vicomte.

At dinner, poor Denis Wilde curses Monsieur D'Arblet; Miss Frampton, and his own fate, indiscriminately and ineffectually. He is sitting exactly opposite to his divinity, but he cannot even enjoy the felicity of staring at her, for Miss Frampton will not let him alone. She chatters unceasingly and gushingly. At an early period of the repast the string of her amber-bead necklace suddenly gives way with a snap. The beads trickle slowly down, one by one; half a dozen of them drop with a cracking noise, like little marbles, upon the polished floor, where there is a general scramble of waiters and gentlemen under the table together after them; two fall into her own soup, three more on to Denis Wilde's table-napkin; as fast as the truants are picked up others are shed down in their wake from the four apparently inexhaustible rows that garnish her neck.

Miss Frampton bears it all with serene and smiling good temper.

"Dear me, I am really very sorry to give so much trouble. It doesn't signify in the least, Mr. Wilde—thanks, that is one more. Oh, there goes another into the sweet-breads; but I really don't mind if they are lost. Jameson, of the 17th, gave them to me. Do you know Jameson? cousin of Jameson, in the 9th; he brought them from Italy, or Turkey, or somewhere. I am sure I don't remember where amber comes from; do you, Mr. Wilde?"

Mr. Wilde, if he is vague as to where it comes from, is quite decided as to where he would desire it to go. At this moment he had crunched a tender tooth down upon one of these infernal beads, having helped himself to it unconsciously out of the sweetbread dish.

Is he doomed to swallow amber beads for the remainder of the repast? he asks himself.

"Did you ever meet Archdale, the man who was in the 16th?" continues Miss Frampton, glibly, unconscious of his agonies; "he exchanged afterwards into the 4th—he is such a nice fellow. I lunched every day at Ascot this year on the 16th's drag. The first day I met Lester—that's the major, you know—and Lester is *such* a pet! He told me to come every day to lunch, and bring any of my friends with me; so, of course, I did, and there wasn't a better lunch on the course; and, on the cup-day, Archdale came up and talked to me—he abused the champagne-cup, though; he said there was more soda-water than champagne in it—the more he drank of it the more dreadfully sober he got. However, I am invited to lunch with the 4th at Goodwood. They are going to have a spread under the trees, so I shall be able to compare notes about the champagne-cup. I know two other men in the 4th; Hopkins and Lambert; do you know them?" and so on, until pretty well half the army list and all the luncheon-giving regiments in the service had been passed under review.

And there, straight opposite to him, was Vera, laughing at his discomfiture, he was sure, but also listening to the flattering rubbish which that odious little Frenchman was pouring into her ears.

Did ever young man sit through such a detestable and abominable repast?

If Denis Wilde had been rash enough to nourish insane hopes with regard to moonlight wanderings in the pleasant garden after dinner, these hopes were destined to be blighted.

They were a party of twelve; the waiting was bad, and the courses numerous; the dinner was a lengthy affair altogether. By the time it was over, and coffee had been discussed on the terrace outside the house, the carriages came round to the door, and the ladies of the party voted that it was time to go home.

Soon everybody stood clothed in summer ulsters or white dust-cloaks, waiting in the hall. The coach started from the door with much noise and confusion, with a good deal of plunging from the leaders, and some jibbing from the wheelers, accompanied by a very feeble performance on that much-abused instrument, the horn, by an amateur who occupied a back seat; and after it had departed, a humble train of neat broughams and victorias came trooping up in its wake.

"You will see," said nonentity number one, in her friend's ear; "you will see that Nevill girl will go back in some man's brougham—that is what she has been waiting for; otherwise, she would have perched herself up on the box-seat of the coach, in the most conspicuous place she could find."

"What a disgraceful creature she must be!" is the indignantly virtuous reply.

The "Nevill girl," however, disappointed the expectations of both these charitable ladies by quietly taking her place in Mrs. Hazeldine's brougham, by her friend's side, amid a shower of "Good-nights" from the remainder of the party.

"Ah!" said the nonentity, with a vicious gasp, "you may be sure she has some disreputable supper of men, and cigars, and brandies and sodas waiting for her up in town, or she would never go off so meekly as that in Mrs. Hazeldine's brougham. Still waters run deep, my dear!"

"She is a horrid, disreputable girl, I am quite sure of that," is the answer. "I am very thankful, indeed, that I haven't the misfortune of knowing her."

CHAPTER XXVIII.

MRS. HAZELDINE'S "LONG ELIZA."

Now will I show myself to have more of the serpent than thedove; that is, more knave than fool.

CHRISTOPHER MARLOWE.

For every inch that is not fool is rogue.

DRYDEN.

The scene is Mrs. Hazeldine's drawing-room, in Park Lane, the hour is four o'clock in the afternoon, and the *dramatis personæ* are Miss Nevill, very red in the face, standing in a corner, behind an oblong velvet table covered with china ornaments, and Monsieur Le Vicomte D'Arblet, also red in the face, gesticulating violently on the further side of it.

Miss Nevill, having retired behind the oblong table, purely from prudential motives of personal safety, is devoured with anxiety concerning the too imminent fate of her hostess' china. There is a little Lowestoft tea-service that was picked up only last week at Christie and Manson's, a turquoise blue crackle jar that is supposed to be priceless, and a pair of "Long Eliza" vases, which her hostess loves as much as she does her toy terrier, and far better than she loves her husband.

What will become of her, Vera Nevill, if Mrs. Hazeldine comes in presently and finds these treasures lying in a thousand pieces upon the floor? And yet this is what she is looking forward to, as only too probable a catastrophe.

Vera feels much as must have felt the owner of the proverbial bull in the crockery shop—terror mingled with an overpowering sense of responsibility. All personal considerations are well-nigh merged in the realization of the danger which menaces her hostess' property.

"Monsieur D'Arblet, I must implore you to calm yourself," she says, desperately.

"And how, mademoiselle, I ask you, am I to be calm when you speak of shattering the hopes of my life?" cries the vicomte, who is dancing about frantically backwards and forwards, in a clear space of three square yards, between the different pieces of furniture by which he is surrounded, all equally fragile, and equally loaded with destructible objects.

"*Pray* be careful, Monsieur D'Arblet, your sleeve nearly caught then in the handle of that Chelsea basket," cries Vera, in anguish.

"And what to me are Chelsea baskets, or china, or trash of that kind, when you, cruel one, are determined to scorn me?"

"Oh, if you would only come outside and have it out on the staircase," murmurs Vera, piteously.

"No, I will never leave this room, never, mademoiselle, until you give me hope; never will I cease to importune you until your heart relents towards the *miserable* who adores you!"

Here Monsieur D'Arblet made an attempt to get at his charmer by coming round the end of the velvet table.

Vera felt distracted. To allow him to execute his maneuver was to run the chance of being clasped in his arms; to struggle to get free was the almost certainty of upsetting the table.

She cast a despairing glance across the room at the bell-handle, which was utterly beyond her reach. There was no hope in that direction. Apparently, moral persuasion was her only chance.

"Monsieur D'Arblet, I *forbid* you to advance a step nearer to me!"

He fell back with a profound sigh.

"Mademoiselle, I love you to distraction. I am unable to disobey your commands."

"Very well, then, listen to me. I cannot understand this violent outburst of emotion. You have done me the honour to propose to marry me, and I have, with many thanks for your most flattering distinction, declined your offer. Surely, between a lady and a gentleman, there can be nothing further to say; it is not incumbent upon you to persecute me in this fashion."

"Miss Nevill, you have treated me with a terrible cruelty. You have encouraged my ardent passion for you until you did lift me up to Heaven." Here Monsieur D'Arblet stretched up both his arms with a suddenness which endangered the branches of the tall Dresden candelabra on the high mantelpiece behind him. "After which you do reject me and cast me down to hell!" and down came both hands heavily upon the velvet table between them. The blue crackle jar, the two "Long Eliza" vases, and all the Lowestoft cups and saucers, literally jumped upon their foundations.

"For Heaven's sake!" cried Vera.

"Ah!" in a tone of deep reproach, "do not plead with me, mademoiselle; you have broken my heart."

"And you have nearly broken the china," murmured Vera.

"What is this miserable china that you talk about in comparison with my happiness?" and the vicomte made as though he would tear his hair out with both hands.

The comedy of the situation began to be too much for Vera's self-control; another ten minutes of it, and she felt that she should become hysterical; all the more so because she knew very well that the whole thing was nothing but a piece of acting; with what object, however, she was at a loss to imagine.

"For goodness sake, do be reasonable, Monsieur D'Arblet; you know perfectly well that I never encouraged you, as you call it, for the very good reason that there has never been anything to encourage. We have been very good friends, but never anything more."

"Mademoiselle, you do me injustice."

"On the contrary, I give you credit for a great deal more common sense, as a rule, than you seem disposed to evince to-day. I am quite certain that you have never entertained any warmer feeling towards me than friendship."

This was an injudicious statement. Monsieur D'Arblet felt that his reputation as a *galant homme* and an adorer of the fair sex was impugned; he instantly flew into the most violent passion, and jumped about amongst the gipsy tables and the *étagères*, and the dainty little spindle-legged cabinets more vehemently than ever.

"*I*, not love you! Lucien D'Arblet profess a sentiment which he does not experience! *Ah! par exemple, Mademoiselle, c'est trop fort!* Next you will say that I am a *menteur*, a *fripon*, a *lâche*! You will tell me that I have no honour, and no sense of the generosity due to a woman; that I am a brute and an imbecile," and at every epithet he dashed his hands violently out in front of him, or thrust them wildly through his disordered locks. The whole room shook, every ornament on every table shivered with the strength of his agitation.

"Oh, I will say any single thing you like," cried Vera, "if only you will keep still——"

"Do not insult me by denying my affection!"

"I will deny nothing," said poor Vera, at her wits' ends. "If what I have said has pained you, I am sincerely sorry for it; but for Heaven's sake control yourself, and—and—*do* go away!"

Then Monsieur D'Arblet stood still and looked at her fixedly and mournfully; his hands had dropped feebly by his side, there was an air of profound melancholy in his aspect; he regarded her with a searching intensity. He was asking himself whether his agitation and his despair had produced the very slightest effect upon her; and he came to the conclusion they had not.

"*Peste soit de cette femme!*" he said to himself. "She is the first I ever came across who refused to believe in vows of eternal love. As a rule, women never fail to give them credit, if they are spoken often enough and shouted out loud enough the more one despairs and declares that one is about to expire, the more the dear creatures are impressed, and the more firmly they are convinced of the power of their own charms. But this woman does not believe in me one little bit. Love, despair, rage—it is all the same to her—I might as well talk to the winds! She only wants to get rid of me before her friend comes in, and before I break her accursed china. Ah it is these miserable little pots and jugs that she is thinking about! Very well, then, it is by them that I will do what I want. A great genius can bend to small things as well as soar to large ones—Voyons done, ma belle, which of us will be the victor!"

All this time he was gazing at her fixedly and dejectedly.

"Miss Nevill," he said, gloomily, "I will accept your rejection; to-morrow I will say good-bye to this country for ever!"

"We are all going away this week," said Vera, cheerfully: "this is the end of July. You will come back again next year, and enjoy your season as much as ever."

"Never—never. Lucien D'Arblet will visit this country no more. The words that I am about to speak to you now—the request that I am about to make of you are like the words of a dying man; like the parting desire of one who expires. Mademoiselle, I have a request to make of you."

"I am sure," began Vera, politely, "if there is anything I can do for you——
" She breathed more freely now he talked about going away and dying; it would be much better that he should so go away, and so die, than remain interminably on the rampage in Mrs. Hazeldine's drawing-room. Vera had stood siege for close upon an hour. The moment of her deliverance was apparently drawing near; in the hour of victory she felt that she could afford to be generous; any little thing that he liked to ask of her she would be glad enough to do with a view to expediting his departure. Perhaps he wanted her photograph, or a lock of her hair; to either he would be perfectly welcome.

"There is something I am forced to go away from England without having done; a solemn duty I have to leave unperformed. Miss Nevill, will you undertake to do it for me?"

"Really, Monsieur D'Arblet, you are very mysterious; it depends, of course, upon what this duty is—if it is very difficult, or very unpleasant."

"It is neither difficult nor unpleasant. It is only to give a small parcel to a gentleman who is not now in England; to give it him yourself, with your own hands."

"That does not sound difficult, certainly," said Vera, smiling; after all, she was glad he had not asked for a photograph, or a lock of hair; "but how am I to find this friend of yours?"

"Miss Nevill, do you know a man called Kynaston? Captain Maurice Kynaston?" He was watching her keenly now.

Vera turned suddenly very white: then controlling herself with an effort, she answered quietly.

"Yes, I know him. Why?"

"Because that is the man I want you to give my parcel to." He drew something out of his breast coat-pocket, and handed it to her across the oblong table that was still between them. She took it in her hands, and turned it over doubtfully and uneasily. It was a small square parcel, done up in brown paper, fastened round with string, and sealed at both ends.

It might have been a small book; it probably was. She had no reason to give why she should not do his commission for him, and yet she felt a strange and unaccountable reluctance to undertake it.

"I had very much rather that you asked somebody else to do this for you, Monsieur D'Arblet," she said, handing the packet back to him. He did not attempt to take it from her.

"It concerns the most sacred emotions of my heart, mademoiselle," he said, sensationally. "I could not entrust it to an indifferent person. You, who have plunged me into such an abyss of despair by your cruel rejection of my affection, cannot surely refuse to do so small a thing for me."

Miss Nevill was again looking at the small parcel in her hands.

"Will it hurt or injure Captain Kynaston in any way?" she asked.

"Far from it; it will probably be of great service to him. Come, Miss Nevill, promise me that you will give it to him; any time will do before the end of the year, any time that you happen to see him, or to be near enough to visit him; I only want to be sure that it reaches him. All you have to do is to give it him into his hands when no one else is near. After all, it is a very small favour I ask you."

"And it is precisely because it is so small, Monsieur D'Arblet," said Vera, decidedly, "that I cannot imagine why you should make such a point of a trifle like this; and as I don't like being mixed up in things I don't understand, I must, I think, decline to have anything to do with it."

"*Allons donc!*" said the vicomte to himself. "I am reduced to the china."

He took an excited turn up and down the room, then came back again to where she stood.

"Miss Nevill!" he cried, with rising anger, "you seem determined to wound my feelings and to insult my self-respect. You reject my offers, you sneer at my professions of affection; and now you appear to me to throw sinister doubts upon the meaning of the small thing I have asked you to do for me." At each of these accusations he waved his arm up and down to emphasize his remarks; and now, as if unconsciously, his hand suddenly fell upon the neck of one of the "Long Eliza" vases on the table before him. He lifted it up in the air.

"For Heaven's sake, Monsieur D'Arblet, take care—please put down that vase," cried Vera; suddenly returning to her former terrors.

He looked at the object in his hand as though it were utterly beneath consideration.

"Vase! what is a vase, I ask? Do you not suppose, before relinquishing what I ask of you, I would dash a hundred vases such as this into ten thousand fragments to the earth?" He raised his arm above his head as though on the point of carrying his threat into execution.

Vera uttered a scream.

"Good gracious! What on earth are you doing? It is Mrs. Hazeldine's favourite piece of china; she values it more than anything she has got. If you were to break it, she would go half out of her mind."

"Never mind this wretched vase. Answer me, Mademoiselle Nevill, will you give that parcel to Captain Kynaston?"

"I am not at all likely to meet him; I assure you nothing is so improbable. I know him very little. Ah! what are you doing?"

The infuriated Frenchman was whirling the blue-and-white treasure madly round in the air.

"You are, then, determined to humiliate and to insult me; and to prove to you how great is my just indignation, I will dash——"

"No, no, no!" cried Vera, frantically; "for Heaven's sake, do not be so mad. Mrs. Hazeldine will never forgive me. Put it down, I entreat you. Yes, yes, I will promise anything you like. I am sure I have no wish to insult you."

"Ah, then, you will give that to him?" He paused with the vase still uplifted, looking at her.

Vera felt convinced by this time that she had to do with a raving lunatic. After all, was it not better to do this small thing for him, and to get rid of him. She knew that, sooner or later, down at Sutton, or up in London, she and Maurice were likely to meet. It would not be much trouble to her to place the small parcel in his hands. Surely, to deliver herself from this man—to save Cissy's beloved china, and, perchance, her own throat—for what might he not take a fancy to next!—from the clutches of this madman, it would be easier to do what he wanted.

"Yes, I will give it to him. I promise you, if you will only put that vase down and go away."

"You will promise me faithfully?"

"Faithfully."

"On your word of honour, and as you hope for salvation?"

"Yes, yes. There is no need for oaths; if I have promised, I will do it."

"Very well." He placed the vase back upon the table and walked to the door. "Mademoiselle," he said, making her a low bow, "I am infinitely obliged to you;" and then, without another word, he opened the door and was gone.

Three minutes later Mrs. Hazeldine came in. She was just back from her drive. She found Vera lying back exhausted and breathless in an arm-chair.

"My dear, what have you done to Monsieur D'Arblet? I met him running out of the house like a madman, and laughing to himself like a little fiend. He nearly knocked me down. What has happened! Have you accepted him?"

"No, I have refused him," gasped Vera; "but, thank God, I have saved your 'Long Eliza,' Cissy!"

Early the following morning one of Mrs. Hazeldine's servants was despatched in a hansom with a small brown paper parcel and a note to the Charing Cross Hotel.

During the night watches Miss Nevill had been seized with misgivings concerning the mysterious mission wherewith she had been charged.

But the servant, the parcel, and the note all returned together just as they had been sent.

"Monsieur D'Arblet has left town, Miss; he went by the tidal train last night on his way to the Continent, and has left no address."

So Vera tore up her own note, and locked up the offending parcel in her dressing-case.

CHAPTER XXIX.

A WEDDING TOUR.

Thus Grief still treads upon the heels of Pleasure;
Married in haste, we may repent at leisure.

CONGREVE.

We all know that weddings are as old as the world, but who is it that invented wedding tours? Owing to what delusion were they first instituted?

For a wedding feast there is a reasonable cause, just as there is for a funeral luncheon, or a christening dinner. There has been in each instance a trying ordeal to be gone through in a public church. It is quite right that there should be eating and drinking, and a certain amount of jollification afterwards amongst the unoffending guests who have been dragged in as spectators on the occasion. But why on earth, when the day is over, cannot the unhappy couple be left alone to eat a Darby-and-Joan dinner together in the house in which they propose to live, and return peacefully on the morrow to the avocation of their daily lives? Why must they be sent off amid a shower of rice and shabby satin shoes into an enforced banishment from the society of their fellow-creatures, and so thrown upon each other that, in nine cases out of ten, for want of something better to do, they have learnt the way to quarrel, tooth and nail, before the week is out?

I believe that a great many marriages that are as likely as not to turn out in the end very happily are utterly prevented from doing so by that pernicious and utterly childish custom of keeping up the season known as the honeymoon. "Honey," by the way, is very sweet, doubtless; but there is nothing on earth which sensible people get sooner tired of. Three days of an exclusively saccharine diet is about as much as any grown man or woman can be reasonably expected to stand; after that period there comes upon the jaded appetite unlawful longings after strong meats and anchovies, after turtle-soup and devilled bones, such as no sugar-fed couple has the poetic right to indulge in. Nevertheless, like a snake in the grass, the insidious desire will creep into the soul of one or other of the two. There will be, doubtless, a noble struggle to stifle the treacherous thought; a vigorous effort to bring back the wandering mind into the path of duty; a conscientious effort to go on enjoying honeycomb as though no flavour of richer viands had been wafted to the nostrils of the imagination. The sweet and poetical food will be lifted once more resolutely to the lips, but only to create a sickening satiety from which the nauseated victim finally revolts in desperation. Then come yearnings and weariness, loss of appetite, and consequent loss of temper;

tears on the one side, an oath or two on the other, and the "happy couple" come home eventually very much wiser, as a rule, than they started, and certainly in a position to understand several unpleasant truths concerning each other of which they had not a suspicion before they went away.

Now, if this is too often the melancholy finale to a wedding trip, even with regard to persons who start forth on it full of hopes of happiness, of faith in each other, and of fervent affection on both sides, how much worse is not the case when there are small hopes of happiness, no faith whatever on one side, and of affection none at all on the other?

This was how it was with Captain and Mrs. Maurice Kynaston on their six weeks' wedding trip abroad. They went to a great many places they had neither of them seen before. They stayed a week in Paris, where Helen bought more dresses and declared herself supremely happy; they visited the falls of the Rhine, which Maurice said deafened him; and ran through Switzerland, which they both voted detestably uncomfortable and dirty—the hotels, *bien entendu*, not the mountains. They stopped a night on the St. Gothard, which was too cold for them, and a week or two at the Italian lakes, which were too hot. They sauntered through the picture-galleries of Milan and Turin, at which places Maurice's yawns became prolonged and audible; and they floated through the canals of Venice in gondolas, which Helen asserted to be more ragged and full of fleas than any London four-wheeler. And then they turned homewards, and by the time they neared the shores of the Channel once more they had had so many quarrels that they had forgotten to count them, and they had both privately discovered that matrimony is an egregious and, alas! an irreparable mistake. Such a discovery was possibly inevitable; perhaps they would have come in time to the same conclusion had they remained at home, but they certainly found it out all the quicker for having gone abroad.

Helen, perhaps, was the most to be pitied of the two. For Maurice there had been no illusions to dispel, no dreams to be dissipated, no castles built upon the sand to fall shattered into atoms; he had known very well what he had to expect; he did not love the wife he was marrying, and he did love somebody else. It had not, therefore, been a brilliant prospect of bliss. Nevertheless, he had certainly hoped, with that vague kind of hope in which Englishmen are prone to indulge, that things would "come right" in some fashion, and that he and Helen would manage "to get on" together. That they did not do so was an annoyance, but hardly a surprise to him.

But to Helen there was a good deal of unexpected grief and mortification of soul. She, at all events, had loved him; it was her own strength of will, the fervour of her own lawless passion for him that had carried the day, and had, in the end, made her his wife. And she had said to herself that, once married to him, she would make him love her.

Alas, in love there is no such thing as compulsion! The heart that loves, loves freely, spontaneously, unreasonably; and, where love is dead, there neither entreaties nor prayers, nor yet a whole ocean of tears can serve to re-awaken the frail blossom into life.

But Helen had made sure that, once absolutely her own, once irrevocably separated from the girl whom instinct had taught her to regard as her rival, Maurice would return to the old allegiance, and learn to love her once more, as in days now long gone by.

A very short experience served to convince her of the contrary. Maurice yawned too openly, was too evidently wearied and bored with her society, too utterly indifferent to her sayings and her doings, for her to delude herself long with the hope of regaining his affection. It was all the same to him whatever she did. If she showered caresses upon him, he submitted meekly, it is true, but with so evident a distaste to the operation that she learnt to discontinue the kisses he cared for so little; if she tried to amuse him with her conversation, he appeared to be thinking of other things; if she gave her opinion, he hardly seemed to listen to it. Only when they quarrelled did the slightest animation enter into their conjugal relations; and it was almost better to quarrel than to be at peace on such terms as these.

And then Helen got angry with him; angry and sore, wounded in her heart, and hurt in her vanity. She said to herself that she had been ready to become the best and most devoted of wives; to study his wishes, to defer to his opinion, to surround him with loving attentions; but since he would not have it so, then so much the worse for him. She would be no model wife; no meek slave, subservient to his caprices. She would go her own way, and follow her own will, and make him do what she liked, whether it pleased him or not.

Had Maurice cared to struggle with her for the mastery, things might have ended differently, but it did not seem worth his while to struggle; as long as she let him alone, and did not fret him with her incessant jealousies and suspicions, he was content to let her do as she liked.

Even in that matter of living at Kynaston he learnt, in the end, to give way to her. Sir John, who had already started for Australia, had particularly requested him to occupy the house. Lady Kynaston did nothing but urge it in every letter. Helen herself was bent upon it. There was no good reason that he could bring forward against so reasonable and sensible a plan. The house was all ready, newly decorated, and newly furnished; they had nothing to do but to walk into it. It would save all trouble in looking out for a country home elsewhere, and would, doubtless, be an infinitely pleasanter abode for them than any other house could be. It was the natural and rational thing for them to do. Maurice knew of only one argument against it, and that one was in his own heart, and he could speak of it to no one.

And yet, after all, what did it matter, what difference would it make? A little nearer, a little further, how could it alter things for either of them? How lessen the impassable gulf between her and him? It was in the natural course of things that he must meet her at times; there would be the stereotyped greeting, the averted glance, the cold shake of hands that could never hope to meet without a pang; these things were almost inevitable for them. A little oftener or a little seldomer, would it matter very much then?

Maurice did not think it would; bound as he was to the woman whom he had made his wife—tied to her by every law of God and of man, of honour, and of manly feeling—that there should be any actual danger to be run by the near proximity of the woman he had loved, did not even enter into his head. If he had known how to do his duty towards Helen before he had married her, would he not tenfold know how to do so now? Possibly he over-rated his own strength; for, however high are our principles, however exalted is our sense of honour—after all, we are but mortals, and unspeakably weak at the very best.

It did not in any case occur to him to look at the question from Vera's point of view. It is never easy for a man to put himself into a woman's place, or to enter into the extra sensitiveness of soul with which she is endowed.

So it was that he agreed to go straight back to Kynaston, and to make the old house his permanent home according to his wife's wishes.

It was whilst the newly-married couple were passing through Switzerland on their homeward journey that they suddenly came across Mr. Herbert Pryme, who had been performing a melancholy and solitary pilgrimage in the land of tourists.

It was at the table d'hôte at Vevay, upon coming down to that lengthy and untempting repast, chiefly composed of aged goats and stringy hens, which the inventive Swiss waiter exalts, with the effort of a soaring imagination, into "Chamois," and "Salmi de Poulet," that Captain and Mrs. Kynaston, who had scarcely recovered from a passage of arms in the seclusion of their bed-chamber, suddenly descried a familiar face amongst the long array of uncongenial people ranged down either side of the table.

What the print of a hob-nailed boot must be to the lonely traveller across the desert, what the sight of a man from one's own club going down Pall Mall is in mid-September, or as a draught of Giesler's '68 to an epicure who has been about to perish on ginger-beer—so did Herbert Pryme's face shine upon Maurice Kynaston out of the arid waste of that Vevay *salle-à-manger*.

In England he had been only an acquaintance—at Vevay he became his most intimate friend. The delight of having a man to speak to, and a man who knew others of his friends, was almost intoxicating. To think of getting one evening—nay, one hour of liberty from that ever-present chain of matrimonial intercourse which was galling him so sorely, was a bliss for which he could hardly find words to express his gratitude.

Herbert, who could not quite understand the reason of it, was almost overpowered by the warmth of Captain Kynaston's greeting. To have his place removed next to his own, and to grasp him heartily by both hands, wringing them with affectionate fervour, was the work of a few seconds. And then, who so lively, so full of anecdote and laughter, so interested in all that could be said to him, as Maurice Kynaston during that dinner?

It made Helen angry to hear him. He could be agreeable enough, she thought, bitterly, to a chance acquaintance, picked up nobody knew where; he could find plenty of conversation for this almost unknown young man; it was only when they were alone together that he sat by glumly and silently, without a smile and without a word!

She did not take it into account how surfeited the man was with his honeycomb. Herbert Pryme, individually, was nothing much to him; but he came as the sight of a distant sail is to a shipwrecked mariner. It is doubtful, indeed, whether, under the circumstances, Maurice would not have been equally delighted to have met his tailor or his bootmaker. After dinner was over the two men went out and smoked their cigars together. This was a fresh offence to Mrs. Kynaston; usually she enjoyed an evening stroll with her husband after dinner, but when he asked her to come out with him on this occasion, she refused, shortly and ungraciously.

"No, thank you; if you and Mr. Pryme are going to smoke, I could not possibly come; you know that I hate smoke."

Poor Herbert was about to protest that nothing would induce him to smoke; but Maurice passed his arm hurriedly through his.

"Come along, then, and have a cigar in the garden," he said, with scarcely concealed eagerness; he felt like a schoolboy let out of school.

Helen went up to her bedroom, and sat sulkily by her open window, looking over the lake on to the mountains. Long after it was dark she could see the two red specks of their cigars wandering about like fire-flies in the garden, and could hear the crush of the rough gravel under their footsteps, and the low murmur of their voices as they talked.

"You are coming into Meadowshire, are you not?" asked Maurice, ere they parted.

Herbert shook his head.

"Not to the Millers?"

"No, I am afraid I shall never be asked to Shadonake again," answered the younger man, gloomily.

"Why, I thought you and Beatrice—forgive me—but is it not the case?"

"Her parents have stopped all that, Kynaston."

"But I am sure Beatrice herself will never let it stop; I know her too well," said Maurice, cheerily.

"There are laws in connection with minors," began Mr. Pryme, solemnly.

"Fiddlesticks!" was Maurice's rejoinder. "There are no laws to prevent young women falling in love, or the world would not be in such a confounded muddle as it frequently is. Don't be downhearted, Pryme; you stick to her, and it will all come right; and look here, if they won't ask you to Shadonake, I ask you to Kynaston; drop me a line, and come whenever you like—as soon as you get home."

"You are exceedingly kind; I shall be only too delighted."

"When will you be home?"

"I can be home at any time—there is nothing to keep me."

"Well, then, come as soon as you like, the sooner the better. And now I must say good-night and good-bye too, I fear, for we are off early to-morrow. I shall be glad enough to be home; I'm dead sick of the travelling. Good-night, old fellow; it has been a real pleasure to meet you."

And, positively, this was the only evening out of his whole wedding-trip that Maurice had thoroughly enjoyed.

"What on earth kept you out so late with that solemn young prig?" says his wife to him as he opens her door.

"I find him a very pleasant companion, and I have asked him to come to Kynaston," answers Maurice, shortly.

"Umph!" grunts Helen, and inwardly determines that his visit shall be a short one.

Four days later they were in England again.

It was only when the train had actually stopped at Sutton, and he was handing his wife into her own carriage under the arch of greenery across the road, and amid the ringing cheers of the rustics, who had gathered to see them arrive, that Maurice began to realise how powerfully that home-coming was to be tinged in his own mind with thoughts of her who was once so nearly going as a bride to the same house where now he was taking Helen.

All along the lane, as they drove under the arches of flags and flowers that had been put up from the station to the park gates, and as they responded to the hearty welcome from the village-folk who lined the road, Maurice was asking himself, with a painful anxiety, whether *she* was at Sutton now; whether her eyes had rested upon these rustic decorations, whether her steps had passed along under these mottoes of welcome and of happiness. And then, as they neared the church, the clang of the bells burst forth loudly and jarringly.

Was *she*, perchance, there in the house, kneeling alone, white and stricken by her bedside, whilst those joy-bells rang out their deafening clamour from the church hard by?

For the life of him, Maurice could not help casting a glance at the vicarage as they drove swiftly by it.

The windows were wide open, but no one looked out of them, the muslin blinds fluttered in the wind, the Gloire de Dijon roses nodded upon the wall, the Virginia creeper hung in crimson festoons over the porch; but there was not a living creature to be seen.

He had caught no glimpse of the woman that was ever in his heart; and it was a great pity that he had looked for her, because his wife, whose sharp eyes nothing ever escaped, had seen him look.

CHAPTER XXX.

"IF I COULD DIE!"

Why cannot I forgo, forget
That ever I loved thee, that ever we met?
There is not a single link or sign
To bind thy life in this world with mine.

M. W. Praed.

But it was not until Captain and Mrs. Maurice Kynaston had been at home for more than a fortnight that Vera came back to her brother-in-law's house.

She had kept away, poor girl, as long as she could. She had put off the evil hour of her return as long as possible. The Hazeldines had gone to Scotland, and Vera had, in desperation, accepted an invitation to stay with some acquaintances whom she neither knew very well nor liked overmuch. It had kept her from Sutton a little longer. But the visit had come to an end at last, and what was she to do? She had no other visits to prolong her absence, and her sister wrote to her perpetually, urging her to return. Her home was at Sutton; she had no other place to go to. She had told Sir John that in absence from his brother lay her only hope of safety. But where was she to seek that safety? Where find security, when he; reckless, or, perchance, heedless of her danger, had come to plant himself at her very doors? They should have been far as the poles asunder, and a malevolent fate had willed that the same parish should contain them.

For whatever Maurice did, Vera in no way underrated the danger. Too well she knew her own heart; too surely she estimated the strength of a passion which, repressed and thwarted, and half-smothered, as it had been within her, yet burnt but the fiercer and the wilder. For that is the way with love: if it may not flourish and thrive openly and bravely before the eyes of the world, it will eat into the very heart and life, till all that is fair and sweet in the garden of the soul is choked and blighted and overgrown, till the main-spring of life becomes poisoned, and all things that are happy, withered and dried up.

In Vera's love for Maurice there had been nothing of joy, and all of pain. There had never been for her that sweet illusion of dawning affection—that intangible sense of delight in the consciousness of an unspoken sympathy that is the very essence of a happy love. She had no memories that were serene and untroubled—no days of calm and delicious happiness to recall. His first conscious look had been a terror to her; his words of hopeless love had given her a shock that had been almost physical; and his few passionate kisses had burnt into her very soul till they had seemed to have been printed upon her lips in fire. Vera's love had brought her no good thing that she could count. But it had done one thing for her: if it had cursed her life, it had purified her soul.

The Vera who had come back to Sutton Vicarage in August was no longer the same woman who had stood months ago on the terrace at Kynaston among the falling autumn leaves, and who had told herself that it was money alone that was worth living for.

She came back to everything that was full of pain, and to much in which there was absolute fear.

Five minutes after she had entered the vicarage drawing-room her tortures began.

"You have not asked after the bride and bridegroom," says old Mrs. Daintree, as she sits in her corner, darning everlastingly at those brown worsted socks of her son's. Vera thinks she must have been sitting there darning incessantly, day and night, ever since she had been away. "We are all full of it down here. Such a pretty welcome home they had—arches across the road, and processions with flags, and a band inside the lodge-gates. You should have been here to have seen it. Everybody is making much of Mrs. Kynaston; she is a very pretty woman, I must say, and called here three days ago in the most beautiful Paris gown."

"She seemed very sorry not to see you," says Marion, "and quite disposed to be friendly. I do hope you and she will get on, Vera, in spite of the awkwardness of her being in your place, as it were."

"What do you mean?" rather sharply.

"Only, of course, dear, that it will be rather painful to you just at first to see anybody else the mistress at Kynaston, where you yourself might have been——"

"If you had not been a fool," interpolated the old lady, bluntly.

"I don't think I shall mind that much," says Vera, quietly. "Where is Eustace?"

"Oh, he will be in presently; he has gone up to the Hall about the chancel. The men have made all kinds of mistakes about the tesselated pavement; the wrong pattern was sent down from town, and we have had so much trouble about it, and there has been nobody to appeal to to set things right. Captain Kynaston is all very well, and now he is back, I hope we may get things into a little order; but I am sorry to say he takes very little interest in the church or the parish; he is not half so good a squire as poor dear Sir John." And there was a whole volume of unspoken reproach in the sigh with which Marion wound up her remarks.

"Decidedly," said Vera, to herself, as she went slowly upstairs to her own little room; "decidedly I must get away from all this. I shall have to marry." She leant out of her open window in a frame-work of roses and jessamine, and looked out over the lime-trees towards the Hall. Now that the trees were in full leaf, she could catch no glimpse of its red-stacked chimneys and its terraced gardens; but, by-and-by, when the leaves were down and the trees were bare, she knew she should see it. Every morning when she got up the sun would be shining full upon it; every night when she went to bed she would see the twinkling lights of the many windows gleaming through the darkness; she would be in her room alone, and *he* would be out there, happy with his wife.

"I shall not be able to bear it," said Vera, slowly, speaking aloud to herself. "I had better marry, and go away; there is nothing else to be done. Poor Denis! He is worthy of a better woman; but I think he will be good to me."

For it had come to this now, that when Vera thought about marrying, it was upon Denis Wilde that she also pondered.

To be at Sutton, and not to come face to face with Maurice, was of course an impossibility. Carefully as Vera confined herself to the house and garden for the next three days, she could not avoid going to church when Sunday came. And at church were Captain and Mrs. Kynaston. During the service she only saw his back, erect and broad-shouldered, in the seat in front of her, for the pews had been cleared away, and open sittings had been substituted all through the church. Maurice looked neither to the right nor to the left; he stood, or sat, or knelt, and scarcely turned his head an inch, but Helen's butterfly bonnet was twisted in every direction throughout the service. It is certain that she very soon knew who it was who had come into the vicarage seat behind her.

When Vera came out of church, having purposely lingered as long as she could inside, until the rest of the congregation had all gone out, she found the bride and bridegroom waiting for her in the churchyard.

Helen stood with her hand twined with easy familiarity round her husband's arm; possibly she had studied the attitude with a view to impressing Vera with the perfection of her conjugal happiness. She turned quite delightedly to greet her.

"Oh, here you are at last, Miss Nevill. We have been waiting for you, have we not, Maurice dear? We both felt how pleased we should be to see you. I am very glad you have come back; it will make it much more pleasant for me at Kynaston; you will come up to see me, won't you? I should like you to see my boudoir, it is lovely!"

"You forget that Miss Nevill has seen it all long ago," said Maurice, gravely; their hands had just met, but he had not looked at her.

"Oh, yes, to be sure; how stupid I am! Of course, I remember now, it was all done up for *you* by poor dear old John. Doesn't it seem funny that I should be going to live in the house? Ah, how d'ye do, Mr. Daintree?" as Eustace came out of the vestry door; "here we are, chattering to your sister. What a delightful sermon, dear Mr. Daintree, and what a treat to be in a Christian church—I mean a Protestant church—again after those dreadful Sundays on the Continent."

Vera had turned to Maurice.

"Have you any news of Sir John yet?"

"No; we cannot expect to hear of his arrival till next month. I dare say you will like to hear about him. I will let you know as soon as he writes."

"Thank you; I should like to know about him very much."

Helen, in the middle of Eustace's polite acknowledgment of her compliment to his sermon, was casting furtive glances at her husband; even the two or three grave words he had exchanged with Vera were sufficient to make her uneasy. She desired to torture Vera with envy and with jealousy; she had forgotten to take into account how very easily her own suspicious jealousy could be aroused. She interrupted the vicar in the very middle of his speech.

"Now, really, we must run away. Come, Maurice, darling, we shall be late for lunch; you and Miss Nevill must finish your confidences another day. You will come up soon, won't you? Any day at five I am in—good-bye." She shook hands with them, and hurried her husband away.

"What an odd thing it is that you and that girl never can meet without having all sorts of private things to say to each other," she said, angrily, as soon as they were out of earshot.

"Private things! what can you possibly mean, Helen? Miss Nevill was asking me if I had heard of John's arrival."

"I wonder she has the face to mention John's name!"

"Why, pray?"

"After her disgraceful conduct to him."

"I think you know very little about Miss Nevill's conduct, Helen."

"No, I dare say not. And *you* have always known a great deal more about it than anybody else. That I have always understood, Maurice."

Maurice looked very black, but he was silent.

"I am very glad I told her about the boudoir," continued Helen, spitefully. "How mortified she must feel to think that it has all slipped through her fingers and into mine. I do hope she will come up to the house. I shall show her all over it; she will wish she had not been such a fool!"

Maurice was looking at his wife with a singular expression.

"I begin to think you have a very bad heart, Helen," he said, with a contempt in his voice that was very near akin to disgust.

She looked up, a little startled, and put her hand back, caressingly, under his arm.

"Oh, don't look at me like that, Maurice; I don't want to vex you. You know very well how much I love you—and—and"—looking up with a little smile into his face that was meant as a peace offering—"I suppose I am jealous!"

"Suppose you wait to be jealous until I give you cause to be so," answered her husband, gravely and coldly, but not altogether unkindly, for he meant to do his duty to her, God helping him, as far as he knew how.

But all the way home he walked silently by her side, and wondered whether the sacrifice he had made of his love to his duty had been, indeed, worth it.

It had been hard for him, this first meeting with Vera. He had felt it more than he had believed possible. Instinctively he had realized what she must have suffered; and that her sufferings were utterly beyond his power to console. It began to come into his mind that, meaning to deal rightly by Helen, he had dealt cruelly and badly by Vera. He had sacrificed the woman he loved to the woman he did not love.

Had it, indeed, been such a right and praiseworthy action on his part? Maurice lost himself in speculation as to what would have happened had he broken his faith to Helen, and allowed himself to follow the dictates of his heart rather than those of his conscience.

That was what Vera had done for his sake; but what he had been unable to do for hers.

There was a certain hardness about the man, a rigid sense of honour that was almost a fault; for, if it be a virtue to cleave to truth and good faith above everything, to swear to one's neighbour and disappoint him not—even though it be to one's own hindrance—it is certainly not a fine or noble thing to mistake tenderness for a weakness only fit to be crushed out of the soul with firm hands and an iron determination.

Guilty once of one irreparable action of weakness, Maurice had set himself determinedly ever after to undo the evil that he had done.

To be true to his brother, to keep his faith with Helen, these had been the only objects he had steadily kept in view: he had succeeded in his efforts, but had scarcely realized that, in doing so, he had not only wrecked his own life, but also that of the woman whom he had so infinitely wronged.

But when he saw her once again—when he held for an instant the cold hand within his own—when he marked, with a pang, the dark circles round the averted eyes that spoke so mutely and touchingly of sleepless vigils and of many tears—when he noted how the lovely sensitive lips trembled a little as she spoke her few common-place words to him—then Maurice began to understand what he had done to her; and, for the first time, something that was almost remorse, with regard to his own conduct towards her, came into his soul.

Such meditations were not, however, safe or profitable to indulge in for long. Maurice recalled his wandering thoughts with an effort, and with something of repentance for having given them place, turned his attention resolutely to his wife's chatter during the remainder of the walk home.

Meanwhile Vera and the vicar are walking back, side by side, to the vicarage.

"Something," says Eustace, with solemn displeasure, "something must really be done, and that soon, about Ishmael Spriggs; that man will drive me into my grave before my time! Anything more fearfully and awfully out of tune than the Te Deum I never heard in the whole course of my life. I can hear his voice shouting and bellowing above the whole of the rest of the choir; he leads all the others wrong. It is not a bit of use to tell me that he is the best behaved man in the parish; it is not a matter of conduct, as I told Mr. Dale; it is a matter of voice, and if the man can't be taught to sing in tune, out of the choir he shall go; it's a positive scandal to the Service. Marion says we shall turn him into an enemy if we don't let him sing, and that he will go to the dissenting chapel, and never come to church any more. Well, I can't help that; I must give him up to the dissenters. As to keeping him in the choir, it is out of the question after that Te Deum. I shall never forget it. It will give me a nightmare to-night, I am convinced. Wasn't it dreadful, Vera?"

"Yes, very likely, Eustace," answered Vera, at random. She has not heard one single word he has said.

Eustace Daintree looks round at her sharply. He sees that she is very white, and that there are tears upon her cheeks.

"Why, Vera!" he cries, standing still, you have not listened to a word I have been saying. "What is the matter, child? Why are you crying?"

They are in the vicarage garden now; among the beds of scarlet geraniums, and the tall hollyhocks, and the glaring red gladioli; a whole bank of greenery, rhododendrons and lauristinas, conceals them from the windows of the house; a garden bench sheltered beneath a nook of the laurel bushes is close by.

With a sudden gesture of utter misery Vera sinks down upon it, and bursts into a passion of tears.

"My dear child; my poor Vera! What is it? What has happened? What can be the reason of this?"

Mr. Daintree is infinitely distressed and puzzled; he bends over her, taking her hand between his own. There is something in this wild outburst of grief, from one habitually so calm and self-contained as Vera, that is an absolute shock to him. He had learnt to love her very dearly; he had thought he had understood all the workings of her candid maiden soul; he had fancied that the story of her broken engagement was no secret to him, that it was but the struggle of a conscientious nature after what was true and honest. It had seemed to him that there had been no mystery in her conduct, for he could appreciate all her motives. And surely, as she had done right, she must be now at peace. He had told himself that the pure instincts of a naturally stainless soul had triumphed in Vera over the carelessness and worldliness of her early training; and lo, here was the passionate weeping of a tempest-tossed woman, whose agony he could not fathom, and whose sorrows he knew not how to divine.

"Vera, will you not tell me?" he asked her, in his distress. "Will you not make a friend of me? My dear, forget that I am a clergyman; remember only that I am your brother, and that I shall know how to feel for you—for you, my dear sister."

But she could not tell him. There are some troubles that must be kept for ever buried within our own souls; to speak of some things is only to make them worse. Only she choked back her sobs, and lifted her face, white and tear-stained; there was a look of hunted despair in her eyes, that bewildered, and even half-terrified him.

"Tell me," she said, with a sort of anger, "tell me, you that are a clergyman— Do you think God has made us only to torment us? You have got a daughter, Eustace; pray God, night and morning, that she may have a hard heart, and that she may never have one gleam of womanly tenderness within her; for only so are women happy!"

He did not answer her wild words. Instinctively he felt that common-place speeches of rebuke or of consolation would be trivial and out of place before the great anguish of her heart. The man's soul was above the narrow limits of his training; he felt, dimly, that here was something with which it were best not to intermeddle, some trouble for which he could offer no consolation.

She rose and stood before him, holding his hands and gazing earnestly at his anxious face.

"It has come to this with me," she said, below her voice, "that there are times when there is but one good thing in all the world that I know any longer how to desire. God has so ordered my life that there is no road open for me that does not lead to sin or to misery. Surely, if He were merciful, He would take back the valueless gift."

"Vera! what do you mean?"

"I mean," she exclaimed, wearily, "that if I could die, I should be at peace."

She had walked slowly on; her voice, that had trembled at first with a passionate wildness, had sunk into the spiritless apathy of despair; her head was bent, her hands clasped before her; her dress trailed with a soft rustle across the grass, sweeping over a whole wilderness of white daisies, that bent their heads beneath its folds as she walked. A gleam of sunshine fell upon her hair, and a bird sang loud and shrill in the lime trees overhead.

Often and often, in the after days, Eustace Daintree thought of her thus, and remembered with a pang the sole sad gift that she had craved at Heaven's hands. Often and often the scene came back to him; the sunny garden, the scarlet geraniums flaring in the borders, the smooth green lawn, speckled with shadows from the trees, the wide open windows of his pleasant vicarage beyond, and the beautiful figure of the girl at his side, with her bent head, and her low broken voice—the girl who, at twenty-three, sighed to be rid of the life that had become too hard for her; that precious gift of life which, too often, at three-score years and ten, is but hardly resigned!

"If I could die, I should be at peace," she had said. And she was only twenty-three!

Eustace Daintree never forgot it.

CHAPTER XXXI.

AN EVENTFUL DRIVE.

Ill blows the wind that profits nobody.

SHAKESPEARE, "Henry IV."

I imagine that the most fretting and wearing of all the pains and penalties which it is the lot of humanity to undergo in this troublesome and naughty world are those which, by our own folly, our own shortsightedness, and our own imprudence, we have brought upon ourselves.

There is a degree of irritation in such troubles which adds a whole armoury of small knife-cuts to intensify the agony of the evil from which we suffer. It is more dreadful to be moaning over our own mistakes than over the inscrutable perversity of an unpropitious fate.

Somebody once has said that most men grieve over the smallest mistake more bitterly than over the greatest sin. This is decidedly a perversion of the moral nature; nevertheless, there is a good deal of truth in it.

"If only I had not been such a fool! If I could only have foreseen such and such results?"

These are more generally the burden of our bitterest self-reproaches.

And this was what Miss Miller was perpetually repeating to herself during the months of August and September. Beatrice, in these days, was a thoroughly miserable young woman. She was more utterly separated than ever from her lover, and that entirely by her own fault. That foolish escapade of hers to the Temple had been fatal to her; her father, who had been inclined to become her lover's friend, had now peremptorily forbidden her ever to mention his name again, and her own lips were sealed as to the unlucky incident in which she had played so prominent a part.

Beatrice knew that, in going alone and on the sly to her lover's chambers, she had undoubtedly compromised her own good name. To confess to her own folly and imprudence was almost beyond her power, and to clear her lover's name at the expense of her own was what she felt he himself would scarcely thank her for.

Mr. Miller had, of course, said something of what he had discovered at Mr. Pryme's chambers to the wife of his bosom.

"The young man is not fit for her," he had said; "his private life will not bear investigation. You must tell Beatrice to put him out of her head."

Mrs. Miller had, of course, been virtuously indignant over Mr. Pryme's offences, but she had also been triumphantly elated over her own sagacity.

"Did I not tell you he was not a proper husband for her? Another time, Andrew, you will, I hope, allow that I am the best judge in these matters."

"My dear, you are always right," was the meekly conjugal reply, and then Mrs. Miller went her way and talked to Beatrice for half-an-hour over the sinful lives which are frequently led by young men of no family residing in the Temple, and the shame and disgrace which must necessarily accrue to any well-brought-up young woman who, in an ill-advised moment, shall allow her affections to rove towards such unsanctified Pariahs of society.

And Beatrice, listening to her blushingly, knew what she meant, and yet had no words wherewith to clear her lover's character from the defamatory evidence furnished against him by her own sunshade and gloves.

"Your father has seen with his own eyes, my dear, that which makes it impossible for us ever to consent to your marrying that young man."

How was Beatrice to say to her mother, "It was I—your daughter—who was there, shut up in Mr. Pryme's bedroom." She could not speak the words.

The sunshine twinkled in Shadonake's many windows, and flooded its velvet lawns. Below, the Bath slumbered darkly in the shadow of its ancient steps and its encircling belt of fir-trees; and beyond the flower-gardens, half-an-acre of pineries, and vineries, and orchard-houses glittered in a dazzling parterre of glass-roofs and white paint. Something new—it was an orchard-house—was being built. There was always something new, and Mr. Miller was superintending the building of it. He stood over the workmen who were laying the foundation, watching every brick that was laid down with delighted and absorbed interest. He held a trowel himself, and had tucked up his shirt cuffs in order to lend a helping hand in the operations. There was nothing that Andrew Miller loved so well. Fate and his Caroline had made him a member of Parliament, and had placed him in the position of a gentleman, but nature had undoubtedly intended him for a bricklayer.

Beatrice came out of the drawing-room windows across the lawn to him. She was in her habit, and stood tapping her little boot with her riding whip for some minutes by her father's side.

"I am going to see uncle Tom, papa," she said; "have you any message?"

"Going to Lutterton? Ah, that's right; the ride will do you good, my dear. No; I have no message."

Beatrice went back into the house; her little bay mare stood at the door. She met her mother in the hall.

"I am going to see uncle Tom," she said, to her also.

Mrs. Miller always encouraged her children in their attentions to her brother. He was rich, and he was a bachelor; he must have saved a good deal one way or another. Who could tell how it would be left? And then Beatrice was undoubtedly his favourite. She nodded pleasantly to her daughter.

"Tell uncle Tom to come over to lunch on Sunday, and, of course, he must come here early for Guy's birthday next week," for there were to be great doings on Guy's birthday. "Ride slowly, Beatrice, or you will get so hot."

Lutterton Castle was a good six miles off. The house stood well, and even imposingly, on a high wooded knoll that overlooked the undulating park, and the open valley at its feet. It was a great rambling building with a central tower and four smaller ones at each corner. When Mr. Esterworth was at home, which was almost always, it was his vanity to keep a red flag flying from the centre tower as though he had been royalty. All the reception-rooms and more than half the bedrooms were permanently shuttered up, and there was a portly and very dignified housekeeper, who rattled her keys at her châtelaine, and went through all the unused apartments daily, followed by a meek phalanx of housemaids, to see that all the rooms were well-aired and well kept in order, so that at any minute they might be fit for occupation. Five or six times during the hunting season the large rooms were all thrown open, and there was a hunt breakfast held in the principal dining-hall; but, with that exception, Mr. Esterworth rarely entertained at all.

He occupied three rooms opening out of each other in the small western tower. They consisted of a bedroom, a dressing-room, and a small and rather inconvenient study, where the huntsman, whips, and other official personages connected with the hunt were received at all hours of the day and night. The room was consequently pervaded by a faint odour of stables and tobacco; there were usually three or four dogs upon the hearthrug, and it was a rare thing to find Mr. Esterworth in it unaccompanied by some personage in breeches and gaiters, wearing a blue spotted neckcloth and a horseshoe pin.

Such an individual was receiving an audience at the moment of Miss Miller's arrival, and shuffled awkwardly and hurriedly out of the room by one door as she entered it by another.

"All right, William," calls the M.F.H. after his departing satellite. "Look in again to-night. I shall have her fired, I think, and throw her up till December. Hallo! Pussy, how are you?"

All the four dogs rose from the hearthrug and wagged their tails solemnly in respectful greeting to her. Beatrice had a pat and a word for each, and a kiss for her uncle, before she sat down on the chair he pulled forward for her.

"What brings you, Pussy? What are you riding?"

"Kitty; they have taken her round to the stable. I thought I'd have lunch with you, uncle Tom."

"Very well; you won't get anything but a mutton-chop."

"I don't ask for anything better."

Beatrice felt that her heart was beating. She had taken a desperate resolution during her six miles' solitary ride; she had determined to take her uncle into her confidence. He had always been indulgent and kind to her; perhaps he would not view her sin in so heinous a light as her mother would; and who knows? perhaps he would help her.

"Uncle Tom, I'm in dreadful trouble, and I want to tell you about it," she began, trembling.

"I'm very sorry, Pussy; what is it?"

"I did a shocking, dreadful thing when I was in London. I went to a young man's rooms, and got shut up in his bedroom."

"The deuce you did!" says Tom Esterworth, opening his eyes.

"Yes," continues Beatrice, desperately, and crimson with shame and confusion; "and the worse of it is, that I left my sunshade in the sitting-room; and papa came in, and, of course, he did not know it was mine, and—and—he thinks—he thinks———"

"That's the best joke I ever heard in my life!" cries Mr. Esterworth, laying his head back in the chair and laughing aloud.

"Uncle Tom!" Beatrice could hardly believe her ears.

"Good lord, what a situation for a comedy!" cries her uncle, between the outbursts of his mirth. "Upon my word, Pussy, you are a good plucked one; there isn't much Miller blood in your veins. You are an Esterworth all over."

"But, uncle, indeed, it's no laughing matter."

"Well, I don't see much to cry at if your father did not find you out; the young man is never likely to talk."

"Oh, but uncle Tom; papa and mamma think so badly of him, and I can't tell them that I was there; and they will never let me marry him."

"Oh! so you are in love, Pussy?"

"Yes, uncle."

Tom Esterworth smote his hand against his corduroy thigh.

"What a mistake!" he exclaimed; "a girl who can go across country as you do—what on earth do you want to be married for? Is it Mr. Pryme, Pussy?"

Beatrice nodded.

"And he can't go a yard," said her uncle, sorrowfully and reproachfully.

"Oh, I think he goes very well, uncle; his seat is capital; it is only his hands that are a bit heavy; but then he has had very little practice."

"Tut—tut, don't talk to me, child; he is no horseman. He may be a good young man in his way, but what can have made you take a fancy to a fellow who can't ride is a mystery to me! Now tell me the whole story, Pussy."

And then Beatrice made a clean breast of it.

"I will see if I can help you," said her uncle, seriously, when she had finished her story; "but I can't think how you can have set your heart upon a fellow who can't ride!"

This was evidently a far more fatal error in Tom Esterworth's eyes than the other matter of her being shut up in Mr. Pryme's rooms. Beatrice began to think she had not done anything so very terrible after all.

"I must turn it over in my mind. Now come and eat your mutton-chop, Pussy, and when we have finished our lunch, you shall come out with me in the dog-cart. I am going to put Clochette into harness for the first time."

"Will she go quietly?"

"Like a lamb, I should say. You won't be nervous?"

"Dear, no! I am never nervous; I shall enjoy the fun."

The mutton-chop over, Clochette and the dog-cart came round to the door. She was a raking, bright chestnut mare, with a coat like satin. Even as she stood at the door she chafed somewhat at her new position between the shafts. This, however, was no more than might have been expected. Mr. Esterworth declining the company of the groom, helped his niece up and took the reins.

"We will go round by Tripton and back by the common," he said, "and talk this matter well over, Pussy; we shall enjoy ourselves much better with nobody in the back seat. A man sits there with his arms crossed and his face like a blank sheet of paper, but one never knows how much they hear, and their ears are always cocked, like a terrier's on the scent of a rat."

Clochette went off from the door with a bound, but soon settled down into a good swinging trot. She kept turning her head nervously from side to side, and there was evidently a little uncertainty in her mind as to whether she should keep to the drive, or deviate on to the grass by the side of it; but, upon the whole, she behaved fairly well, and turned out of the lodge gates into the high road with perfect docility and good breeding.

There was a whole avalanche of dogs in attendance. A collie, rushing on tumultuously in front; a "plum-pudding" dog between the wheels; a couple of fox-terriers snapping joyfully at each other in the rear; and there was also an ill-conditioned animal—half lurcher, half terrier—who killed cats, and murdered fowls, and worried sheep, and flew at the heels of unwary strangers; and was given, in short, to every sort of canine iniquity, and who possessed but one redeeming feature in his character—that of blind adoration to his master.

This animal, who followed uncle Tom whithersoever he went, came skurrying out of the stables as the dog-cart drove off, and joined in the general scamper.

Perhaps the dogs may have been too much for Clochette's nerves, or perhaps the effort of behaving well as far as the park gates with those horrible wheels rattling behind her was as much as any hunter born and bred could be expected to do, or perhaps uncle Tom was too free with that whip with which he caressed her shining flanks; but be that as it may, no sooner was Clochette's head well turned along the straight high-road with its high-tangled hedge-rows on either side than she began to show symptoms of behaving very badly indeed. She bucked and pranced, and stood on her hind legs; she whipped suddenly round, pirouetted upon her own axis with the dexterity of a circus performer, and demonstrated very plainly that, if she only dared, she would like to take to her heels in the reverse direction to that which her driver desired her to go.

All this was, however, equally delightful and exciting both to Tom Esterworth and his niece. There was no apprehension in Beatrice's mind, for her uncle drove as well as he rode, and she felt perfectly secure in the strong, supple hands that guided Clochette's erratic movements.

"There is not a kick in her," uncle Tom had said, as they started, and he repeated the observation now; and kicking being out of the category of Clochette's iniquities, there was nothing else to fear.

No sooner, however, had the words left his lips than a turn of the road brought them within sight of a great volume of black smoke rushing slowly but surely towards them; whilst a horrible roaring and howling, as of an antediluvian monster in its wrath, filled the silence of the summer afternoon with a hideous and unholy confusion.

Talk about there being no wild animals in our peaceful land! What could have been the Megatherium and the Ichthyosaurus, and all the fire-spitting dragons of antiquity compared to the traction engines of the nineteenth century?

"It's a steam plough!" ejaculated Beatrice, below her breath.

"D——n!" cried her uncle, not at all below *his* breath.

As to Clochette, she stood for an instant stock still, with her ears pricked and her head well up, facing the horrors of her situation; next she gave an angry snort as though to say, "No! *this* is too much!" Then she turned short round and began a series of peculiar bounds and plunges, accompanied by an ominous uplifting of her hind quarters, which had plainly but one object in view—the correct conjugation of the verb active "to kick."

There was a crunching of woodwork, a cracking as of iron hoofs against the splash-board. Beatrice instinctively put up her hands before her face, but she did not utter a sound.

"Do you think you could get down, Pussy, and go to her head?"

"Shall I hold the reins, uncle?"

"No, you couldn't hold her; she'll be over the hedge if I let go of her. Get down if you can."

It was not easy. Beatrice was in her habit, and to jump from the vacillating height of a dog-cart to the earth is no easy matter even to a man unencumbered with petticoats.

"Try and get over the back," said her uncle, who was in momentary terror lest the mare's heels should be dashed into her face. And Beatrice, with that finest trait of a woman's courage in danger, which consists in doing exactly what she is told, began to scramble over the back of her seat.

The situation was critical in the extreme; the traction engine came on apace, the man with the red flag having paused at a public-house round the corner, was only now running back into his place. Uncle Tom shouted vainly to him; his voice was drowned in the deafening roar of the advancing monster.

But already help was at hand, unheard and unperceived by either uncle or niece; a horseman had come rapidly trotting up the road behind them. To spring from his horse, who was apparently accustomed to traction engines, and stood quietly by, to rush to the plunging, struggling mare, and to seize her by the head was the work of a moment.

"All right, Mr. Esterworth," shouted the new comer. "I can hold her if you can get down; we can lead her into the field; there is a gate ten yards back."

Uncle Tom threw the reins to his niece and slipped to the ground; between them the two men contrived to quiet the terrified Clochette, and to lead her towards the gate.

In another three minutes they were all safely within the shelter of the hedge. The traction engine passed, snorting forth fire and smoke, on its devastating way; and Clochette stood by, panting, trembling, and covered with foam. Beatrice, safely on the ground, was examining ruefully the amount of damage done to the dog-cart, and Mr. Esterworth was shaking hands with his deliverer.

It was Herbert Pryme.

"That's the last time I ever take a lady out, driving without a man-servant behind me," quoth the M.F.H. "What we should have done without your timely assistance, sir, I really cannot say; in another minute she would have kicked the trap into a thousand bits. You have saved my niece's life, Mr. Pryme."

"Indeed, I did very little," said Herbert, modestly, glancing at Beatrice who was trembling and rather pale; but, perhaps, that was only from her recent fright. She had not spoken to him, only she had given him one bewildered glance, and then had looked hastily away.

"You have saved her life," repeated Mr. Esterworth, with decision. "I hope you do not mean to contradict my words, sir? You have saved Beatrice's life, sir, and it's the most providential thing in this world for you, as Clochette very nearly kicked her to pieces under your nose. I shall tell Mr. and Mrs. Miller that they are indebted to you for their daughter's life. Young people, I am going to lead this brute of a mare home, and, if you like to walk on together to Lutterton in front of me, why you may."

That was how Herbert Pryme came to be once more re-instated in the good graces of his lady love's father and mother.

Mr. Esterworth contrived to give them so terrifying an account of the danger in which Beatrice had been placed, and so graphic and highly-coloured a description of Herbert Pryme's pluck and sagacity in rushing to her rescue, that Mr. and Mrs. Miller had no other course left than to shake hands gratefully with the man to whom, as uncle Tom said, they literally owed her life.

"I could not have saved her without him," said uncle Tom, drawing slightly upon his imagination; "in another minute she must have been kicked to pieces, or dashed violently to the earth among the broken fragments of the cart, and"—with a happy after-thought—"the steam plough would have crushed its way over her mangled body."

Mrs. Miller shuddered.

"Oh, Tom, I never can trust her to you again!"

"No, my dear; but I think you must trust her to Mr. Pryme; that young man deserves to be rewarded."

"But, my dear Tom, there are things against his character. I assure you, Andrew himself saw——"

"Pooh! pooh!" interrupted Mr. Esterworth. "Young men who sow their wild oats early are all the better husbands for it afterwards. I will give him a talking to if you like, but you and your husband must let Pussy have her own way; it is the least you can do after his conduct; and don't worry about his being poor, Caroline; I have nothing better to do with my money, and I shall take care that Pussy is none the worse off for my death. She is worth all the rest of your children put together—an Esterworth, every inch of her!"

That, it is to be imagined, was the clenching argument in Mrs. Miller's mind. Uncle Tom's money was not to be despised, and, by reason of his money, uncle Tom's wishes were bound to carry some weight with them.

Mr. Pryme, who had been staying for a few days at Kynaston, where, however, the cordial welcome given to him by its master was, in a great measure, neutralised by the coldness and incivility of its mistress, removed himself and his portmanteau, by uncle Tom's invitation, to Lutterton, and his engagement to Miss Miller became a recognised fact.

"All the same, it is a very bad match for her," said Mrs. Miller, in confidence, to her husband.

"And I should very much like to know who that sunshade belonged to," added the M.P. for Meadowshire, severely.

"I think, my dear, we shall have to overlook that part of the business, for, as Tom will leave them his money, why——"

"Yes, yes, I quite understand; we must hope the young man has had a good lesson. Let bygones be bygones, certainly," and Mr. Miller took a pinch of snuff reflectively, and wondered what Tom Esterworth would "cut up for."

"But I am *determined*," said Mrs. Miller, ere she closed the discussion, "I am determined that I will do better for Geraldine."

After all, the mother had a second string to her bow, so the edict went forth that Beatrice was to be allowed to be happy in her own way, and the shadow of that fatal sunshade was no longer to be suffered to blacken the moral horizon of her father's soul.

CHAPTER XXXII.

BY THE VICARAGE GATE.

Before our lives divide for ever,
While time is with us and hands are free,
(Time swift to fasten, and swift to sever Hand from hand....)
I will say no word that a man might say
Whose whole life's love goes down in a day;
For this could never have been. And never
(Though the gods and the years relent) shall be.

SWINBURNE.

The peacocks had it all to themselves on the terrace walk at Kynaston. They strutted up and down, craning and bridling their bright-hued necks with a proud consciousness of absolute proprietorship in the place, and their long tails trailed across the gravel behind them with the soft rustle of a woman's garments. Now and then their sad, shrill cries echoed weirdly through the deserted gardens.

There was no one to see them—the gardeners had all gone home—and no one was moving from the house. Only one small boy, with a rough head and a red face, stood below the stone balustrade, half-hidden among the hollyhocks and the roses, looking wistfully up at the windows of the house.

"What am I to do with it?" said Tommy Daintree, half-aloud to himself, and looked sorely perplexed and bewildered.

Tommy had a commission to fulfil, a commission from Vera. He carried a little note in his hands, and he had promised Vera faithfully that he would wait near the house till he saw Captain Kynaston come in from his day's shooting, and give him the note into his own hands.

"You quite understand, Tommy; no one else."

"Yes, auntie, I quite understand."

And Tommy had been waiting there an hour, but still there was no sign of Captain Kynaston's return; he was getting very tired and very hungry by this time, for he had had no tea. He had heard the dressing-bell ring long ago in the house—it must be close upon their dinner hour. Tommy could not guess that, by an unaccustomed chance, the master of the house had gone in by the back-door to-day, and that he had been in some time.

Presently some one pushed aside the long muslin curtains, and came stepping out of the long French window on to the terrace. It was Helen.

She was dressed for dinner; she wore a pale blue dress, cut open at the neck, a string of pearls and a jewelled locket hung at her throat; she turned round, half laughing, to some one who was following her.

"You will see all the county magnates at Shadonake to-morrow. You will have quite enough of them, I promise you; they are neither lively nor entertaining."

A young man, also in evening dress, had followed her out on to the terrace; it was Denis Wilde; he had arrived from town by the afternoon train. Why he should have thrown over several very good invitations to country houses in Norfolk and Suffolk, where there were large and cheerful parties gathered together, and partridge shooting to make a man dream of, in order to come down to the poor sport of Kynaston and the insipid society of a newly married couple, with whom he was not on very intimate terms, is a problem which Mr. Wilde alone could have satisfactorily solved. Being here, he was naturally disposed to make himself extremely agreeable to his hostess.

"You can't think how anxious I am to inspect the *élite* of Meadowshire!" he said, laughing. "My life is an incomplete thing without a sight of it."

"You will witness the last token of mental aberration in a decently-brought up young woman in the person of Beatrice Miller. You know her. Well, she has actually engaged herself to a barrister whom nobody knows anything about, and who—*bien entendu*—has no briefs—they never have any. He was staying here for a couple of days; a slow, heavy young man, who quoted Blackstone. Maurice took a fancy to him abroad; however, he was clever enough to save Beatrice's life by stopping a run-away horse. Some people say the accident was the invention of the lovers' own imaginations; however, the parents believed in it, and it turned the scales in his favour; but he has taken himself off, I am thankful to say, and is staying at Lutterton with her uncle. Beatrice might have married well, but girls are such fools. Hallo, Topsy, what are you barking at?"

Mrs. Kynaston's pug had come tearing out of the house with a whole chorus of noisy yappings. The peacocks, deeply wounded in their tenderest feelings, instantly took wing, and went sailing away majestically over the crimson and gold parterre of flowers below.

"What can possess her to bark at the peacocks?" said Helen. "Be quiet, Topsy."

But Topsy refused to be tranquillized.

"She is barking at something below the terrace; perhaps there is a cat there," said Denis.

"If so, it would be Dutch courage, indeed," answered Helen, laughing. They went to the edge of the stone parapet and looked over; there stood Tommy Daintree below them, among the hollyhocks.

"Why, little boy, who are you, and what do you want? Why, are you not Mr. Daintree's little boy?"

"Yes."

"Then what are you waiting for?"

"I want to give a note to Captain Kynaston," said Tommy, crimson with confusion. "Is he ever coming in?"

"He is in now; give me the note."

"I was to give it to himself, to nobody else."

"Who told you?"

"Aunt Vera."

"Oh!" There was a whole volume of meaning in the simple exclamation. Mrs. Kynaston held out her hand. "You can give it to me, I am Captain Kynaston's wife, you know. Give it to me, Tommy. Your name is Tommy, isn't it? Yes, I thought so. Mr. Wilde, will you be so kind as to fetch Tommy a peach off the dinner-table? Give the note to me, my dear, and you can tell your aunt that it shall be given to Captain Kynaston directly."

When Denis returned from his mission to the dining-room he only found Tommy waiting for his peach upon the terrace steps. Mrs. Kynaston had gone back into the house.

Tommy went off devouring his prey with, it must be confessed, rather a guilty conscience over it. Somehow or other, he felt that he had failed in the trust his aunt had placed in him; but then, Mrs. Kynaston had been very kind and very peremptory; she had almost taken the letter out of his hand, and she had smiled and looked quite like a fairy princess out of one of Minnie's story-books in her pretty blue silk dress and shining locket—and then, peaches were so very nice!

What happened to Denis Wilde after the small boy's departure was this. He sauntered back to the drawing-room windows and looked in; no one was there. He then wandered further down the terrace till he came opposite the window of the boudoir—Mrs. Kynaston's own boudoir—which Sir John's loving hands had once lined with blue and silver for his Vera. Here he caught sight of Mrs. Kynaston's fair head and slender figure. Her back was turned to him; he was on the point of calling out to her, when suddenly the words upon his lips were arrested by something which he saw her doing. Instead of speaking, he simply stood still and stared at her.

Mrs. Kynaston, unconscious of observation, held the note which Tommy had just given her over the steam of a small jug of hot water, which she had hastily ordered her maid to bring to her. In less than a minute the envelope unfastened of itself. Helen then deliberately took out the note and read it.

What she read was this:—

"Dear Captain Kynaston,—I have something that I have promised to give to you when you are alone. Would you mind coming round to the vicarage after dinner to-night, at nine o'clock? You will find me at the gate.—Sincerely yours,

"VERA NEVILL."

Then Helen lit a candle, and fastened the letter up again with sealing-wax.

And Denis Wilde crept away from the window on tip-toe with a sense of shocked horror upon him such as he never remembered having experienced in his life before.

All at once his pretty, pleasant hostess, with whom he had been glad enough to banter, and with whom even he had been ready to enter upon a mild and innocent flirtation, became horrible and hateful to him; and there came into his mind, like an inspiration, the knowledge of her enmity to Vera; for it was Vera's note that she had opened and read. Then his instincts were straightway all awake with the acuteness of a danger, to something—he knew not what—that threatened the woman he loved.

"Thank God, I am here," he said to himself. "That woman is her foe, and she will be dangerous to her. I would not have come to her house had I known it; but now I am here, I will stay, for it is certain that she will need a friend."

At dinner-time the note lay by Maurice's side on the table. Whilst the soup was being helped he took it up and opened it. He little knew how narrowly both his wife and his guest watched him as he read it.

But his face was inscrutable. Only he talked a little more, and seemed, perhaps, in better spirits than usual; but that is what a stranger could not have noticed, although it is possible that Helen may have done so.

"By the vicarage gate," she had said, and it was there that he found her. Behind her lay the dark and silent garden, beyond it the house, with its wide-open drawing-room windows, and the stream of yellow light from the lamp within, lying in a golden streak across the lawn. She leant over the gate; an archway of greenery, dark in the night's dim light, was above her head, and clusters of pale, creamy roses hung down about her on every side.

It was that sort of owl's light that has no distinctness in it, and yet is far removed from darkness. Vera's perfect figure, clad in some white, clinging garment that fell about her in thick, heavy folds, stood out with a statue-like clearness against the dark shrubs behind her. She seemed like some shadowy queen of the night. Out of the dimness, the clear oval of her perfect face shone pale as the waning moon far away behind the church tower, whilst the dusky veil of her dark hair lost itself vaguely in the shadows, and melted away into the background. A poet might have hymned her thus, but no painter could have painted her.

And it was thus that he found her. For the first time for many weary weeks and months he was alone with her; for the first time he could speak to her freely and from his heart. He knew not what it was that had made her send for him, or why it was that he had come. He did not remember her note, or that she had said that she had something for him. All he knew was, that she had sent for him, and that he was with her.

There was the gate between them, but her white soft hands were clasped loosely together over the top of it. He took them feverishly between his own.

"I am late—you have waited for me, dear? Oh, Vera, how glad I am to be with you!"

There was a dangerous tenderness in his voice that frightened her. She tried to draw away her hands.

"I had something for you, or I should not have sent—please, Captain Kynaston—Maurice—please let my hands go."

He was alone under the star-flecked heavens with the woman he loved, there was all the witchery of the pale moonlight about her, all the sweet perfumes of the summer night to intensify the fascination of her presence. There was a nameless glamour in the luminous dimness—a subtle seduction to the senses in the silence and the solitude; a bird chirruped once among the tangled roses overhead, and a soft, sighing breeze fluttered for one instant amid its long, trailing branches. And then, God knows how it came to pass, or what madness possessed the man; but suddenly there was no longer any faith, or honour, or truth for him—nothing on the face of the whole earth but Vera.

He caught her passionately in his arms, and showered upon her lips the maddest, wildest kisses that man ever gave to woman.

For one instant she lay still upon his heart; all the fury of her misery was at rest—all the storm of her sorrow was at peace—for one instant of time she tasted of life's sublimest joy ere the waters of blackness and despair closed in once more over her soul. For one instant only—then she remembered, and withdrew herself shudderingly from his grasp.

"For God's sake, have pity upon me, Maurice!" she wailed. It was the cry of a broken heart that appealed to his manhood and his honour more surely and more directly than a torrent of reproach or a storm of indignation.

"Forgive me," he murmured, humbly; "I am a brute to you. I had forgotten myself. I ought to have spared you, sweet. See, I have let you go; I will not touch you again; but it was hard to see you alone, to be near you, and yet to remember how we are parted. Vera, I have ruined your life; it is wonderful that you do not hate me."

"A true woman never hates the man who has been hard on her," she answered, smiling sadly.

"If it is any comfort to you to know it, I too am wretched; now it is too late: I know that my life is spoilt also."

"No; why should that comfort me?" she said, wearily. She leant half back against the gate—if he could have seen her well in the uncertain light, he would have been shocked at the worn and haggard face of his beautiful Vera.

Presently she spoke again.

"I am sorry that I asked you to come—it was not wise, was it, Maurice? How long must you stop at Kynaston? Can you not go away? We are neither of us strong enough to bear this—I, I cannot go—but you, *must* you be always here?"

"Before God," he answered, earnestly, "I swear to you that I will go away if it is in my power to go."

"Thank you." Then, with an effort, she roused herself to speak to him: "But that is not what I wanted to say; let me tell you why I sent for you. I made a promise, a wretched, stupid thing, to a tiresome little man I met in London— a Monsieur D'Arblet, a Frenchman; do you know him?"

"D'Arblet! I never heard the name in my life that I know of."

"Really, that seems odd, for I have a little parcel from him to you, and, strangely enough, he made me promise on my word of honour to give it to you when no one was near. I did not know how to keep my promise, for, though we may sometimes meet in public, we are not often likely to meet alone. I have it here; let me give it to you and have done with the thing; it has been on my mind."

She drew a small packet from her pocket, and was about to give it to him, when suddenly his ear caught the sound of an approaching footstep; he looked nervously round, then he put forth his hand quickly and stopped her.

"Hush, give me nothing now!" he said, in a low, hurried voice. "To-morrow we shall meet at Shadonake; if you will go near the Bath some time during the day after lunch is over, I will join you there, and you can give it to me; it can be of no possible importance; go in now quickly; good-night. It is my wife."

She turned and fled swiftly back to the house through the darkness, and Maurice was left face to face with Helen.

CHAPTER XXXIII.

DENIS WILDE'S LOVE.

A mighty pain to love it is,
And 'tis a pain that love to miss;
But, of all pains, the greatest pain
Is to love, but love in vain.

Cowley.

He had not been mistaken. It was Helen who had crept out after him in the darkness, and whose slight figure, in her pale blue dress, stood close by him in an angle of the road.

How long she had stood there and what she had heard he did not know. He expected a torrent of abuse and a storm of reproaches from her, but she refrained from either. She passed her arm within his, and walked beside him for several minutes in silence. Maurice, who felt rather guilty, was weak enough to say, hesitatingly,

"The night was so fine, I strolled out to smoke——"

"*Qui s'excuse s'accuse*," quoted Helen; "only you are not smoking, Maurice!"

"My cigar has gone out; I—I met Miss Nevill at the gate of the vicarage."

"So I saw," rather significantly.

"I stopped to have a little talk to her. There is no harm, I suppose, in that!" he added, irritably.

Helen laughed shortly and harshly.

"Harm! oh dear, no; whoever said there was? By the way, is not this freak of yours of going out into the roads to smoke, as you say, alone, rather a slight on your guest? Here is Mr. Wilde; how very amusing! we all seem to be drawn out towards the vicarage to-night."

Denis Wilde, in fact, had followed in the wake of his hostess, and they met him now by the lodge gates.

"How very strange!" called out Helen to him, in her scornful, bantering voice; "how strange that we should all have gone out for solitary rambles, and all meet in the same place; and there was Miss Nevill out in the vicarage garden, also on a solitary ramble."

"Is Miss Nevill there? I think I will go on and call upon her," said Denis.

"You too, Mr. Wilde!" cried Helen. "Have you fallen a victim to the beauty? We heard enough of her in town; she turned all the men's heads; even married men are not safe from her snares, and yet it is singular that none of her admirers care to marry her; there are some women whom all men make love to, but whom none care to make wives of!"

And Maurice was a coward, and spoke no word in her defence; he did not dare; but young Denis Wilde drew himself up proudly.

"Mrs. Kynaston," he said, sternly, "I must ask you not to speak slightingly of Miss Nevill."

"Good gracious, why not? I suppose we are all free to use our tongues and our eyes in this world! Why should you become the woman's champion?"

"Because," answered Denis, gravely, "I hope to make her my wife."

Maurice was man enough to hold out his hand to him in the darkness.

"I am glad of it," he said, rather hoarsely; "make her happy, Denis, if you can."

"Thanks. I shall go on to see her now."

Helen murmured an unintelligible apology, and Denis Wilde passed onwards towards the vicarage.

He had taken her good name into his keeping, he had shielded her from that other woman's slandering tongue; but he had done so in his despair. He had spoken no lie in saying that he hoped to make her his wife; but it was no doubt a fact that Helen and her husband would now believe him to be engaged to her. Would Vera be induced to verify his words, and to place herself and her life beneath the shelter of his love, or would she only be angry with him for venturing to presume upon his hopes? Denis could not tell.

Ten minutes later he stood alone with her in the vicarage dining-room; he had sent in his card with a pencilled line upon it to ask for a few minutes' conversation with her.

Vera had desired that her visitor might be shown into the dining-room. Old Mrs. Daintree had been amazed and scandalized, and even Marion had opened her eyes at so unusual a proceeding; but the vicar was out by a sick bedside in the village, and no one else ever controlled Vera's actions.

Nevertheless, she herself looked somewhat surprised at so late a visit from him. And then, somehow or other, Denis made it plain to her how it was he had come, and what he had said of her. Her name, he told her, had been lightly spoken of; to have defended it without authority would have been to do her more harm than good; to take it under his lawful protection had been instinctively suggested to him by his longing to shield her. Would she forgive him?

"It was Mrs. Kynaston who spoke evil things of me," said Vera, wearily. She was very tired, she hardly understood, she scarcely cared about what he was saying to her; it mattered very little what was said to her. There was that other scene under the shadow of the roses of the gateway so vividly before her; the memory of Maurice's passionate kisses upon her lips, the sound of his beloved voice in her ears. What did anything else signify?

And meanwhile Denis Wilde was pouring out his whole soul to her.

"My darling, give me the right to defend you now and always," he pleaded; "do not refuse me the happiness of protecting your dear name from such women. I know you don't love me, dear, not as I love you, but I will not mind that; I will ask you for nothing that you will not give me freely; only try me—I think I could make you happy, love. At any rate, you shall have anything that tenderness and devotion can give you to bring peace into your life. Vera, darling, answer me."

"Oh, I am very tired," was all she said, moaningly and wearily, passing her hand across her aching brow like a worn-out child.

It was life or death to him. To her it was such a little matter! What were all his words and his prayers beside that heartache that was driving her into her grave! He could do her no good. Why could he not leave her in peace?

And yet, at length, something of the fervour and the passion of his love struck upon her soul and arrested her attention. There is something so touching and so pitiful in that first boy-love that asks for nothing in return, craves for no other reward than to be suffered to exist; that amongst all the selfish and half-hearted passions of older and wiser men, it must needs elicit some response of gratitude at least, if not of answering love, in the heart of the woman who is the object of such rare devotion.

It dawned at length upon Vera, as she listened to his fervent pleading, and as she saw the tears that rose in poor Denis's earnest eyes, and the traces of deep emotion on his smooth, boyish face, that here was, perchance, the one utterly pure and noble love that had ever been laid at her feet.

There arose a sentiment of pity in her heart, and a vague wonder as to his grief. Did he suffer, she asked herself, as she herself suffered?

"Vera, Vera, I only ask you to be my wife. I do not ask you for your heart; only give me your dear self. Only let me be always with you to brighten your life and to take care of you."

How was she to resist such absolute unselfishness?

"Oh, Denis, how good you are to me!" burst from her lips. "How can I take you at your word? Do you not know that my heart is gone from me? I have no love to give you."

"Yes, yes, darling," he said, quickly, pressing her hand to his lips. "Do not pain yourself by speaking of it. I have guessed it. I have always seemed to know it. But it is hopeless, is it not? And I—I would so gladly take you away and comfort you if I could."

And so, in the end, she half yielded to him. What else was she to do? She gave him a sort of promise.

"If I can, it shall be as you wish," she said; "but give me till to-morrow night. I will think of it all day, and if you will come here again to-morrow evening, I will answer you. Give me one more day—only one," she repeated, with a dull reiteration, out of her utter weariness.

"One day will soon be gone," he said, joyfully, as he bade her good night.

Alas, how little he knew what that day was to bring forth!

That night the heavens were overcast with heavy clouds, and torrents of rain poured down upon the face of the earth, and peal after peal of thunder boomed through the heavy heated air. Helen could not sleep; she rose, feverish and unrested from her husband's side, and paced wildly and miserably about the room. Then she went to the window and drew back the curtain, and looked out upon the storm-driven world. The clouds racked wildly across the sky; the trees bent and swayed before the howling wind; the rain beat in floods upon the ground; yet greater and fiercer still was the tempest that raged in Helen Kynaston's heart. Hatred, jealousy, and malice strove and struggled within her, and something direr still—a terror that she could not quench nor stifle; for late that night her husband had said to her suddenly, without a word of warning or preparation—

"Helen, do you know a Frenchman called D'Arblet?"

Helen had been at her dressing-table—her back was turned to him—he did not see the livid pallor which blanched her cheeks at his question.

A little pause, during which she busied herself among the trifles upon the table.

"No, I never heard the name in my life," she said, at length.

"That is odd—because neither have I—and yet the man has sent me a parcel." It was of so little importance to him, that it did not occur to him that there could possibly be any occasion for secresy concerning Vera's commission. What could an utter stranger have to send to him that could possibly concern him in any way?

It did not strike him how strained and forced was the voice in which his wife presently asked him a question.

"And the parcel! You have opened it?"

"No, not yet," began Maurice, stifling a yawn; and he would have gone on to explain to her that it was not yet actually in his possession, although, probably, he would not have told her that it was Vera who was to give it to him; only at that minute the maid came into the room, and he changed the subject.

But Helen had guessed that it was Vera who was the bearer of that parcel. How it had come to pass she could not tell, but too surely she divined that Vera had in her possession those fatal letters that she had once written to the French vicomte; the letters that would blast her for ever in her husband's estimation, and turn his luke-warmness and his coldness into actual hatred and repulsion.

And was it likely that Vera, with such a weapon in her hands, would spare her? What woman, with so signal a revenge in her power, would forego the delight of wreaking it upon the woman who had taken from her the man she loved? Helen knew that in Vera's place she would show no mercy to her rival.

It was all clear as daylight to her now; the appointment at the vicarage gate, the something which she had said in her note she had for him; the whole mystery of the secret meeting between them—it was Vera's revenge. Vera, whom Maurice loved, and whom she, Helen, hated with such a deadly hatred!

And then, in the silence of the night, whilst her husband slept, and whilst the thunder and the wind howled about her home, Helen crept forth from her room, and sought for that fatal packet of letters which her husband had told her he had "not yet" opened.

Oh, if she could only find them and destroy them before he ever saw them again! Long and patiently she looked for them, but her search was in vain. She ransacked his study and his dressing-room; she opened every drawer, and fumbled in every pocket, but she found nothing.

She was frightened, too, to be about the house like a thief in the night. Every gust of wind that creaked among the open doors made her start, every flash of lightning that lighted up the faces of the old family portraits, looking down upon her with their fixed eyes, made her turn pale and shiver, lest she should see them move, or hear them speak.

Only her jealousy and her hatred burnt fiercely above her terror; she would not give in, she told herself, until she found it.

Denis Wilde, who was restless too, had heard her soft footsteps along the passage outside his door; and, with a vague uneasiness as to who could be about at such an hour, he came creeping out of his room, and peeped in at the library door.

He saw her sitting upon the floor, a lighted candle by her side, an open drawer, out of her husband's writing-table, upon her lap, turning over papers, and bills, and note-books with eager, trembling hands. And he saw in her white, set face, and wild, scared eyes, that which made him draw back swiftly and shudderingly from the sight of her.

"Good God!" he murmured to himself, as he sought his room again, "the woman has murder in her face!"

And at last she had to give it up; the letters were not to be found. The storm without settled itself to rest, the thunder died away in the far distance over the hills, and Helen, worn out with fatigue and emotion, sought a troubled slumber upon the sofa in her dressing-room.

"She cannot have given it to him," was the conclusion she came to at last. "Well, she will do so to-morrow, and I—I will not let her out of my sight, not for one instant, all the day!"

CHAPTER XXXIV.

A GARDEN PARTY.

I have done for ever with all these things:
The songs are ended, the deeds are done;
There shall none of them gladden me now, not one.
There is nothing good for me under the sun
But to perish—as these things perished.

A. L. GORDON.

Mr. Guy Miller is a young gentleman who has not played an important part in these pages; nevertheless, but for him, sundry events which took place at Shadonake at this time would not have had to be recorded.

It so happened that Guy Miller's twenty-first birthday was in the third week of September, and that it was determined by his parents to celebrate the day in an appropriate and fitting manner. Guy was a youth of no particular looks, and no particular manners; he had been at Oxford, but his father had lately taken him away from it, with a view to his travelling, and seeing something of the world before he settled down as a country gentleman. He had had no opportunity, therefore, of distinguishing himself at college; but as he was not overburdened with brains, and had, moreover, never been known to study with interest any profounder literature than "Handley Cross" and "Mr. Sponge's Sporting Tour," it is possible that, even had he been left undisturbed to pursue his studies at the university, he would never have developed into a bright or shining ornament at that seat of learning.

As it was, Guy came home to the paternal mansion an ignorant but amiable and inoffensive young man, with a small, fluffy moustache, and no particular bent in life beyond smoking short pipes, and loafing about the premises with his hands in his trousers pockets.

He was a tolerable shot, and a plucky, though not a graceful horseman. He hated dancing because he trod on his partner's toes, and shunned ladies' society because he had to make himself agreeable to them. Nevertheless, having been fairly "licked into shape" by a course successively of Eton and of Oxford, he was able to behave like a gentleman in his mother's house when it was necessary for him to do so, and he quite appreciated the fact of his being an important personage in the Miller family.

It was to celebrate the coming of age of this interesting young gentleman that Mr. and Mrs. Miller had settled to give a monster entertainment to several hundreds of their fellow-creatures.

The proceedings were to include a variety of instructive and amusing pastimes, and were to last pretty nearly all day. There was to be a country flower-show in a big tent on the lawn; that was pure business, and concerned the farmers as much as the gentry. There were also to be athletic sports in a field for the active young men, lawn-tennis for the active young women, an amateur polo match got up by the energy and pluck of Miss Beatrice and her uncle Tom; a "cold collation" in a second tent to be going on all the afternoon; the whole to be finished up with a dance in the large drawing room, for a select few, after sunset.

The programme, in all conscience, was varied enough; and the day broke hopefully, after the wild storm of the previous night, bright and cool and sunny, with every prospect of being perfectly fine.

Beatrice, happy in the possession of her lover, was full of life and energy; she threw herself into all the preparations of the *fête* with her whole heart. Herbert, who came over from Lutterton at an early hour, followed her about like a dog, obeying her orders implicitly, but impeding her proceedings considerably by a constant under-current of love-making, by which he strove to vary and enliven the operation of sticking standard flags into the garden borders, and nailing up wreaths of paper roses inside the tent.

Mrs. Miller, having consented to the engagement, like a sensible woman, was resolved to make the best of it, and was, if not cordial, at least pleasantly civil to her future son-in-law. She had given over Beatrice as a bad job; she had resolved to find suitable matches for Guy and for Geraldine.

By one o'clock the company was actually beginning to arrive, the small fry of the neighbourhood being, of course, the first to appear. By-and-by came the rank and fashion of Meadowshire, and by three o'clock the gardens were crowded.

It was a brilliant scene; there was the gaily-dressed crowd going in and out of the tents, groups of elderly people sitting talking under the trees, lawn-tennis players at one end of the garden, the militia band playing Strauss's waltzes at the other, the scarlet and white flags floating bravely over everybody in the breeze, and a hum of many voices and a sound of merry laughter in every direction.

Mr. and Mrs. Miller, and Guy, the hero of the day, moved about amongst the guests from group to group. Guy, it must be owned, looking considerably bored. Beatrice, with her lover in attendance, looking flushed and rosy with the many congratulations which the news of her engagement called forth on every side; and the younger boys, home from school for the occasion, getting in everybody's way, and directing their main attention to the ices in the refreshment-tent. Such an afternoon party, it was agreed, had not been held in Meadowshire within the memory of man; but then, dear Mrs. Miller had such energy and such a real talent for organization; and if the company *was* a little mixed, why, of course, she must recollect Mr. Miller's position, and how important it was for him, with the prospect of a general election coming on, to make himself thoroughly popular with all classes.

No one in all the gay crowd was more admired or more noticed than "the bride," as she was still called, young Mrs. Kynaston. Helen had surpassed herself in the elaboration of her toilette. The country dames and damsels, in their somewhat dowdy home-made gowns, could scarcely remember their manners, so eager were they to stare at the marvels of that wondrous garment of sheeny satin, and soft, creamy gauze, sprinkled over with absolute works of art in the shape of wreaths of many-hued embroidered birds and flowers, with which the whole dress was cunningly and dexterously adorned. It was a masterpiece of the great Worth; rich without being gaudy, intricate without losing its general effect of colour, and, above all, utterly and absolutely inimitable by the hands of any meaner artist.

Mrs. Kynaston looked well; no one had ever seen her look better; there was an unusual colour in her cheeks, an unusual glitter in her blue eyes, that always seemed to be roving restlessly about her as though in search of something even all the time she was saying her polite commonplaces in answer to the pleasant and pretty speeches that she received on all sides from men and women alike.

But through it all she never let Vera Nevill out of her sight; where Vera moved, she moved also. When she walked across the lawn, Mrs. Kynaston made some excuse to go in the same direction; when she entered either of the tents, Helen also found it necessary to go into them. But the crowd was too great for any one to remark this; no one saw it save Denis Wilde, whose eyes were sharpened by his love.

Once Helen saw that Maurice and Vera were speaking to each other. She could not get near enough to hear what they said, but she saw him bend down and speak to her earnestly, and there was a sad, wistful look in Vera's upturned eyes as she answered him. Helen's heart beat with a wild, mad jealousy as she watched them; and yet it was but a few words that had passed between them.

"Vera, young Wilde says you are going to marry him; is it true?"

"He wants me to do so, but I don't think I can."

"Why not? It would be happier for you, child; forget the past and begin afresh. He is a good boy, and by-and-by he will be well off."

"You, too—you advise me to do this?" she answered with unwonted bitterness. "Oh, how wise and calculating one ought to be to live happily in this miserable world!"

He looked pained.

"I cannot do you any good," he said, rather brokenly. "God knows I would if I could. I can only be a curse to you. Give me at least the credit of unselfishly wishing you to be less unhappy than you are."

And then the crowd, moving onwards, parted them from each other.

"Do not forget to meet me at the Bath," she called out to him as he went.

"Oh, to be sure! I had forgotten. I will be there just before the dancing begins."

And then Denis Wilde took his place by her side.

If Mrs. Kynaston surpassed herself in looks and animation that day, Vera, on the contrary, had never looked less well.

Her eyes were heavy with sleepless nights and many tears; her movements were slower and more languid than of wont, and her face was pale and thin.

Meadowshire generally, that had ceased to trouble itself much about her when she had thrown over the richest baronet in the county, considered itself, nevertheless, to be somewhat aggrieved by the falling off in her appearance, and passed its appropriate and ill-natured comments upon the fact.

"How ill she looks," said one woman to another.

"Positively old. I suppose she thought she could whistle poor Sir John back again whenever she chose; now he is out of the country she would give her eyes for him!"

"I daresay; and looks as if she had cried them out; but he must be glad to have escaped her! Well, it serves her right for behaving so badly. I'm sure I don't pity her."

"Nor I, indeed."

And the two amiable women passed onwards to discuss some other ill-fated victim.

But to the two men who loved her Vera that day was as beautiful as ever; for love sees no flaw in the face that reigns supreme in the soul. And Vera sat still in her corner of the tent where she had taken refuge, and leant her tired, aching head against a gaudy pink-and-white striped pillar. It was the tent where the flower-show was going on. From her sheltered nook there was not much that was lovely to be seen, not a vestige of a rose or a carnation to refresh her tired eyes, only a counter covered with samples of potatoes and monster cauliflowers; and there was a slab of white wood with pats of yellow butter, done up in moss and ferns, which had been sent from the principal dairy-farms of the county, and before which there was a constant succession of elderly and interested housewives tasting and comparing notes. There seemed some difficulty in deciding to whom the butter prize was to be awarded, and at last a committee of ladies was formed; they all tasted, solemnly, of each sample all round, and then they each gave their verdict differently, so that it had all to be done over again amidst a good deal of laughter and merriment.

Vera was vaguely amused by this scene that went on just in front of her. When the knotty point was settled, the committee moved on to decide upon something else, and she was left again to the uninterrupted contemplation of the Flukes and the York Regents.

Denis Wilde had sat by her for some time, but at last she had begged him to leave her. Her head ached, she said; if he would not mind going, and he went.

Presently, Beatrice, beaming with happiness, found her out in her corner.

"Oh, Vera!" she said, coming up to her, all radiant with smiles, "you are the only one of my friends who has not yet wished me joy."

"That is not because I have not thought of you, Beatrice, dear," she answered, heartily grasping her friend's outstretched hands. "I was so very glad to hear that everything has come right for you at last. How did it all happen?"

"I will come over to the vicarage to-morrow, and tell you the whole story. Oh! do you remember meeting Herbert and me, that foggy morning, outside Tripton station?"

Would Vera ever forget it?

"I little thought then how happily everything was to end for us. I used to think we should have to elope! Poor Herbert, he was always frightened out of his life when I said that. But we have had a very narrow escape of being blighted beings to the end of our lives. If it hadn't been for uncle Tom and that dear darling mare, Clochette, whom I should like to keep in a gold and jewelled stall to the end of her ever-blessed days!——Ah, well! I've no time to tell you now—I will come over to Sutton to-morrow, and I may bring him, may I not?"

"Him," of course, meaning Mr. Herbert Pryme. Vera requested that he might be brought by all means.

"Well, I must run away now—there are at least a hundred of these stupid people to whom I must go and make myself agreeable. By the way, Vera, how dull you look, up in this corner by yourself. Why do you sit here all alone?"

"My head aches; I am glad to be quiet."

"But you mean to dance by-and-by, I hope?"

"Oh, yes, I daresay. Go back to your guests, Beatrice; I am getting on very well."

Beatrice went off smiling and waving her hand. Vera could watch her outside in the sunshine, moving about from group to group, shaking hands with first one and then another, laughing at some playful sally, or smiling demurely over some graver words of kindness. She was always popular, was Beatrice, with her bright talk and her plain clever face, and there was not a man or woman in all that crowd who did not wish her happiness.

And so the day wore away, and the polo match—very badly played—was over, and the votaries of lawn-tennis were worn out with running up and down, and the flowers and the fruits in the show-tent began to look limp and dusty. The farmers and those people of small importance who had only been invited "from two to five," began now to take their departure, and their carriage wheels were to be heard driving away in rapid succession from the front door. Then the hundred or so of the "best county people," who were remaining later for the dancing, began to think of leaving the lawns before the dew fell. There was a general move towards the house, and even the band "limbered up," and began to transfer itself from the garden into the hall, where its labours were to begin afresh.

Then it was that Vera crept forth out of her sheltered corner, and, unseen and unnoticed save by one watchful pair of eyes, wended her way through the shrubbery walks in the direction of the Bath.

CHAPTER XXXV.

SHADONAKE BATH.

A jolly place—in times of old,
But something ails it now:
The spot is cursed!

WORDSWORTH.

Calm and still, like the magic mirror of the legend, Shadonake Bath lay amongst its everlasting shadows.

The great belt of fir-trees beyond it, the sheltering evergreens on the nearer side, the tiers of grey, moss-grown steps that encompassed it about, all found their image again upon its smooth and untroubled surface. There was a golden light from the setting sun to the west, and the pale mist of a shadowy crescent moon had risen in the east.

It was all quiet here—faint echoes of distant voices and far-away laughter came up in little gusts from the house; but there was no trace of the festivities down by the desolate water, nothing but the dark fir-trees above it, and the great white heads of the water-lilies that lay like jewels upon its silent bosom.

Vera sat down upon the steps, and rested her chin in her hands, and waited. The house and the gardens behind her were shut out by the thick screen of laurels and rhododendrons. Before her, on the other side, were the fir-trees, with their red, bronzed trunks, and the soft, dark brown carpet that lay at their feet; there was not even a squirrel stirring among their branches, nor a bird that fluttered beneath their shadows.

Vera waited. She was not impatient nor anxious. She had nothing to say to Maurice when he came—she did not mean to keep him, not even for five minutes, by her side; she did not want to run any further risks with him—it was better not—better that she should never again be alone with him. She only meant just to give him that wretched little brown paper parcel that weighed upon her conscience with the sense of an unfulfilled vow, and then to go back with him to the house at once. They could have nothing more to say to each other.

Strangely enough, as she sat there musing all her life came back in review before her. The old days at Rome, with the favourite sister who was dead and gone; her own gay, careless life, with its worldly aims and desires; her first arrival at Sutton, her determination to make herself Sir John Kynaston's wife, and then her fatal love for his brother; it all came back to her again. All kinds of little details that she had long forgotten came flooding in upon her memory. She remembered how she had first seen Maurice standing at the foot of the staircase, with the light of the lamp upon his handsome head; and then, again, how one morning she and he had stood together in this very place by the Bath, and how she had told him, shuddering, that it would be dreadful to be drowned there, and she had cried out in a nameless terror that she wished she had not seen it for the first time with him by her side; and then Helen had come down from the house and joined them, and they had all three gone away together. She smiled a little to herself over that foolish, reasonless terror. The quiet pool of water did not look dreadful to her now—only cool, and still, and infinitely restful.

By-and-by other thoughts came into her mind. She recalled her interview with old Lady Kynaston at Walpole Lodge, when she had so nearly promised her to give back her hand to her eldest son, when she would have done so had it not been for that sight of Maurice's face in the adjoining room. She wondered what Lady Kynaston had thought of her sudden change of mind; what she had been able to make of it; whether she had ever guessed at what had been the truth. It seemed only yesterday that the old lady had told her to be wise and brave, and to begin her life over again, and to make the best of the good things of this world that were still left to her.

"There is a pain that goes right through the heart," Maurice's mother had said to her; "I who speak to you have felt it. I thought I should die of it, but you see I did not."

Alas! did not Vera know that pain all too well; that heartache that banishes peace by day and sleep by night, and that will not wear itself out?

And yet other women had borne it, and had lived and been even happy in other ways; but she could not be happy. Was it because her heart was deeper, or because her sense of pain was greater than that of others?

Vera could not tell. She only wished, and longed, and even prayed that she might have the strength to become Denis Wilde's wife; that she might taste once more of peace, if not of joy; and yet all her longings and all her prayers only made her realize the more how utterly the thing was beyond her power.

To Maurice, and Maurice alone, belonged her life and her soul, and Vera felt that it would be easier for her to be true to the sad, dim memory of his love than to give her heart and her allegiance to any other upon earth.

So she sat and mused, and pondered, and the amber light in the east faded away into palest saffron, and the solemn shadows deepened and lengthened upon the still bosom of the water.

Suddenly there came a sharp footstep and the rustle of a woman's silken skirts across the stone flags behind her. She looked up quickly; Helen stood beside her. Helen, in all the sheen of her gay Paris garments, with the evening light upon her uncovered head, and the glow of a passion, fiercer than madness, in her glittering eyes. Some prescience of evil—she knew not of what—made Vera spring to her feet.

Helen spoke to her shortly and defiantly.

"Miss Nevill, you are waiting here for my husband, are you not?"

A faint flush rose in Vera's face.

"Yes," she answered, very quietly. "I am waiting to speak a few words to him."

"You have something to give him, have you not? Some letters that are mine, and which you have probably read."

Helen said the words quickly and feverishly; her voice shook and trembled. Vera looked surprised and even indignant.

"I don't understand you, Mrs. Kynaston," she began, coldly.

"Oh, yes, you understand me perfectly. Give me my letters, Miss Nevill; you have no doubt read them all," and she laughed harshly and sneeringly.

"Mrs. Kynaston, you are labouring under some delusion," said Vera, quietly; "I have no letters of yours, and if I had," with a ring of utter contempt, "I should not be likely to have opened them."

For it did not occur to her that Helen was speaking of Monsieur D'Arblet's parcel; that did not in the least convey the idea of letters to her mind; nor had it ever entered into her head to speculate about what that unhappy little packet could possibly contain; she had never even thought about it.

"I have no letters of yours," she repeated.

"You are saying what is false," cried Helen, angrily. "How can you dare to deny it? You know you have got them, you are here to give them to Maurice, knowing that they will ruin me. You *shall* not give them to him. I have come to take them from you—I *will* have them."

"I do not even know what you are speaking about," answered Vera. "Why should I want to ruin you, if, indeed, such a thing is to be done?"

"Because you hate me as much as I hate you."

"Hate is an ugly word," said Vera, rather scornfully. "I have no reason to hate you, and I do not know why you should hate me."

"Don't imagine you can put me off with empty words," cried Helen, wildly. She made a step forward; her white hands clenched themselves together with a reasonless fury; she was as white as the crescent moon that rose beyond the trees.

"Give me my letters—the letters you are waiting here to give to my husband!" she cried.

"Mrs. Kynaston, do not be so angry," said Vera, becoming almost bewildered by her violence; "you are really mistaken—pray calm yourself. I have no letters: what I was going to give your husband was only a little parcel from a man who is abroad—he is a foreigner. I do not think it is of the slightest importance to anybody. I have not opened it, I have no idea what it contains, and your husband himself said it was nothing—only I have promised to give it him alone; it was a whim of the little Frenchman who entrusted me with it, and whom, I must honestly tell you, I believe to have been half-mad. Only, unfortunately, I have promised to deliver it in this manner."

Mrs. Kynaston was looking at her fixedly; her anger seemed to have died away.

"Yes," she said, "it was Monsieur D'Arblet who gave them to you."

"That was his name, D'Arblet. I did not like the man; but he bothered me until I foolishly undertook his commission. I am sorry now that I did so, as it seems to vex you so much; but I do not think there are letters in the parcel, and I certainly have not opened it."

Helen was silent again for a minute, looking at her intently.

"I don't believe you," she said; "they are my letters, sure enough, and you have read them. What woman would not do so in your place? and you know that they will ruin me with my husband."

"It is you yourself that tell me so!" cried Vera, impatiently, beginning to lose her temper. "I do not even know what you are talking about!"

"Miss Nevill!" cried Helen, suddenly changing her tone; "give that parcel to me, I entreat you."

"I am very sorry, Mrs. Kynaston; I cannot possibly do so."

"Oh yes, you can—you will," said Helen, imploringly. "What can it matter to you now? It is I who am his wife; you cannot get any good out of a mere empty revenge. Why should you spoil my chance of winning his heart? I know well enough that he loves you, but——"

"Mrs. Kynaston, pray, pray recollect yourself; do not say such words to me!" cried Vera, deeply distressed.

"Why should I not say them! You and I know well enough that it is true. I hate you, I am jealous of you, for I know that my husband loves you; and yet, if you will only give me that parcel, I will forgive you—I will try to live at peace with you—I will even pray and strive for your happiness! Let me have a chance of making him love me!"

"For God's sake, Mrs. Kynaston, do not say these things to me!" cried Vera. She was crimson with pain and shame, and shocked beyond measure that his wife should be so lost to all decency and self-respect as to speak so openly of her husband's love for herself.

"I will not and cannot listen to you!"

"But you will not be so cruel as to ruin me?" pleaded Helen; "only give me that parcel, and I shall be safe! You say you have not opened it; well, I can hardly believe it, because in your place I should have read every word; yet, if you will give them to me, I will forgive you."

"You do not understand what you are saying!" cried Vera, impatiently. "How can I give you what is not mine to give? I have no right to dispose of this parcel"—she held it in her hand—"and I have given my word that I will give it to your husband alone. How could I be so false as to do anything else with it? You are asking impossibilities, Mrs. Kynaston."

"You will not give it to me?" There was a sudden change in Helen's voice— she pleaded no longer.

"No, certainly not."

"And that is your last word?"

"Yes."

There was a silence. Helen looked away over the water towards the fir-trees. She was pale, but very quiet; all her angry agitation seemed to have died away. Vera stood a little beneath her on the lowest step, close down to the water; she held the little parcel that was the object of the dispute in her hands, and was looking at it with an expression of deep annoyance; she was wishing heartily that she had never seen either it or the wretched little Frenchman who had insisted upon confiding it to her care.

Neither of them spoke; for an instant neither of them even moved. There was a striking contrast between them: Helen, slight and fragile in her bird-of-paradise garments, with jewels about her neck, and golden chains at her wrist; her pretty piquant face, almost childish in the contour of the small, delicate features. Vera, in her plain, tight-fitting dress, whose only beauty lay in the perfect simplicity with which it followed the lines of her glorious figure; her pure, lovely face, laden with its burden of deep sadness, a little turned away from the other woman who had taken everything from her, and left her life so desolate. And there was the silent pool at their feet, and the darkening belt of fir-trees beyond, and the pale moon ever brightening in the shadowy heavens. It was a picture such as a painter might have dreamt of.

Not a sound—only once the faint cry of some wild animal in the far-off woods, and the flutter of a night-moth on the wing. Helen's face was turned eastwards towards the fast-fading evening glow.

What is it that sends the curse of Cain into the human heart?

Did some foul and evil thing, wandering homeless around that fatal spot, enter then and there, unbidden, into her sin-stained soul? Or had the hellish spirit been always there within her, only biding its time to burst forth in all its naked and hideous horror?

God only knows.

"Vera, gather me a water-lily! See how lovely they are. I am going back to dance; I want a water-lily."

Vera looked up startled. The sudden change of manner and the familiar mention of her name struck her as strange. Helen was leaning towards her, all flushed and eager, pointing with her glistening, jewelled fingers over the water.

"Don't you see how white they are, and how they gleam in the moonlight like silver? Would not one of them look lovely in my hair?"

"I do not think I can reach them," said Vera, slowly. She was puzzled and half-frightened by the quick, feverish words and manner.

"Yes, yes, your arms are long—much longer than mine; you can reach them very well. See, I will hold the sleeve of your dress like this; it is very strong. I can hold you quite safely. Kneel down and reach out for it, Vera. Do, please, I want it so much. There is one so close there, just beyond your hand. Stoop over a little further; don't be afraid; I have got you tightly."

And Vera knelt and stretched out over the dark face of the waters.

Then, all at once, there was a cry—a wild struggle—a splash of the dark, seething waves—and Helen stood up again in her bright raiment alone on the margin of the pool; whilst ever-widening circles stretched hurriedly away and away, as though terror-stricken, from the baleful spot where Vera Nevill had sunk below the ill-fated waters.

Someone came madly rushing out of the bushes behind her. Helen screamed aloud.

"It was an accident! She slipped forward—her footing gave way!" gasped the unhappy woman in her terror. "Oh, Maurice, for pity's sake, believe me; it was an accident!" She sunk upon her knees, with wildly outstretched arms, and trembling, and uplifted hands.

"Stand aside," he said, hoarsely, pushing her roughly from him, so that she almost fell to the earth, and he plunged deep into the still quivering waters.

It was the water-lilies that brought her to her death. The long clinging stems amongst which she sank held her fair body in their cold, clammy embraces, so that she never rose again. It was long before they found her.

And, oh! who shall ever describe that dreadful scene by the margin of Shadonake Bath, whilst the terrified crowd that had gathered there quickly waited for her whom all knew to be hopelessly gone from them for ever!

The sobbing, frightened women; the white, stricken faces of the men; the agony of those who had loved her; the distress and dismay of those who had only admired her; and there was one trembling, shuddering wretch, in her satin and her jewels, standing white and haggard apart, with knees that shook together, and teeth that clattered, and tearless sobs that shook her from head to foot, staring with a half-maddened stare upon the fatal waters.

Then, when all was at an end and the worst was known, when the poor dripping body had been reverently covered over and borne away by loving arms amid a torrent of sobs and wailing tears towards the house, then some one came near her and spoke to her—some one off whom the water came pouring in streams, and whose face was white and wild as her own.

"Get you away out of my sight," said the man whom she had loved so fruitlessly to her.

"Have pity! have pity!" was the cry of despair that burst from her quivering lips. "Was it not all an accident?"

"Yes, let it be so to the world, because you bear my name, and I will not have it dragged through the mire—to all others it is an accident—but never to me, for I *saw you let her go*! There is the stain of murder upon your hands. I will never call you wife, nor look upon your face again; get yourself away out of my sight!"

With a low sobbing cry she turned and fled away from him, and away from the place, out among the shadows of the fir-trees. Once again some one stopped her in her terror-stricken flight.

It was Denis Wilde, who came striding towards her under the trees, and caught her roughly by the wrist.

"It is *you* who have killed her!" he said, savagely.

"What do you mean?" she murmured, faintly.

"I saw it in your face last night when you were wandering about the house during the thunderstorm; you meant her death then. I saw it in your eyes. My God! why did I not watch over her better, and save her from such a devil as you?"

"No, no, it is not true; it was an accident. Oh, spare me, spare me!" with a piteousness of terror, was all she could say.

"Yes; I will spare you, poor wretch, for your husband's sake—because she loved him—and his burden, God help him! is heavy enough as it is. Go!" flinging her arm rudely from him. "Go, whilst you have got time, lest the thirst for your blood be too strong for me."

And this time no one saw her go. Like a hunted animal, she fled away among the trees, her gleaming many-hued dress trailing all wet and drabbled on the sodden earth behind her, and the darkness of the gathering night closed in around her, and covered her in mercy with its pitiful mantle.

CHAPTER XXXVI.

AT PEACE.

Open, dark grave, and take her:
Though we have loved her so,
Yet we must now forsake her:
Love will no more awake her:
Oh bitter woe!
Open thine arms and take her
To rest below!

A. PROCTER.

So Vera was at peace at last. The troubled life was over; the vexed question of her fate was settled for her. There was to be no more struggling of right against wrong, of expediency against truth, for her for evermore. She had all—nay, more than all she wanted now.

"It was what she desired herself," said the vicar, brokenly, as he knelt by the side of her who had been so dear and precious to him. "Only a Sunday or two ago she said to me 'If I could die, I should be at peace.'"

And Maurice, with hidden face at the foot of the bed, could not answer him for tears.

It was there, by that white still presence, that lay so calm and so lovely amongst the showers of heavy-scented waxen flowers, wherewith loving hands had decked her for her last long sleep; it was there that Eustace learnt at last the secret of her life, and the fatal love that had so wrecked her happiness. It was all clear to him now. Her struggles, her temptations, her pitiful moments of weakness and misery, her courageous strife against the hopelessness of her fate—all was made plain now: he understood her at last.

In Maurice Kynaston's passion of despairing grief he read the story of her sad life's trouble.

Truly, Maurice had enough to bear; for he alone, and one other, who spoke no word of it to him, knew the terrible secret of her death; to all else it was "an accident;" to him and to Denis Wilde alone it was "murder." To him, too, the motive of the foul, cowardly deed had been revealed; for, tightly clasped in that poor dead hand, true to the last to the trust that had been given her, was the fatal packet of letters that had been the cause of her death. They were all blotted and blurred, and sodden with the water, but there were whole sentences in the inner folds that were sufficient for him to recognize his wife's handwriting, and to see what was the drift and the meaning of them.

Whom they were written to, when they had been penned, he neither knew nor cared to discover; it was enough for him that they had been written by her, and that they were altogether shameful and sinful. With a deep and sickened disgust, he set fire to the whole packet, and scattered the blackened and smouldering ashes into the empty grate. They had cost a human life, those reckless, sinful letters; but for them, Vera would not have died.

The terrible tragedy came to an end at last. They buried her beneath the coloured mosaic floor of the new chancel, which Sir John had built at her desire; and Marion smothered herself and her children in crape, and people shook their heads and sighed when they spoke of her; and Shadonake was shut up, and the Millers all went to London; and then the world went its way, and after a time it forgot her; and Vera Nevill's place knew her no more.

After Christmas there was a wedding in Eaton Square; a wedding small and not at all gay. Indeed, Geraldine Miller considered her sister next door to a lunatic, and she told herself it would be hardly worth while to be married at all if there was to be no more fuss made over her marriage than over Beatrice's. For there were no bridesmaids and no wedding guests, only all the Millers, from the eldest down to the youngest, uncle Tom, and an ancient Miss Esterworth, unearthed from the other end of England for the occasion; and there were also a Mr. and Mrs. Pryme, a grave and aged couple—uncle and aunt to the bridegroom.

There was, however, one remarkable feature at this particular wedding: when the family party came down into the dining-room to take their places for the conventional breakfast upon the plate of the bride's father were to be seen some very curious things.

These were a faded white lace parasol with pink bows; a pair of soiled grey *peau de suède* gloves, and a little black wisp of a spotted net veil.

"Bless my soul!" said the member for Meadowshire, putting up his eye-glasses; "what on earth is all this?"

"I think you have seen them before, papa," says the bride, demurely, whilst uncle Tom bursts into a loud and hearty guffaw of laughter.

"Good gracious me!" says Mr. Miller, turning rather red, and looking bewilderedly from his daughter to his wife: "I don't really understand. Caroline, my dear, do you know the meaning of these—these—most extraordinary objects?"

Mrs. Miller draws near and examines the little heap of faded finery critically. "Why, Beatrice!" she exclaims, in astonishment, "it is your last summer's sunshade, and a pair of your old gloves: how on earth did they come here on your papa's plate?"

"I put them there; I thought papa would like to see them again," cries Beatrice, laughing; "he met them in Herbert's rooms in the Temple one day last summer."

"*Beatrice!*" falters her father, staring in amazement at her.

"Yes, papa, dear, don't be too dreadfully shocked at me; it was I, your very naughty daughter, who had gone on the sly to see Herbert in the Temple, and I ran into the next room to hide myself when I heard you come in, and left those stupid tell-tale things on the table! I don't think, now I am Herbert's wife, that it matters very much how much I confess of my improprieties, does it?"

"Good gracious me!" says Mr. Miller, solemnly, and then turns round and shakes hands with his son-in-law. "And I might have retained you for that libel case after all, instead of getting in a young fool who lost it for me!" was all he said. And then the sunshade and the gloves were swept away, and they all sat down and ate a very good breakfast, and drank to the bride and bridegroom's health none the less heartily for that curious little explanatory scene at the beginning of the feast.

Maurice Kynaston has joined his brother in Australia, where, report says, they are doing very well, and rapidly making a large fortune; although no one thinks that either brother will ever leave the country of his adoption and return to England.

Old Lady Kynaston lives on alone at Walpole Lodge; she is getting very aged, and is a dull, solitary old woman now, with an ever-present sadness at her heart.

Before he left England Maurice told her the story of his love for Vera, and the whole truth about her death. The old lady knows that Vera and her fatal beauty has wrecked the lives of both her sons. There will be no tender filial hands to close her dying eyes, no troops of merry grandchildren to cheer and brighten her closing years. They will live away from her, and she will die alone. She knows it—and she is very, very sad.

In South Kensington there lives a gay, world-loving woman who keeps open house, and entertains perpetually. She has horses and carriages, and a box at the opera, and is always to be seen faultlessly dressed and the gayest of the gay at every race meeting, and at every scene of pleasure.

People admire her and flatter her, and speak lightly of her too, sometimes, for it is generally known that Mrs. Kynaston is "separated" from her husband; and though a separation is a perfectly respectable thing, and has no possible connection with a divorce, yet there are ugly whispers in this case as to what is the cause of the dissension between the husband in Australia and the wife in London; whispers that often do not fall very far short of the truth. And, gay as she is, and light-hearted as she seems to be, there are times when pretty Mrs. Kynaston is more to be pitied than any wretched beggar who toils along the streets, for always there is the terror of detection at her heart, and the fear that her dreadful secret, known as it is to at least two persons on earth, may ooze out—be guessed by others.

There are things Mrs. Kynaston can never do: to read of some dreadful murder such as occasionally fills all the papers for days with its sickening details makes her shut herself in her own room till the horrible tragedy is over and forgotten; to hear of such things spoken of in society causes her to faint away with terror. To walk by a pond, or even to speak of being rowed upon a lake or river, fills her with such horror of soul that none of her friends ever care to suggest a water-party of any kind to her.

"She saw that poor Miss Nevill drowned," say her compassionate acquaintances; "it has upset her nerves, poor dear; she cannot bear the sight of water." And there are a few who think, and who are not ashamed to whisper their thoughts with bated breath, that she saw Miss Nevill's sad death too near and too well to be utterly spotless in the matter.

That she allowed her to perish without attempting to save her, because she was jealous of her, is the generally received impression; but there is no one who has quite realized that she was actually guilty of her death.

Did they think so, they could not eat her dinners with decency. And they do eat her dinners, which are uncommonly good ones; and they flock to her house, and they sit in her carriage and her opera-box, and they take all they can get from her, although at their hearts they do not care to be intimate with her. But then money covers a multitude of sins. And a great many crimes may be glossed over if we are only rich enough and popular enough, and sufficiently the fashion.

As to Denis Wilde, he was young, and in time he got over it and married an amiable young lady who bore him three children and loved him devotedly, so that after a while he forgot his first love.

Shadonake Bath has been drained. Mr. Miller has at last been allowed to have his own way about it. It is an ill wind that blows nobody any good, and there could be found no voice to plead for its preservation after that terrible tragedy of which it was the scene.

So the old steps have all been cleared away, and brick walls line the straight deep sides, whereon grow the finest peaches and nectarines in the county, whilst a parterre of British Queens and Hautboys cover the spot where Vera died with their rich red fruit and their luxuriant foliage.

And at Sutton things go on much the same as of old. Old Mrs. Daintree is dead, and no one sorrowed much for her loss, whilst the domestic harmony is decidedly enhanced by her absence. Tommy and Minnie are growing big and lanky, and the subject of schools and education is beginning to occupy the minds of Marion and her husband.

But the vicar has grown grey and old; his back is more bent and his face more careworn than it used to be. He has never been quite the same since Vera's death.

There is a white marble monument in the middle of the chancel, raised by the loving hands of two brothers far away in Australia. It is by the best sculptor of the day, and on it lies a pale white figure, with a pure delicate profile, and hands always meekly crossed upon the bosom.

Every Sunday, as Eustace Daintree passes from his place at the reading-desk up to the altar to read the Communion Service, there falls upon it a streak of sunshine from the painted window above, which he himself and his wife had put up to her memory, lighting up the pale marble image with a chequered glory of gold and crimson. And the vicar's eye as he passes alights for a moment with a never-dying sadness upon the simple words carved at the foot of her tomb—

VERA NEVILL, AGED 23.

AT PEACE.